AUTHENTICITY AND EARLY MUSIC

D0165431

Authenticity and Early Music

A SYMPOSIUM

EDITED BY

Nicholas Kenyon

Oxford   New York

OXFORD UNIVERSITY PRESS

Oxford University Press, Walton Street, Oxford OX2 6DP

Oxford New York Toronto
Delhi Bombay Calcutta Madras Karachi
Petaling Jaya Singapore Hong Kong Tokyo
Nairobi Dar es Salaam Cape Town
Melbourne Auckland
and associated companies in
Berlin Ibadan

Oxford is a trade mark of Oxford University Press

Published in the United States
by Oxford University Press, New York

British Library Cataloguing in Publication Data
Authenticity and early music: a symposium.
1. Music, 1500–1750. Performance
I. Kenyon, Nicholas, 1951–
781.6'3
ISBN 0–19–816153–0 (pbk)

Library of Congress Cataloging in Publication Data
Authenticity and early music: a symposium / edited by Nicholas Kenyon.
1. Music—Performance—Congresses. 2. Style, Musical—Congresses. 3. Music—
History and criticism—Congresses. I. Kenyon, Nicholas. 1951–
ML457.A98 1988   781.6'3—dc19   18–15464
ISBN 0–19–816153–0 (pbk)

Printed in Great Britain by
Biddles Ltd, Guildford and King's Lynn

For
William Glock

CONTENTS

PREFACE

This symposium has a somewhat complicated history. When Oxford University Press asked me to take over the editorship of the journal *Early Music* in 1983, one of the first things I wanted to do was to assemble a group of articles which looked at, and perhaps questioned, the basis of the so-called 'authenticity' movement. There was on the one hand such wide acceptance of the evident (and indeed moral) rightness of an approach to performance which 'respected the composer's original intentions', and on the other hand such a violent dismissal of the end results by many thinking and articulate musicians that it was time for a reappraisal of the situation. For the argument had not paid enough attention to what exactly was happening in attempts to 'revive' past performance styles, nor had it addressed itself to the practical results of the historical performance movement.

A couple of important articles appeared in 1982 and 1983 (by Richard Taruskin in the *Journal of Musicology* and by Laurence Dreyfus in the *Musical Quarterly*), and then in the February 1984 issue of *Early Music* a group of pieces was published under the title 'The Limits of Authenticity'. They included a fierce and brilliant article by Richard Taruskin, and caused something of a storm. As editor, I was accused of pulling the rug out from under the early music movement, or (to use an alternative metaphor) of giving aid and succour from within the citadel to those who wished to attack the movement. The argument continued, and achieved some notoriety. When Joseph Kerman's highly stimulating book, published in America as *Contemplating Music* and in England as *Musicology*, appeared in 1985, we were able to read that the historical performance movement was 'in the greatest turmoil', and that articles questioning received wisdom in this field had 'even been fostered by the new editor of *Early Music*'.

As a result of that issue of the journal, Sir William Glock, the former Controller of Music at the BBC (where he had been a strong promoter not only of new music but of earlier music from Machaut to Rameau), who was then the editor of

Eulenburg Books, asked me if I would put together a volume for him on 'the whole nature of authenticity'. After much delay, spurred on by the ever-increasing heat if not light in the debate, I agreed to edit a symposium. I put together a plan, wrote to the authors, and they, much to my agreeable surprise, accepted.

At this point I was telephoned by a friend, Lisa Goode Crawford of the Oberlin Conservatory of Music, Ohio. She planned to put together for the 1986–7 academic year a series of conferences about the historical performance movement, and wanted to discuss possible speakers. I outlined the proposed book to her, and it soon became clear that our ideas matched very closely. The eventual result was that Oberlin invited all the contributors to the book to speak during the conferences, and generously invited me to the final session. (The coincidence that all the authors I had approached worked in America was purely a matter of my initial choice.)

Oberlin's series of meetings, entitled 'Musical Interpretation: The Influence of Historically Informed Performance', were far larger than this book. They included panel discussions, concerts, and addresses both formal and informal. This, alas, cannot be a full 'proceedings' of that valuable event, though we did decide to include Will Crutchfield's address (published here in a form which retains its nature as a spoken introduction to the conference). It pithily raises the issues in the debate from an American point of view, complementing the British-based view in my own introduction. The main Oberlin sessions, however, were based around the other papers being prepared for this book by Howard Mayer Brown, Robert Morgan, Philip Brett, Gary Tomlinson, and Richard Taruskin. The discussion I was able to take part in at Oberlin in March 1987 was an exceptionally lively and fruitful one, and the authors had the opportunity to revise their papers in the light of comments received. So the Oberlin experience was highly beneficial to this book, and I am very grateful to the Dean, David Boe, and to Lisa Goode Crawford for all their help.

This, then, is a highly topical exploration of views and attitudes to the problems of authenticity in early music which have become current over the last few years. It aims to represent the present state of this debate and will undoubtedly become outdated by change. This topicality presented a problem when, after I had finished gathering the material, it became clear that the parent company of Eulenburg Books (the music publishers Schott) had decided to sell its book list. At this point I was extremely concerned that the book should not be delayed further. So I am very indebted to the authors, to John Harper, managing director of Eulenburg, to Sir William Glock, and to Patrick Carnegy of Faber, for their understanding of the fact that I felt it should be published quickly by Oxford University Press. Bruce Phillips of OUP has speeded the acceptance and the production of the book, and both I and the authors are most grateful for that. In the end, the volume perhaps belongs back with the publishers and constant supporters of *Early Music*, where it all started. For help in the preparation of the material, I am very grateful to Jane Ruthven, Caroline Prior, Audrey Twine and Mary Worthington.

N. K.

January 1988

NOTES ON CONTRIBUTORS

NICHOLAS KENYON read Modern History at Balliol College, Oxford. He worked for BBC Radio 3 and in 1979 was invited to join Andrew Porter as a music critic for *The New Yorker*. He returned to England as a music critic for *The Times*, and in 1983 was appointed Editor of *Early Music* magazine. In 1985 he joined the London *Observer*, where in 1987 he became chief music critic. He is the author of two previous books, a regular broadcaster, and a member of the Music Advisory Panel of the Arts Council of Great Britain.

WILL CRUTCHFIELD was born in North Carolina and studied political science at Northwestern University. He joined the staff of the *The New York Times* in 1984, and has written for other journals in the United States and Britain. His scholarly work has centred on nineteenth-century performance practice and on early recordings. He has published papers on ornamentation in the operas of Verdi, on the performing style of Brahms's colleagues, and on the prosodic appoggiatura in the music of Mozart and his contemporaries. He is the author of chapters on nineteenth-century operatic staging and on Classical and Romantic singing style for forthcoming *New Grove* publications.

HOWARD MAYER BROWN, Ferdinand Schevill Distinguished Service Professor of Music at the University of Chicago, has written extensively on Renaissance music, and on the conventions of performing early music. His books include *Music in the Renaissance*; *Embellishing Sixteenth-Century Music*; *Sixteenth Century Instrumentation*; *Music in the French Secular Theater, 1400–1550*; *Instrumental Music Printed Before 1600*; and, most recently, a two-volume edition of *A Florentine Chansonnier from the Time of Lorenzo the Magnificent*, which won the Otto Kinkeldey Prize given by the American Musicological Society for the best book of the year. He is a past President of the American Musicological Society, and Vice-President of the International Musicological Society.

Robert P. Morgan is Professor of Music at the University of Chicago. He is the author of *Twentieth-Century Music*, forthcoming from W. W. Norton, and of numerous articles on the history, theory and aesthetics of nineteenth- and twentieth-century music. He is editing a volume of essays on the music of Alban Berg for Oxford University Press, which will contain his own essay 'The Eternal Return: Retrograde and Circular Form in Berg'. He is a member of the Editorial Board of *Critical Inquiry*, and has also been active as a composer, pianist, and critic.

Philip Brett was born in England and studied at Cambridge University under Thurston Dart. He became a Fellow of King's College, Cambridge, and in 1966 joined the faculty of music at the University of California, Berkeley, where he is now Professor of Music. He is the General Editor of *The Byrd Edition*, and editor of the Masses, *Gradualia*, and several volumes of songs in that series as well as of *Consort Songs* (*Musica Britannica*, Volume 22). He is editor of the Cambridge Opera Handbook on Benjamin Britten's *Peter Grimes*, and has published articles on many aspects of English music.

Gary Tomlinson studied at Dartmouth College and the University of California, Berkeley, and teaches at the University of Pennsylvania. He is the author of *Monteverdi and the End of the Renaissance* and the editor of *Italian Secular Song 1606–1636*. He has also written on nineteenth-century Italian opera and music historiography; his article 'The Web of Culture: A Context for Musicology' appeared in *Nineteenth-Century Music*. In 1982 he won the Alfred Einstein Award of the American Musicological Society. He is presently at work on a study of the relations of music and the occult sciences in Renaissance thought, and in July 1988 was awarded a MacArthur Fellowship.

Richard Taruskin is Professor of Music at the University of California, Berkeley. His performing activities have included choral conducting, notably with Cappella Nova in New York, which he founded in 1975, and playing the viola da gamba as a soloist and with the Aulos Ensemble. As a scholar he is best known for his work on fifteenth-century music, Russian opera in the nineteenth century, and Stravinsky, on whom he has recently completed a book. As a critic he has been actively engaged in the questions surrounding 'authenticity' for several years. He has been the recipient of the Alfred Einstein and Noah Greenberg Awards of the American Musicological Society, and the Dent Medal of the Royal Musical Association.

INTRODUCTION
Authenticity and Early Music: Some Issues and Questions

NICHOLAS KENYON

No change has more profoundly influenced the development of our music-making during the last two decades than the growth of the historical performance movement. The search for original methods and styles of performance has brought about a sea-change in our listening habits, and indeed in our approach to the whole question of repertory and tradition in classical music.

On the face of it, this is an odd state of affairs. We might expect the composition and performance of new music to carry forward the development of our cultural life, but the impetus seems to have shifted inexorably. I vividly remember a contemporary composer, in the course of an American sympo-sium on this subject a few years ago, giving as one of his objections to the 'authenticity' movement that it was 'the one musical activity these days which has the passion of the new . . . the latest step forward in authentic performance practice draws the sort of attention previously reserved for new music'. He concluded honestly: ' . . . and if you want to think there's some sour grapes there you're absolutely right'.

As far as I am concerned, as a listener and as a critic, the development of new performing styles for the music of the past has been perhaps the most stimulating part of concert-going and record-listening over the last couple of decades. New contem-porary music has continued to have its rich rewards, but they have been individual revelations within an unclear picture of myriad styles and jostling schools. A sense of continuity, a sense of advancement, has been more fruitfully provided by the rediscovery of old music, old instruments, and unfamiliar playing styles for them. The central question of the extent to which the authenticity movement represents a retreat from an engagement with the music of our own time is fully discussed in Robert Morgan's contribution to this symposium (Chapter 3). Why is old music more readily accessible to us now than it was in previous ages? Why has the single, developing tradition of

classical music broken down? Does this fact necessarily betoken
a state of cultural decay and collapse?

It is perhaps worth reminding ourselves in this introduction
just how rapid these changes have been in recent years. Howard
Mayer Brown's contribution (Chapter 2) fascinatingly charts
the growth of what has become known, rather misleadingly, as
the early music movement. Several strands interweave in the
story: an interest in old music itself, an interest in period
performing techniques, musicological work, instrument
building—a complex of scholarly and practical considerations
which together formed a bedrock for the movement's eventual
popular success. But for many years, indeed for most of this
century, these activities took place among a small coterie of
committed and enthusiastic converts to the cause. Of course,
some 'early music' had always maintained its popularity here:
the Elizabethan madrigals, nurtured by the choral groups of the
1920s, and the whole of the English church music tradition,
fostered by our cathedrals and larger churches. And some
important personalities whose work Mayer Brown surveys—
Dolmetsch, Landowska, Boulanger—made their presence felt
far beyond the specialist world. But there is a significant
difference between such occasional attention and the sudden
irruption of 'early music' into professional concert-giving and
on to the record turntable. Everyone's experience of when that
began to happen will be essentially autobiographical: to some
Noah Greenberg or Thomas Binkley, Julian Bream or Alfred
Deller, August Wenzinger, Gustav Leonhardt, or Frans Brüggen will represent the moment when things really began to
move. Will Crutchfield in his contribution (Chapter 1) identifies
some more recent trends in America. Howard Mayer Brown in
his chapter rightly shies away from any attempt to evaluate
these more recent phenomena, but some more detailed pointers
around this contemporary period are necessary (even though, as
Sir Walter Raleigh put it, 'whosoever, in writing a modern
history, shall follow truth too near the heels, it may haply strike
out his teeth').

The last two decades will serve as a rough and ready period
during which, in one personal perspective from England, early
music has acquired its huge popular following. For two very
different activities can be seen as achieving popular recognition

at almost exactly the same time around 1968: first the revival of forgotten repertories played on unfamiliar instruments, and second the performance of familiar repertories from the past in a radically different manner.

In 1968 the work of David Munrow's Early Music Consort of London was taking on an international dimension with its first tours and recordings, and over the next few years it succeeded in galvanizing audiences with its highly professionalized skills and invigorating performance style. Munrow had burst upon an unsuspecting world in May 1965, when he first assembled a Renaissance dance band to play Susato's *Danserye* at Birmingham University, and from then on his professional career, powered by driving enthusiasm and hard work, made remarkable strides. It is chronicled in the recordings he made for EMI—first of Morley and Susato, and then *Ecco la primavera* in 1969, *Music of the Crusades* in 1971, *The Triumphs of Maximilian I* in 1973, *The Art of Courtly Love*, and, as vocal music became more important to him, two major projects which appeared only after his death in 1976, *Music of the Gothic Era* and *The Art of the Netherlands*.

One has only to compare Munrow's performances of Machaut, for example, with more recent recordings by Gothic Voices, or his whole approach to the early medieval repertory with that of a group such as Sequentia, to see how quickly the field has developed and how precarious were some of its scholarly tenets. But—to state an obvious but important fact—it was not as purveyors of 'authentic performance' that the Consort won such a following among audiences. It was because they made music with a conviction and an enthusiasm that won people over; because their concerts were skilfully programmed, well prepared, professionally organized, and animated by Munrow's unique personal skills. Almost at a stroke, early music was removed from the realms of a specialist activity for which special pleading had to be made, and put in a forum where it could compete on equal terms with any kind of music-making. It would be fair to characterize it as an approach in which scholarly certainty came second to the performer's instinct— and given the repertory, that was probably inevitable. Christopher Hogwood, a founder-member of the Consort, said later of their work: 'There just wasn't enough evidence for all the things we were doing . . . It was just one invention on top of another all the time.' As the early music movement advanced into the public domain, immense areas of old music were being opened up again, but there was not perhaps quite enough information to go round. Of some other performances of medieval music, one felt tempted to quote Catherine Morland in Jane Austen's *Northanger Abbey*: 'I often think it odd that it should be so dull, for a great deal of it must be invention.'

In 1968, too, Nikolaus Harnoncourt made his first recording of Bach's B minor Mass. His Concentus Musicus of Vienna had already been active for over a decade: the Brandenburg Concertos and the Suites, as well as the St John Passion under Hans Gillesberger's direction, had already appeared. In Holland Gustav Leonhardt, Anner Bylsma, and Frans Brüggen were also making records for the same company, Telefunken, of smaller-scale repertory during the late 1950s and 1960s (very early on, Leonhardt had recorded the 'Agnus Dei' of the B minor Mass with the counter-tenor Alfred Deller and a small consort of baroque instruments). But it was the Harnoncourt Mass that made the most controversial impact, for it used not only 'original' instruments, but boys' voices in the choir and new approaches to phrasing, balance, and articulation. (It is of course ironic, and a comment on the whole 'authenticity' business, that most of its artefacts are in the extremely inauthentic form of recordings without audience which sound the same every time one plays them.)

Harnoncourt had written an important statement of his views as early as 1954 ('Zur Interpretation historischer Musik', an essay not published in book form until as late as 1982), but it was not until this recording that his principles became widely read in English. 'An interpretation must be attempted in which the entire romantic tradition of performance is ignored . . . Today we only want to accept the composition itself as a source, and present it as our own responsibility. The attempt must thus again be made today, with Bach's masterpieces in particular, to hear and perform them as if they had never been interpreted before, as though they had never been formed nor distorted.'

That is a magisterial statement of the approach which was to gain so much favour over the succeeding years. The argument which has swirled around this theory is one that is firmly nailed down by Richard Taruskin in Chapter 6: can a performance style really be reinvented from scratch? Is there any evidence that Harnoncourt and others did such a thing? Taruskin proceeds to question the idea of a historically 'authentic' style and demonstrates the continuity of modern performing styles in certain repertories. It is revealing to look back at the arguments which surrounded Harnoncourt's recording at the time, and to read again Paul Henry Lang's attack on it in *High Fidelity* magazine: 'All this music-making by the book is a bit pitiful . . . [Harnoncourt's] own musicology is altogether romantic in its effusiveness and lack of realism. All right, his strings carefully avoid all modern appurtenances: they have flat bridges and gut strings, they use light bows, and so forth, and for all I know their players may take a pinch of snuff during the pauses before the last chords (which, incidentally, are *not* in the book); but they also sound flat and have no guts'.

In fact, the success of this recording and of Harnoncourt's later work in this field was surely the result of the fact that, technically and interpretatively, his performances were very strong ones, convincing on their own terms—whether those in fact could be shown to be 'authentic' or not. Lang may well have been right about the romantic character of Harnoncourt's musicology, and he has been one of the few coherently outspoken critics of the movement, continuing to comment in the editorial columns of the *Musical Quarterly* and elsewhere. But he was quite wrong if he thought the public would not accept the results. As the movement gathered steam, audiences and record buyers (as with Munrow's success) responded instinctively to performances they enjoyed, and did not argue the finer points of faithfulness to the past. The same point could be made about Frans Brüggen's influential recorder playing and Leonhardt's similarly influential harpsichord playing: each had a strong sense of personal conviction behind it, and could either be strongly liked or strongly disliked—but the impetus was never purely historical.

Many of the performers in this field did not make wild claims for their activity: it was the disciples and the publicists who did that. Gustav Leonhardt, for example, wrote in the notes to his recording of the Brandenburg Concertos (one of those discussed by Richard Taruskin in Chapter 6): 'If one strives only to be authentic, it will never be convincing. If one is convincing, what is offered will leave an authentic impression.' Brüggen said in a throwaway remark that historical information could not account for more that 30–40 per cent of his performance style. Nevertheless, it quickly became clear to the record companies that the legend 'Performed on Authentic Instruments' was regarded as some sort of seal of Good Musical Housekeeping, and the implication of much of their activity was that the use of such instruments guaranteed or at least went some considerable way to ensuring an 'authentic' performance. Eventually we reached the absurd situation where the American company releasing the Academy of Ancient Music's recording of the Pachelbel Canon affixed a sticker to the disc proclaiming: 'Authentic Edition. The famous Kanon as Pachelbel heard it'. Those of us who had difficulty knowing what Pachelbel looked like, never mind what he heard like, had some problems with this.

There was no doubt at all that the basis of the work of the early ensembles in the field—Christopher Hogwood's Academy of Ancient Music, Trevor Pinnock's English Concert, Sigiswald Kuijken's Petite Bande—was the claim of historical faithfulness to the past. Hogwood, one of the most articulate writers and speakers on the subject, quoted Dr Johnson: 'Nothing shall be imposed . . . without notice of the alteration, nor shall conjecture be wantonly or unnecessarily indulged'; the implication was that performers should follow only the historical evidence, should withhold their own personalities, and not overlay what resulted with any present-day gloss. The Florilegium series of recordings claimed to present 'performances of music from the Renaissance to the Romantic periods on original instruments or authentic copies, based on the most recent research into the original texts, instrumentation and performing styles of each period'. (Pinnock, while always more sceptical of the idea of historical authenticity, believed firmly in the claims of old instruments as such, and in letting them create a performing style.)

The many questions raised by these declarations remained, on the whole, unasked. I think those of us who judged, sometimes fiercely, sometimes enthusiastically, the early products of the period-instrument revival on record and in concert did so on the basis of whether we liked the noise and not on whether the historical evidence used was either plausible, sufficient, or correctly interpreted. Many critics and musicians hated the noise and said so (I recall one writer suggesting that we needed a revival of period strings as much as we needed a revival of period dentistry), but they too were involved in what one might call gut reactions. For some of us, there were many revelations to be had from the timbres, textures, and balances of these performances; we displayed an enthusiasm which perhaps helped to build up an unhealthy mystique surrounding the use of old instruments. We certainly criticized old-instrument performances for their lack of artistry and sometimes their lack of competence, but this was perhaps overlooked. The whole movement was swept along in a wave of popular enthusiasm which was only aided and abetted by the occasional controversy. By the time Hogwood made best-selling recordings of Handel's *Water Music* and *Messiah*, performing both at the Proms in London in the late 1970s, the bandwagon was well and truly rolling and not much would stand in its way.

Looking back on it, this is strange. Those professional musicians—and there were many of them—who loathed the whole period-instrument movement did not actually dispute its claims to historical faithfulness. They disputed firstly its arrogance, and secondly its competence. A strong and detailed attack was not mounted, as it might have been, on the whole philosophical basis of the undertaking. Instead there was the implication that it was not very well done, or that it was absurd to argue that an 'authentic' approach was the only way—points with which it was easy to agree. Not surprisingly, many of the strongest objections came from those who had made the biggest contributions to the revival of baroque music on what were becoming known quaintly as 'modern' instruments. Most preferred word-of-mouth to the written denunciation, but one who was brave enough to express his reservations in print was the conductor and scholar Raymond Leppard, whose revivals of Monteverdi and Cavalli in his own editions had opened up the area of early baroque opera for modern audiences in much the same way as Munrow had opened up the Middle Ages.

In an article in *Keynote* magazine, New York, in October 1982 (subsequently adapted for the Glyndebourne Festival programme book of 1984), Leppard laid into those who claim 'that the actual playing of these specialised instruments is the only way for the music to be performed . . . It is then that we enter the world of cult and bigotry that is as offensive to the art of music as it is inhibiting and unattractive at a human level.' He did not argue against players taking up old playing techniques, but he did go so far as to assert that 'many of them who take this *droict chemin* do so because their road must, otherwise, be very stony'—a strong accusation of sheer unprofessionalism which was typical of many musicians' views on the subject. This changed as standards improved rapidly and the very notion of baroque strings as 'specialized instruments' now reads like a period remark. Indeed it is arguable that, just as the insights of the baroque performance style of Raymond Leppard and Neville Marriner in the 1950s and 1960s were gradually absorbed by other performing groups, so the same process is now happening with the Hogwood and Pinnock style of the 1970s.

The success of David Munrow on the one hand and of the original instrument players on the other had pushed into the limelight many smaller early music activities that might have remained of only specialist concern. In particular it gave a new high profile to the burgeoning company of instrument builders, whose work had been developing for very many years. Their harpsichords, lutes, viols, baroque-style violins and oboes, crumhorns, racketts, and shawms (not to mention the elusive cornamuse) now assumed a crucial and central role in bringing this music to the public. Early music instrument makers acquired new status and importance; instrument fairs became an integral part of several large early music festivals. And all the activity in studying and playing these instruments which had remained in the wings suddenly came to the centre of the stage. There had been specialist societies for the recorder since 1937, for the viola da gamba since 1948, for the lute since 1956, and so on. Nothing could have happened so quickly in the professional field had it not been for their quieter activities over the years.

In the field of Renaissance music, Anthony Rooley's ensemble the Consort of Musicke began to record for Florilegium, and it was a sign of the times that after one bold anthology, *Musicke of Sundrie Kindes* (1975), he was able to embark from 1976 on a complete recording of John Dowland's music, setting new standards for ensemble singing. Many other groups benefited from the high profile Rooley obtained for this area of work in both concerts and discussions—notably the 1977 conference 'The Future of Early Music in Britain', a watershed in the post-Munrow period—and small specialist groups proliferated, devoting themselves to particular areas of music-making: the Medieval Ensemble of London with fourteenth-century French music, L'École d'Orphée with the French baroque, and so on. The York Early Music Week flourished in the North of England.

But it was in the field of baroque and then classical music that activity really accelerated: over a number of years Roger Norrington explored major choral works—Bach's St Matthew Passion (1975), the St John Passion (1977), Handel's *Messiah* (1978), and others—in performances that made ever-increasing use of the rapidly increasing arsenal of period-instrument players, wedded to the stalwart and ever-adaptable skills of English singers, many of them products of choir schools or Oxford and Cambridge colleges. Andrew Parrott's Taverner Choir and Players gave exploratory accounts of pieces from Machaut's *Messe de Notre Dame* to Bach's B minor Mass—though they did not begin to record them, and thus achieve an international reputation, until some years later. As the skills of period-instrument players became greater, so conductors who had been previously sceptical were converted: after 1976, John Eliot Gardiner formed the English Baroque Soloists which has since been one of the most active of these ensembles.

Probably in each centre of the early music revival there was a similar ferment of activity: a properly detailed survey remains to be written. Will Crutchfield's introductory chapter here gives a feeling of the advancing tide in New York; when I was there several years ago I encountered spectacular achievements in the earlier repertory: Alexander Blachly's Pomerium Musices in Dufay, John Blackley's Schola Antiqua in plainchant, and Richard Taruskin's Cappella Nova in Renaissance choral music. Not all these groups are now active, and others have succeeded them. In the baroque field, Albert Fuller's dedicated work with Aston Magna and the growth of groups such as the Aulos Ensemble, Banchetto Musicale in Boston, and the Smithsonian

Players in Washington gave America some distinguished performances, but Europe continued to make the running, at least until the briefly brilliant Boston Early Music Festival Orchestra assembled all the best American East Coast players between 1985 and 1987.

One could go on cataloguing the developments endlessly, but a general point needs to be made in this essentially personal perspective. It is a commercial one: as the old-instrument bands became big business, the large record companies' interest in what we have characterized as the Munrow strand—the revival of forgotten repertories—tended to evaporate, and only small record companies, or broadcasting organizations such as the BBC in London and WDR in Cologne continued to plough neglected furrows. This has been one of the most unfortunate by-products of early music's recent success. Pressure began to come from the record companies and concert promoters: it was far easier to sell another *Water Music* or another Mozart symphony with the *frisson* of the period-instrument label than to work away at Biber and Schmelzer (of whom Harnoncourt's group had made some of their most impressive records). Controversy was welcome too, and when as in the case of Joshua Rifkin's recording of Bach's B minor Mass (1981) a well-known masterpiece could be allied to a full-scale musicological dust-up over the basis of his performance, so much the better. 'First Recording in the Original Version', reads the sleeve of that record: the selling points remained unchanged.

It is partly those commercial considerations, then, which have stimulated the move forward into classical and romantic music, which is currently absorbing so much attention. Both the players and the audiences, one suspects, were ready for the challenge, but, more importantly, the record companies have given their enthusiastic support because the composers' names involved are ones that every record purchaser knows. Again it was Christopher Hogwood's Academy of Ancient Music which made the running with its complete Mozart symphony cycle (Florilegium, from 1979), and whatever the reservations about its musical achievements, it was an enormous popular success which created a new market for classical music on period instruments. Other ideas were waiting in the wings for their time to come: the early piano was ready, for example, after years of work by players and makers to which little public attention had been paid, to make its reappearance as a viable concert instrument in the hands of players such as Malcolm Bilson and Melvyn Tan. In the wake of this advancing chronology the Beethoven symphonies have followed, and Berlioz was explored in a Norrington weekend in London in March 1988, which included successful performances of both the *Symphonie fantastique* and *Romeo and Juliet* using not only period instruments but adapted 'period' seating plans for orchestra and chorus. The excitement of the new, to which I referred at the start of this introduction, is found in breaking the next chronological barrier. Finally, period instruments are now reaching far within the musical Establishment: from 1989 Glyndebourne Festival Opera will be using an old–instrument band (the Orchestra of the Age of Enlightenment) for some of its Mozart performances at the insistence of the conductor Simon Rattle. The future is wide open.

All this chronological advance has had the incidental effect of destroying one part of the historically orientated performer's argument that there was a chronological limit to the process of rediscovery because for later music there was a continuous performing tradition. (This was an argument used by Harnoncourt in that first introduction to the B minor Mass recording in 1968; for him at that time there was no need to re-imagine Beethoven because continuity of performance ensured that 'the traditional interpretation that has arisen is sure to have a high degree of authenticity'.) This change has been rapid: Robert Morgan in Chapter 3 of this book quotes Howard Mayer Brown's article on performing practice published in 1980 in *The New Grove*. In the section 'after 1750' this claims:

Continuity of tradition. The study of performing practice in music since 1750 is fundamentally different from the study of earlier performing practice . . . there is no 'lost tradition' separating the modern performer from the music of Haydn, Mozart and their successors.

In the early 1970s, this was an orthodoxy. But by the time of the appearance in 1984 of *The New Grove Dictionary of Musical Instruments*, this section had been subtly and subversively revised by Robert Winter. It now read:

Apparent continuity of tradition. Superficially, there is a fundamental difference between the study of performing practice before 1750 and the study of it after that date . . . But on closer examination neither the assumption of an unbroken performing history nor the corollary of an unbroken performing tradition stands up . . .

So the process of rediscovering a historical approach has now no time limits, though Robert Morgan expresses here his suspicions about that change. Perhaps surprisingly, the principle of historically orientated performance styles has been widely accepted. Conductors such as Harnoncourt, Hogwood, and Norrington are now widely employed by conventional orchestras who wish to acquire some of the received wisdom in this area. Cross-fertilization is extensive. But ironically, at the same time that the cause of period-performance styles appears to have been largely won in the musical world, increasingly loud questions have begun to be asked about the aims and the means of the 'authentic' approach from within its own ranks. It is those questions which form the thinking behind this book.

It was always naïve to assume that a supposedly historical faithful manner of performance *guaranteed* anything at all about the artistry of the end result. But there was certainly in some minds an assumption that an approach which respected the composer's intentions and attempted to re-create the sound-world which he had in mind was more likely to result in a 'good' performance than one which did not. It has taken a long time to dispose of the fallacy behind this reasoning, and I will not anticipate here the arguments with which Richard Taruskin in Chapter 6 attempts so to do. But it may be useful to indicate some of the ways in which this symposium—which is not a random group of essays but was planned carefully as a set of interlocking, though not always congruent, pieces—raises recurring themes about the nature of 'authenticity'. This will risk over-simplifying some complex arguments, but at least the problems are clear. Some of them were formulated in the questions I asked authors in gathering the articles for *Early Music*'s 'The Limits of Authenticity' in 1983.

Is the use of period instruments in re-creating the music of the past really a significant factor compared with musical understanding, cultural and social context, acoustical conditions, concert-giving situations?

Can the composer expect any influence over how his music is performed after he has written it, and is there any moral obligation on us to fulfil his original intentions? If so, how can these be discerned and what kind of evidence is relevant?

Are we more likely to understand a composer's piece of music by restricting ourselves to the means he had available when he wrote it, or does such a restriction inhibit our full expression of the piece?

What is the relation between a performer's and a scholar's work in this area? How can the scholar reconcile the need for an open verdict with the performer's need to make a practical decision; for the performer, what happens at the moment when the cautious conclusions of musicological enquiry have to be turned into action?

Over the whole discussion hangs the spectre of Ranke's stirring phrase in the 1830s about the purpose of historical investigation: *wie es eigentlich gewesen*—simply to show how it really was. The notion that one could, simply or otherwise, show how the past really was, has come in for some battering from historians in recent decades. We cannot make contact with the past, we cannot reconstitute the past, nor can we pin it down as an objective reality. It must exist only through our eyes— which is not to imply, as some historians such as Collingwood have done, a stance of total subjectivity, but to argue that there is a continuing dialogue between past and present, between subject and object, in a way that makes it impossible to separate the two.

This whole matter has been elegantly and wittily discussed by E. H. Carr in his 1961 Trevelyan Lectures at Cambridge, subsequently printed as *What is History?*. The choice of what is a historical fact depends on the historian's point of view and is thus essentially a matter of interpretation. A historian may have more or less regard for the value of his evidence, but the evidence is inextricably bound in with the historian's selection and presentation of it. Now the claim of a musician to reconstruct, for example, the essentials of a past playing technique for a baroque sonata looks pretty shady in this context. What is the nature of the evidence? Treatises? How do we interpret the content of a treatise or assess its importance at the time it was written? Was it typical of its time? Or a reaction

to some abuse of the time? Against what background of
performance style was it written? Without knowing most of
these things, we are left with the remark of Lytton Strachey that
the first requisite in these circumstances is ignorance: 'ignorance
which simplifies and clarifies, which selects or omits'. Otherwise few performing decisions would ever be made.

If the facts of history refuse to be pinned down, how much
more so a piece of music which is, of its essence, utterly
unfactual. Even a composer does not give a definitive form to a
piece, however precisely he may realize it in notational language
(unless he creates it as an electronic piece, and then conditions of
'performance' can vary). Once composers have written their
music, they 'let go' of it, and it is up to posterity to do what it
wants with it. But is posterity likely to get more out of it if it
respects what the composer originally thought of doing with it?
This central problem of the composer's intention, which
underlies so much argument about authentic performance
practice, is dealt with fully in Philip Brett's chapter. His point of
view is that of the editor, who must transmit his understanding
of a piece to the prospective performer. The philosophical basis
of this handing-down of a text is one of Brett's central concerns,
and it is illuminated by both musical and literary examples. In
that process of transmission are all the problems of historical
discrimination and understanding of which Carr wrote. It
certainly would be an arrogance on the part of a performer to
claim to overleap that process and claim that he had suddenly
arrived at an 'original' understanding of the piece. Will
Crutchfield here makes the strongest claim for the performer's
autonomy in this area. We might all be said to be searching—
and as Mayer Brown and Taruskin both argue from very
different points of view, older, pre-authentic performers seem
to have been no less concerned with claiming a closeness to the
composer's vision—but there is certainly no 'thing' at the end of
the rainbow which can be found.

The problem of historical context is one that has preoccupied
many musicologists over the last couple of decades, and is a
complex matter. Articles by Joseph Kerman, Leo Treitler, and
Carl Dahlhaus, cited by Philip Brett, are required reading in this
area; the question boils down to whether pieces of music are
'significant in some transhistorical way, or [whether they] can

be approached only as products of their context'. Gary Tomlinson in his chapter develops themes from his article on contextual scholarly work 'The Web of Culture: A Context for Musicology' in *Nineteenth-Century Music,* April 1984, and comes up with a startling conclusion. He suggests that performance is not the most appropriate way of achieving or communicating those 'authentic meanings' that a scholar discovers in a piece of music. The meaning of a piece involves factors other than the piece itself; therefore it cannot be fully communicated by a performance. For a performer this is perhaps a discouraging point of view, but it is one that must be addressed. The question of how to incorporate contextual understanding into a perfor- mance is also one faced by Philip Brett, since it involves the problem that the composer's 'original intention' was formed within a context that we now cannot fully re-create.

One central problem here has been the moral imperativeness of the need to respect the composer's intention. This was a stance attacked by Nicholas Temperley in his contribution to the *Early Music* symposium: 'I do not recognize that the mode of performance that suited the composer is necessarily the best for all time.' He cited the transformation of Handel's *Messiah* into *The Messiah* of the Victorian age. 'Others can build on what one has created, even if they change its meaning in the process.' Some musicians have different perspectives: I once asked the pianist Jorge Bolet how he could justify changing passages in Chopin and he said that he did it because Chopin was concerned with the piece only for a few months, but he had played it for years and thought he knew more about what worked and what did not. The late Hans Keller argued characteristically in *Early Music* (November 1984) that our understanding of Beethoven was far greater than that of his contemporaries: 'as far as the authentic evidence at our disposal goes, there wasn't a single musician in Beethoven's lifetime, however mature, who had the remotest understanding of these masterpieces [the late string quartets] . . . We understand a past genius's music better than they did—*a priori,* we are the more authentic players of it.'

The relationship there between understanding and authen- ticity is a crucial one, and it comes down to the unavoidable mediation of the performer. Music operates through perfor- mances, and we cannot abstract ourselves from that process.

(For more on the notion of 'the work itself', and of what that consists, see Richard Taruskin's review of period-instrument recordings of Beethoven symphonies, in *Opus* magazine, October 1987.) Even if you choose to do as little as possible you make an interpretative decision. Eric van Tassel, reviewing a volume of Christopher Hogwood's Mozart symphony cycle in *Early Music* (February 1984), made the remarkable observation that 'a performance not merely "under-interpreted" but un-interpreted offers potentially an experience of unequalled authenticity, using that word in a sense as much existential as musicological'. He was strongly criticized for that statement by, among others, Malcolm Bilson, but one suspects that it accurately represented what Hogwood was trying to achieve.

That notion now seems to have been scotched: Beethoven was in any case likely to call into question any notion that under-interpretation could be musically effective. But the problem of forming the performer's understanding—which is the only channel through which an 'authentic' interpretation can possibly emerge—has not been solved. When Taruskin wrote positively in his contribution to 'The Limits of Authenticity' that the special task of performers in this area was 'to foster an approach to performance that is founded to an unprecedented degree on personal conviction and on individual response to individual pieces', that was ignored in the rush to denounce his claim that the search for historical authenticity was in many ways a spurious pursuit. How convincingly, to borrow Will Crutchfield's telling phrase, can a historical performer assume a floppy-disc mentality in which various style complexes stand ready for use in the brain? How does a conventionally trained performer re-form his imagination in the light of recent research?

Many would answer: precisely through the use of old instruments and through renouncing expressive possibilities which are foreign to them. It may be wrong to assume that a restriction of stylistic possibilities in performance is actually a limitation: it can in fact free the performer to operate without any restraint at all within a given framework (compare playing Mozart on a Steinway piano and Mozart on a Walter). In his chapter in this volume Richard Taruskin acknowledges the 'improvement and refreshment' of personal choice which has been brought about by 'old instruments, historical treatises and all the rest'. He writes of the 'value of the old instruments in freeing minds and hands to experience old music newly'. This is to value them for the discontinuity they bring with traditional performing practices, but it is arguable that this relegates to incidental status the quite extraordinary developments which these resources have stimulated in our current performance styles (whether or not these are truly historical). It is easy to agree that instruments and treatises are no guarantee of historical faithfulness, but surely their effect has been far deeper and far more radical in the hands of good performers than some are now prepared to admit.

There had to be a swing of the pendulum. There had, on the one hand, to be a period when performers, trying to come to terms with a new approach, emptied themselves to a self-negating extent of their own tastes and prejudices, and tried to let the historical materials simply work on them. And that was a process more easily tried with a totally unfamiliar instrument under one's fingers. 'Just letting it happen' in musical terms was unattainable in theory and probably undesirable in practice, but it was an inevitable stage in the attempt to escape the expressive reflexes with which one had been brought up. So now, on the other hand, the pendulum has swung back and a strong personal taste is now accepted; expressive instincts can now be unleashed without any danger of their being proved unhistorical. Perhaps it has already swung too far: only in the last year have we been able to hear period-instrument Mozart performances in neo-Furtwängler style or neo-Toscanini style, with voluptuous rhythmic rubati or driven like a rhythmic bulldozer, played with Schumann's 'Grecian lightness and grace' or Abert's demonic fury. Where does this leave the historical faithfulness of authentic performance style? Well, the choice is ours, as indeed it has been all along. We are twentieth-century music-ians, performing for a twentieth-century audience, but the conviction we seek—perhaps because of the insecurity so tellingly described here by Robert Morgan—is one that can be 'authenticated' not just by our own limited experiences, but also, and valuably, by the evidence of the past. Many performers—I have heard this view expressed recently by players as diverse as Gustav Leonhardt and Reinhard Goebel—

do wish to attempt to recapture the insights of a past age in as uncompromising and as precise a manner as possible, so that the music can speak with its own special eloquence to today's audiences. Within the framework of this continuing dialogue between past and present, it is surely possible to agree with Philip Brett's conclusion that when a strong intuitive feeling for the music can again be reflected 'without self-consciousness, then the early music movement will have achieved maturity, and authenticity will no longer be an issue'.

I

FASHION, CONVICTION, AND PERFORMANCE STYLE IN AN AGE OF REVIVALS

WILL CRUTCHFIELD

It is startling to note how far the 'authentic performance' movement, once so insular and gentle of cast, has come to resemble a juggernaut, a steamroller, a conquering army. As record companies skim the cream of their LP catalogues for transfer to compact disc, they now choose original-instrument performances by about two to one over those on modern instruments for their Handel, Bach, and Vivaldi. Christopher Hogwood sells more records than Luciano Pavarotti. (Mind you, he has to spend vastly more time in the studios to produce all those records, and no doubt the profits from them are smaller, but he does sell more.) The record clubs that advertise in general-circulation magazines still offer Ormandy and the Philadelphia or Solti and the Chicago for their Tchaikovsky, but for the Brandenburg Concertos or *Messiah*, it's Pinnock and the English Concert, Hogwood and the Academy of Ancient Music, Harnoncourt or Hans-Martin Linde. There are very few modern-instrument recordings of baroque on those lists.

Nor is it by any means a phenomenon whose hard-currency manifestations are limited to recordings. 'Mozart on Original Instruments' ranks up there with Alicia de Larrocha and Pinchas Zukerman among the strongest sellers for the Mostly Mozart Festival in New York—even though they present it in a hall far too big for the instruments to be heard properly. Most shoestring opera groups in Manhattan put on an esoteric work and are happy if they draw an audience in triple figures for one performance; Concert Royal puts on baroque-style stagings and has to turn people away for five-performance runs. The Baltimore Symphony—a major, conservative orchestra in the most traditional role of providing a plush culture product to an old Eastern city—is embarking on a Beethoven cycle using modern instruments for the most part, but with an intensive study of classical bowing techniques, articulations, and the like, and with Beethoven's controversial metronome marks observed. They are trying to head off the enemy at the pass: more than one orchestra has begun to contemplate what the future might be like if each big city shared its orchestral life between two major ensembles—and the Beethoven symphonies belonged to the other one.

Most seriously, historically informed performance has captured the spotlight of critical and scholarly discussion. The issues posed by the Rifkin, Parrott, and Gardiner versions of Bach's B minor Mass, and of the Norrington and Hogwood versions of Beethoven's symphonies, are discussed at length and in detail in numerous journals; when Handel's *Messiah* is recorded, as it recently has been, by Sir Georg Solti and Sir Colin Davis, the level of discussion is simply not comparable; these projects are not received as musical events of serious interest.

All this wakens feelings raging from curiosity through distrust to open hostility in what we call 'traditional' musicians. Their anxiety is eminently well justified. No matter how reticent we are about asserting the radical implications of historically informed performance, these folks are not naïve and the implications are felt. They know it will not stop with Beethoven any more than it stopped with Bach ten years ago. The movement not only hits them in the pocketbook, but questions the very basis of their art. It is as though we told a generation of scientists that their Ph.D.s were based on a now discredited body of theory—say, Ptolemaic astronomy—and now, sorry, the degrees are no good. Worse: it is as though we are told Ptolemy had been right after all. When the opera director Frank Corsaro feels some dramatic need has been thwarted by dogmatic application of something or other from the musicological rulebook, he has a word for it: 'We got gesellschafted.' I have seen otherwise reasonable professional pianists become red with anger in an ostensibly unprovoking situation as they mock the tinkly, puny sounds they think they hear from the predecessors of their sleek modern instruments. Conductors are especially threatened because no matter how much they are told that these strange new performance practices will be worked out in collaboration with the maestro, they know or sense that it all points to a time when the conductor, or pre-conductor, was subject to the will of the soloist. A mezzo-soprano interested in matters of performance practice recently wrote to me about an incident when she added a few passing elaborations to 'Voi che sapete' at a rehearsal. The distinguished conductor stopped the orchestra and enquired, 'Who is the great composer here, you or Mozart?' At this point we reach the politics of confrontation.

The high temperature of the reaction against historically informed performance is intensified by the fact that the 'traditional' performance community is at the moment defending itself from a position of weakness. No complaint has been heard more often in recent years than that there is a dearth of really interesting new violinists, pianists, singers, and conductors for the standard repertory. The complaint is valid. In the general run of sober young conservatory graduates and hot (sober) young competition winners whose débuts I regularly hear in New York, cautious correctness is the rule. In the work of the mid-career touring soloists, a deadly sense of get-the-job-done often compounds the lack of a purposeful musical message. Of course there are exceptions; the rule, though, is discouraging.

This brings us to the questions of performing *style*, and how it is formed—territory a little less well trod and more troublesome than that of original instruments. Take, for a starting-point, the Beethoven symphonies recently recorded by Christopher Hogwood on period instruments. There are differences, but in questions like what is a phrase, what does tempo mean, where is the symphony going, Hogwood is much closer to Karajan than he is to, say, Artur Nikisch, who was born in 1855 and recorded Beethoven's Fifth in 1913. How is one to assess the degrees of 'authenticity' these performances possess? Have we been getting progressively *more* authentic—Karajan and Hogwood alike—over the course of the century? If so, then why do we feel as though the authenticity movement is a revolution? Or do we have a style related in some way to the rationalist composers and strict notation of our day—a style that Hogwood and his players retain even with the original instruments in front of them?

The background to these questions lies in a familiar strand of musical history, dating roughly from the beginning of the nineteenth century: the historicization of the repertory and the alienation of musicians and audiences from contemporary music. The trend towards the increased individualization of each musical work which inclined the public to hold on to particular favourites instead of discarding them with each passing generation, joined hands with the trend to increased chromaticism and complexity, which disinclined the public towards quick acceptance of the new. The upshot is a snowballing accumulation of masterpieces from the past and a swelling audience of music-lovers unwilling to follow the composers of their own times: a vast public for old music only.

What has this got to do with performance style? Two things, which are everything. First, since within this musical community that is primarily interested in old music there still exists some urge towards novelty, we have entered an age of revivals. The twentieth century, and especially the second half of it, has revived more forgotten music of the past than any other era; we have actively attempted, and for the most part the attempt has been successful, to define a repertory in which the music of any generation is equally available—not just the B minor masses and works of that stature, but the whole run of music. The idea of historically informed performance could hardly have arisen without this huge infusion of music from the past, which prompted questions. Second, by the fact of our revivalist orientation, we have strained—perhaps broken, and certainly weakened—the link that used to exist between the compositional style and the performing style of a thriving musical culture. The nature of this link is difficult even to understand today, but if you were an Italian singer in 1888, you did not think of singing Rossini style for Rossini and Mozart style for Mozart and Verdi style for Verdi. You just *sang*. The way you sang—how you felt a crescendo, where you would instinctively accelerate, where you would feel the need to make an ornament, what a good pianissimo note sounded like to you—would have been in the style of the cultural situation of 1888, a style that developed in symbiosis with the middle and late operas of Verdi, along with the secondary composers such as Ponchielli who were active at the time. Rossini you would have sung only in edited, abridged versions; Mozart, except for that great late

Romantic tragedy *Don Giovanni*, you would most likely not have sung at all. The concept did not yet exist of different style-complexes that could be stuck into the heads of performers like a floppy disc into a word processor depending on what program was desired that evening. The great benefit of this close, narrow correspondence between contemporary composition and performing style—as we can still observe it in popular music, on historic recordings, in a very few elder statesmen among today's artists, and in specialists centring their work in the music of today—is that the performer can be so confident in the basic grammar and syntax of his stylistic language that true improvisation, true spontaneity of utterance, becomes possible within it. If the thriving triangular relationship between composers, performers, and the public had not broken down, historically informed performance would be neither likely nor desirable today.

That may seem to put the endeavour on a pessimistic basis. I hope that looking at it from this perspective can instead point in directions that are at least partly optimistic. What, after all, is authenticity in performance? From what is it derived? The idea of an authentic or authoritative performance is much older than the movement we now associate with it, and the term has had various meanings. It was once used in the sense we now reserve for idiomatic: if you wanted to hear authentic Lehár you had to go to Vienna. At other times, as in Toscanini's heyday, it meant a realization of the composer's intentions, a concept that was understood not historically but ideally: progress in musical performance was a motion *away* from the style of the composer's period towards the ultimate goal of authenticity, and Toscanini was the embodiment of authentic Beethoven.

It is fun to skim through the *Oxford English Dictionary*'s multiple definitions of authenticity and the venerable citations given for each. Another 'authentic' idea associated with Toscanini is that of fidelity to the score, and the *OED* has just the thing for it: John Wyclif, who defied the doctrine of transubstantiation much as Toscanini defied the German mystical conductors and their implied claims of a spiritual understanding that transcended the printed page, wrote in 1382 that 'no goostli vnderstondyng is autentik, no but it be groundid in the text opynli'. This is one of the strongest ideas in late twentieth-century musicological thought; the thrust of it (though this is an over-simplification from which some textual scholars would disassociate themselves) is that a musical performance is an inevitably imperfect approximation of a fixed, though unknowable, ideal embodied in the score (or lying behind it in the composer's thought). It is important to realize that there is no inherent logic in this. It is just as reasonable to conceive of the text as an inevitably imperfect approximation of an *unfixed* ideal, knowable only and instantly in the moment of realization, embodied in the act of music itself—in each individual performance. The first, conventional conception assumes that the composers imagined the music they wrote in all its elements, details, and nuances, but either failed to write all of these down or consciously, as part of the compositional plan, left some of them open to the performer's choice. It also assumes that only composers have the right to thoughts about those details, or in any event that their thoughts necessarily supersede anyone else's. This conception is lent seeming credibility by a greater specificity in the notation of details as composers gradually claimed ground that had once been the performer's.

Neither of the two assumptions is susceptible of proof or disproof, but both are suspect because performances that proceed from them are not necessarily perceived by musical listeners as attaining to greater authenticity because of having done so. The point here is not to reopen the perennial debate about composers' intentions versus performers' liberties, but to refine the idea of authentic performance. The authenticity of a text is to be assessed in terms of the sources of the text; the authenticity of a performance is to be understood in terms of the sources of the performance: and these lie within the person who is performing. They are, with due respect to Wyclif, 'goostli', of the spirit.

This authenticity is what the standee at the opera means when he says he has heard 'the real thing', 'the genuine article'. It is the *Ausstrahlung* of the performer; it joins hands with the genius of the composer and in the greatest performances seems to merge so that we feel music and musician are one, yet it is distinct. The Irish theologian William Fitzgerald supplied *Oxford* with the right citation for this: 'That is called Authentic, which is sufficient unto itself, which commends, sustains, proves itself, and hath credit and authority from itself.'

The performers of the early music movement I have hardly mentioned thus far. Many of them embrace in large measure the intention-of-composer idea of authenticity, augmenting it with the notion that the conventions the composer was accustomed to, even though it never occurred to him to specify them, ought to be present as well in authentic performance: timbre, articulation, ornamentation, tempo, and dynamics. This gives rise to the museum model, the precise reconstruction of sounds as near as possible to those heard by the composer.

But we must also keep in view the third idea. One of the unthought-of things the great composers assumed, wanted, and needed was the conviction and passion of great performers. Or, in works other than heaven-storming, the grace, confidence, and stylish freedom of cultivated amateurs. These cannot be reclaimed directly from the treatises nor extrapolated from critical editions. Yet if they are lacking in a scholarly perfor-mance, 'mainstream' musicians will attack it as arid and purposeless. The idea of personal communication between a performer and composer which transcends anything learnt in a book or a treatise is a tricky one, but it must be faced.

The original-instrument players, the authentic-minded per-formers, can go in either of two directions on this question of purpose. If we resurrect historical information on performing style simply to settle on 'correct' ways of playing, to promul-gate and refine rules, to settle questions (the *OED* found Naunton claiming in 1630 that 'we have an authentique Rule to decide the doubt')—if we seek nothing more than to write dozens more programs for the floppy discs we insert in students' brains—then it would be better if we had never started. If instead we seek an immersion in the disciplines of the past because we desire the benefits that both immersion and discipline bring—because we aspire to the freedom and power that can be gained through purposeful accomplishment—then historically informed performance may enable some of our performers to create anew for themselves the life-giving musical culture that swarmed around musicians in healthier times without their having to think about it. This is not a prediction but a hope: the hope is underlined by the sheer aliveness, the interest and passion, of the best of our authentic-instrument, period-style performers. The crucial challenge is to keep that aliveness in mind as the goal; though it can be approached only indirectly, it is more important than the correctness. History is its own reward, and accurate research into past performing styles is a wonderful pursuit. But *for performers* its value lies only in the extent to which it can participate in the quest for aliveness.

The historically informed performance movement poses radical questions for education and concert life, for the specialization of musicians, for our way of looking at the past and the present. My purpose here is not to prove the validity of any one set of answers, nor even to explore them beyond the generalized implications of what I have already said. Rather, I want to assert the centrality of the question. Authenticity implies authority, and ultimately an author. The author of a performance—of a bow stroke, a crescendo, an impulse, a radiant act of absorption—is the performer, with whose condition we must be concerned if authenticity is what we're after.

PEDANTRY OR LIBERATION?
A Sketch of the Historical Performance Movement

HOWARD MAYER BROWN

One central question about 'authentic' performance of early music can be formulated very simply: should we play music in the way the composer intended it, or at the very least in a way his contemporaries could have heard it (bearing in mind that these are not always the same thing)? A whole host of subsidiary questions immediately come to mind. How do we know what the composer intended? How fixed were his intentions? However fixed they were, how closely should we feel obliged to follow them? How should we deal with those elements which the composer himself would have taken to be variable? And how should we deal with those aspects of performance that are not documented (and in many cases not documentable)?

Even if it could be shown that authenticity is the highest ideal to which we can aspire, we cannot reproduce every aspect of past performance, and most musicians probably have no real desire to do so. We know too little about a number of the variables that went into making particular performances: the precise character of the available instruments at a particular time and place, the particular pitch level the musicians used, the vocal technique of a particular set of singers, the kinds of strings or reeds, the precise tempos, and so on. In any case, performers can scarcely buy and learn to play a new instrument for every composition they present in public. And even if we did know all the myriad details about a particular set of performances, the venue and the reasons for performing music in the late twentieth century will almost certainly be different from those prevailing in earlier times. Which compromises are tolerable, and which not, will clearly always be an area where musicians will disagree.

Moreover, performing styles and techniques change rapidly, as we can all now easily hear on recordings made in the course of the present century.[1] The sound of a particular symphony orchestra, for example, evolves and may be quite different from one decade to the next. Unwritten conventions of instrumental playing and even the vocal techniques of the best singers at the beginning of this century differed radically from what is considered ideal today. Technological changes (such as using wire strings on violins) have transformed, though not necess-arily improved, the sound of many kinds of instruments. And recordings, such as those by Igor Stravinsky of the same works conducted at various times in his life, should teach us to be cautious about accepting at face value the strictures concerning fixed intentions of even the most articulate and demanding of composers.[2] In short, musicians in the twentieth century can be shown to have changed their styles of performance frequently. There is no reason to suppose that musical life was ever any different. Moreover, the irrational force of fashion has played as influential a role in the performance of early music in our own time as it has in the performance of the symphonic or operatic repertory.

Some repertories can scarcely be played at all in a convincing way unless musicians use techniques or instruments different from those in current use. Performers in these areas have no choice at all about whether or not to try to revive old instruments and old styles and techniques of playing and singing. Anyone dedicated to the proposal that the music of the thirteenth, fourteenth, and fifteenth centuries merits revival in performance, for example, is virtually forced to take a position

[1] For an evaluation of orchestral recordings from 1920 on, see Robert Philip, 'Some Changes in Style of Orchestral Playing 1920–1950 as Shown by Gramophone Recordings', Ph.D. diss. (Cambridge University, 1974); Philip, 'The Recordings of Edward Elgar (1857–1934)', *Early Music*, 12 (1984), 481–9; and Philip, 'Performance Practice 1900–1940', in Stanley Sadie and Howard Mayer Brown (eds.), *A Handbook of Performance Practice* (forthcoming). For a brief but provocative discussion of the usefulness of recording in studying vocal techniques of the past, see Robert Donington, *A Performer's Guide to Baroque Music* (London, 1973), 58–64. See also Will Crutchfield, 'Vocal Ornamentation in Verdi: The Phonographic Evidence', *Nineteenth-Century Music*, 7 (1983), 3–54, and Crutchfield, 'Brahms by Those Who Knew Him', *Opus*, 2 (1986), 12–21.

[2] For a bibliography of Stravinsky's recordings, see David Hamilton, 'Igor Stravinsky: A Discography of the Composer's Performances', in Benjamin Boretz and Edward T. Cone (eds.), *Perspectives on Schoenberg and Stravinsky* (Princeton, NJ, 1968; 2nd edn., New York, 1972), 268–84.

on the question of authenticity, since it is clear that such music can hardly be played effectively on modern instruments, or sung to good effect using the sort of vocal technique appropriate for twentieth-century opera-houses. Machaut's music can barely be understood without some attempt to use styles and techniques of performance different from those in current use. In the case of medieval music, it is actually easier and certainly more logical to try to find out how the music was performed at that time rather than attempting some sort of translation of very old sounds into modern terms. However, problems immediately arise because the evidence used for documenting medieval performance practice is almost all highly ambiguous and any attempt to duplicate precisely the original performing conditions will inevitably fail for lack of secure information and because of the vast cultural differences between medieval society and our own.

Less obviously, some repertories of much later music will inevitably be lost to us unless we revive the instruments for which they were originally conceived. A particular case is that of the music written in France during the seventeenth and eighteenth centuries—by Lully, Rameau, Couperin, Marin Marais, Forqueray, and others—in which nuances of sonority and a very particular balance among instruments play an essential role in the character of the works. But many other repertories as well from after 1600 seem by their nature to demand some attempt at reconstructing the precise sounds their composers imagined.

It would be fascinating, and perhaps even instructive, to hear symphonies by Schumann, Brahms, Bruckner and Mahler as their contemporaries heard them, but that is a long way from saying that from now on we should only hear such music in period-style performances. To argue that all music should be performed as close to the way the composer conceived it as possible means that we should not tolerate a performance of a Mahler symphony, unless it is played with Viennese winds, extensive use of portamento string playing, and with precisely the size and dimensions of orchestra that Mahler conducted. Surely, most of us would consider such restrictions as unacceptable pedantry, comparable to that of a friend of mine who rejected Peter Maxwell Davies's opera *Taverner* because the

stage band used baroque rather than Renaissance violas da
gamba. And if we took that attitude, what then would become
of our great symphony orchestras? Indeed, if we had so radical a
view of authenticity, we could well ask what should be the
proper repertory for the Chicago Symphony, born almost at the
end of the symphonic age? The truth—although it may seem
controversial to say so now—is that it is more acceptable to play
Bach's music on modern instruments than Rameau's, for it can
be argued that authentic sonorities and old playing techniques
are less important in the one than in the other, and that therefore
the essential nature of Bach's music can emerge in a performance that translates the original into modern terms. In short, it
is possible to defend what might be described as a woolly-
headed liberal approach to the question of repertory: we may
well be enlightened in unexpected ways by performances on
original instruments of much music written in the late eighteenth and nineteenth centuries, and we should keep an open
mind about the interest and importance of such performances.
But at the same time we should encourage rather than
discourage our major cultural institutions—symphony orchestras and opera companies—to broaden their repertories even
though such organizations may perform this music in 'inauthentic' ways. This is a more positive approach than that of declaring
off-limits to any but the specialists more and more of our
musical heritage.

We have all surely exaggerated the extent to which musicians
before the late nineteenth century performed and studied only
the music of their own time. The concept of 'early music'—an
interest and involvement with the music of the past—has been
with us for a long time. Most of the manuscripts containing the
songs of the troubadours, for example, were copied out long
after the music was composed; and so were the anthologies of
Notre-Dame polyphony.[3] The Squarcialupi Codex, prepared in
the fifteenth century, some time after the death of Francesco

---

[3] For a very brief summary of the chronology of troubadour manuscripts,
see *The New Grove Dictionary of Music and Musicians*, ed. Stanley Sadie
(London, 1980) on 'Sources, MS', xvii. 638–9, which lists the principal
manuscripts and cites the most important studies of them. On the sources of
Notre-Dame polyphony, see *The New Grove*, xvii. 649–55, which lists the
principal manuscripts and cites the most important studies of them.

Landini, was intended to celebrate the achievements of the musicians in Florence, evidently as a kind of historical record; and so were several of the other principal anthologies of trecento polyphony.[4] So far as we know, the scribe of the Squarcialupi Codex never supposed that the manuscript would be used for performance. Trecento polyphony and troubadour songs appear for the most part to have circulated among musicians orally, a possibility that suggests we need, too, to revise and refine our distinctions between written and unwritten repertories.

By the second half of the sixteenth century, a number of musicians regularly performed music that was at least fifty years old. Some of the manuscripts prepared at the beginning of the century for the use of the Sistine Chapel in Rome, for example, seem to have been a part of the choir's working library for decades.[5] According to Massimo Troiano, writing in 1569, Lasso's choir at the court of the dukes of Bavaria in Munich normally sang the music of Josquin and his immediate successors at daily mealtimes and religious services.[6] Spanish manuscripts of the seventeenth century are our chief sources of knowledge about music at the Spanish Royal Chapel in the sixteenth century, and motets and Masses by Morales, Victoria, and Guerrero continued to be sung in Spain and in the New World into the eighteenth century and even beyond.[7] It would not be difficult to collect further examples of the great interest in the music of the early sixteenth century shown by musicians during the next several generations, even though such examples may all reveal not so much an attempt to revive old music that had been forgotten as a continuing involvement with music that had never been dropped from the active repertory.

[4] For a summary of views about the date of compilation of the Squarcialupi Codex and other trecento manuscripts, see *The New Grove*, xvii. 665–8, which cites the most important studies of them.

[5] On the longevity of the repertories sung at the Sistine Chapel, see, among other studies, Jeffrey J. Dean, 'The Scribes of the Sistine Chapel, 1501–1527', Ph.D. diss. (The University of Chicago, 1984), 189–214.

[6] See *Die Münchner Fürstenhochzeit von 1568, Massimo Troiano: Dialogo*, facs. edn. with German translation by Horst Leuchtmann (Munich and Salzburg, 1980), 40–1. Troiano writes that Lasso's choir mostly sang music by Clemens non Papa, Josquin, Morales, Rore, and Willaert, along with modern music, especially that written by members of the choir, above all compositions by Lasso himself.

[7] On the late date of most Spanish court manuscripts, see *The New Grove*, xvii. 700, which lists the sources and cites the most important studies of them.

In the second half of the sixteenth century, Girolamo Mei in
Rome and Vincenzo Galilei in Florence, among others, were
deeply concerned to learn about the nature of music in the
ancient world.[8] A purely scholarly interest in the history of
music grew in the seventeenth and eighteenth centuries. Both
Giovanni Battista Doni (1595–1647) and Athanasius Kircher
(1601–80), for example, studied various aspects of music in
antiquity.[9] In 1761, the great teacher, composer, historian, and
music collector, Padre Giovanni Battista Martini (1706–84)
published the first of his three volumes on the history of music,
a work that remains but the torso of what was to be a
monument, since he never progressed beyond the ancient
Greeks.[10] And in England Sir John Hawkins (1719–89) brought
out his general history of music in 1776, the same year that
Charles Burney (1726–1814) issued the first volume of his rival
work.[11] What may well be the first scholarly editions of old
music were edited during the following several decades by John
Stafford Smith.[12]

During the late eighteenth and early nineteenth centuries, too,
there began to be sporadic performances of 'early music'. In
London, both the Academy of Ancient Music and the Concerts
of Antient Music organized performances centred partly around
early English church music, and partly around the music of

[8] On the correspondence between Mei and Galilei about the nature of
ancient music, see Claude V. Palisca, *Girolamo Mei (1519–1594): Letters on
Ancient and Modern Music to Vincenzo Galilei and Giovanni Bardi* (American
Institute of Musicology, 1960; 2nd edn., 1977). On the widespread interest in
the music of antiquity among Italian theorists from the late fifteenth century
on, see Palisca, *Humanism in Italian Renaissance Musical Thought* (New Haven
and London, 1985).

[9] On Doni, see Palisca, *Humanism*, 320–32. On Kircher, see Ulf Scharlau,
Athanasius Kircher (1601–1680) als Musikschriftsteller (Marburg, 1969).

[10] Giovanni Battista Martini, *Storia della musica*, 3 vols. (Bologna, 1761–81;
repr. Bologna, 1967). Martini's letters, which reveal his abiding interest in
historical questions, are listed in Anne Schnoebelen, *Padre Martini's Collection of
Letters in the Civico Museo Bibliografico Musicale in Bologna* (New York, 1979).

[11] Sir John Hawkins, *A General History of the Science and Practice of Music*,
with an introduction by Charles Cudworth, 2 vols. (New York, 1963), and
Charles Burney, *A General History of Music From the Earliest Ages to the Present
Period* (1789), ed. Frank Mercer, 4 vols. in 2 (New York, 1957).

[12] On John Stafford Smith, his own collection of books and manuscripts and
his editions of early music (*A Collection of English Songs . . . Composed about the
year 1500*, published in 1779, and *Musica Antiqua*, published in 1812), see
Nicholas Temperley, 'Smith', *The New Grove*, xvii. 416–17.

Handel and Purcell.[13] At least one concert in early nineteenth-century London offered as its second half a condensed survey of the entire history of music.[14] And in Germanic countries, the music of Bach and Handel was avidly studied and performed by various circles of connoisseurs, among them Mozart and the Baron van Swieten in Vienna.[15] This interest led, among other things, to the publication of the first biography of Bach by Johann Nikolaus Forkel in 1802, to the famous revival in Berlin of the St Matthew Passion, conducted by Mendelssohn in 1829, and eventually to the decision to prepare a scholarly edition of all Bach's music.[16] In France and Belgium, too, there were sporadic concerts of early music during the nineteenth century, among others by François-Joseph Fétis, whose Concerts historiques were presented in Paris from 1832 and in Brussels from 1839.[17]

Most of the performances of early music before the late

[13] On the Academy of Ancient Music, see Sir John Hawkins, *An Account of the Institution and Progress of the Academy of Ancient Music* (London, 1770). On the Concerts of Antient Music, see James E. Matthew, 'The Antient Concerts, 1776–1848', *Proceedings of the Musical Association*, 33 (1906–7), 55–79. See also William Weber, 'Intellectual Bases of the Handelian Tradition, 1759–1800', *Proceedings of the Royal Musical Association*, 108 (1981–2), 100–14 and the studies he cites, for a broader view of the idea of 'ancient music' in the eighteenth century.

[14] The second half of a concert given at the Theatre Royal, Drury Lane on 24 February 1836 (advertised on a playbill in my possession) begins with excerpts from *Messiah* and is followed by 'a popular selection from The Historical Records of Vocal and Instrumental Music'. The historical survey began with Josquin's *Stabat mater* and Gastoldi's *Il Bell'Humore* sung by five singers, and was followed by Luther's Prayer *Nos verbo serva Domine* sung as a solo, an 'Anthem, in Eleven distinct Parts' by Giovanni Gabrieli performed by three singers, two cornets, viols (*sic*), and four trombones, and various other compositions. The concert was arranged by 'Mr Bochsa', evidently Nicholas Charles Bochsa, whose career as a brilliant harpist, organizer of concerts, bigamist, and forger is summarized briefly in *The New Grove*, ii. 831–2.

[15] On Baron van Swieten and his interest in the music of Bach, Handel, and other earlier composers, see Edward Olleson, 'Gottfried van Swieten, Patron of Haydn and Mozart', *Proceedings of the Royal Musical Association*, 89 (1962–3), 63–74; and Olleson, 'Swieten', *The New Grove*, xviii. 414–15.

[16] On the Bach revival, see, among other studies, Hans T. David and Arthur Mendel (eds.), *The Bach Reader: A Life of Johann Sebastian Bach in Letters and Documents* (rev. edn., New York, 1966), 358–86, and Nicholas Temperley, 'Bach Revival', *The New Grove*, i. 883–6.

[17] Robert Wangermée, 'Les premiers concerts historiques à Paris', in *Mélanges Ernest Closson* (Brussels, 1948), 185–96. On early music in Brussels, see Margaret Campbell, *Dolmetsch: The Man and his Work* (London, 1975), 9–13, 21–2.

nineteenth century were probably quite un-selfconscious about
authenticity. The question has never really been studied, but no
evidence known to me suggests that the Sistine Chapel at the
end of the sixteenth century, the Spanish Royal Chapel in the
seventeenth century, or Lasso's choir in Munich in the 1560s
and 1570s, for example, sang Josquin or Morales in a manner
different from that they used for music by their contemporaries.
Whatever attempts musicians in London made in the eighteenth
century to use unfamiliar instruments must have been sporadic.
When Bach performed Palestrina's music he added, at least on
occasion, wind instruments, double bass, and organ accompaniment.[18] And the concerts on historical instruments organized in
Brussels at the end of the nineteenth century cannot have
involved the musicians in any very elaborate attempt to recover
older playing techniques. Either the older music had never been
dropped from the active repertory and was therefore performed
in the same manner as any other music (presumably the case
with sacred vocal music), or else concerts were designed to
introduce audiences to unfamiliar music or unfamiliar sonorities, and once the primary aim was satisfied the necessary
adjustments were made to ensure the success of the enterprise,
without any finicky regard for authentic details. In short, the
history of the idea of authenticity in the performance of early
music seems to begin in a significant way only in the late
nineteenth and early twentieth centuries, with the careers of
Arnold Dolmetsch and Wanda Landowska and with the
foundation of various Collegia Musica in German universities.

   In 1908 Hugo Riemann, the distinguished theorist and
musicologist, decided to call the institute for musicology he
headed at the University of Leipzig ' Collegium Musicum',
apparently in order to make clear his devotion to music as an art
as well as an academic discipline.[19] Riemann's Collegium was
not established to present old music in concert; but he and his
contemporaries did begin to make the music of the Middle
Ages, the Renaissance and the Baroque era available in modern
editions, and especially in the series of monumental volumes

---

[18] See *The Bach Reader*, 27.
[19] On Riemann's Collegium, see 'Riemann', in *Riemann Musiklexikon*, 12th
edn., ed. Wilibald Gurlitt, Personenteil L–Z (Mainz, 1961), 505–10, and
Hellmuth Christian Wolff, 'Riemann', in *Die Musik in Geschichte und
Gegenwart*, xi. 480–5.

published in Germany, among them the *Denkmäler Deutscher Tonkunst*, and the *Denkmäler der Tonkunst in Bayern* that had begun to appear about that time and to which Riemann contributed.[20] His activities, therefore, probably centred more on making editions of hitherto unknown music than in presenting that music in authentic performances.

Riemann's example in calling his institute Collegium Musicum was soon followed at other German universities, although at least some of the later Collegia were organized in the first place as societies within an institute to perform earlier music, both in concert and for the enjoyment and education of the student performers. Probably the best known of these Collegia was that led by Wilibald Gurlitt at the University of Freiburg im Breisgau, founded about 1920.[21] Gurlitt seems not to have written about his activities as a Collegium director, although his concern for authenticity in performance is well known in connection with his efforts to revive the so-called baroque organ, as a part of the 'Organ Revival' (*Orgelbewegung*). Unlike Albert Schweitzer, whose ideals led him to seek to have organs built that were capable of doing justice to J. S. Bach's music, Gurlitt wished to revive the organ of the early seventeenth century, and his efforts culminated in the Praetorius Organ built for Freiburg in the early 1920s.[22] If that instrument (destroyed in 1944 and rebuilt in 1954–5) seems to us today too full of compromises to be considered an acceptable copy of an early baroque instrument, it was nevertheless an important landmark in the history of the idea of authenticity in performance. Its makers had the same ideals as we have today, but a quite different notion of the extent to which the details of construction of an

[20] For a list of monumental editions, see 'Editions, historical', *The New Grove*, v. 854–62, which does not differentiate between scholarly and so-called 'practical' editions.

[21] For scholarly reviews of some of the performances by Gurlitt's Collegium, see Friedrich Ludwig, 'Musik des Mittelalters in der Badischen Kunsthalle Karlsruhe, 14.–16. September 1922', *Zeitschrift für Musikwissenschaft*, 5 (1922–3), 434–60, and Heinrich Besseler, 'Musik des Mittelalters in der Hamburger Musikhalle, 1.–8. April 1924', *Zeitschrift für Musikwissenschaft*, 7 (1924–5), 42–54.

[22] On the Organ Revival in Freiburg, see Wilibald Gurlitt, *Musikgeschichte und Gegenwart. Eine Aufsatzfolge*, ed. Hans Heinrich Eggebrecht, 2 vols. (Wiesbaden, 1966), vol. 2: *Orgel und Orgelmusik*, 3–100. On the Organ Revival in general, and on the history of the idea of a baroque organ, see Peter Williams, 'Organ', *The New Grove*, xiii. 769–78.

original instrument could be modified without changing its essential character.

Gurlitt's Collegium and the musical activities at other German universities in the first quarter of the present century introduced audiences to a vast amount of music they would not otherwise have heard, and taught students of musicology how important it is to have some direct contact with the music they were studying. These university groups were the direct fore-runners of the numerous Collegia Musica that flourished from the 1950s in American universities, and the German scholars responsible for organizing and directing them established the scholarly study of performance in the past—the subdiscipline of *Aufführungspraxis*—as a legitimate branch of historical research. Some of the earliest general histories of performance practice, notably Arnold Schering's and Robert Haas's surveys, grew out of their authors' experiences in German and Austrian universi-ties, and in this way, rather than through more direct contact by means of concerts, these first Collegia Musica exerted their greatest influence on our ideas about how old music should be performed.[23]

In Germany (as in other countries) the growing interest in old music in the first third of the present century was inspired partly by a reaction against the overheated emotionalism of late romanticism and against the increasing secularism of the age. The Wandervogel, the adherents of the German Youth Move-ment (*Jugendbewegung*), members of the various amateur choral societies (*Singbewegung*), and the pious Christians who wished to revive older church music all hearkened back nostalgically to a simpler past, and to a life at one with nature or with God. Men such as Peter Harlan revived the recorder partly as a historical instrument and partly to play folk-songs and other simple music in amateur ensembles; and Karl Vötterle founded Bärenreiter Verlag partly to publish music suitable for the Wandervogel and partly in order to further the revival of old church music and to encourage the composition of new church music. The appeal to nationalism and the German past left some of these movements

[23] Robert Haas, *Aufführungspraxis der Musik* (Potsdam, 1931; repr. 1949), and Arnold Schering, *Aufführungspraxis alter Musik* (Leipzig, 1931). A bibliography of other general (and more specialized) studies on performance practice may be found in Howard Mayer Brown, 'Performing practice', *The New Grove*, xiv. 390–3.

open, of course, to being pre-empted by the Nazis when they came to power in the 1930s, a possible explanation for the fact that the cultivation of early music was relatively slow to revive in Germany after the Second World War.[24]

In German amateur circles, questions of authenticity were relegated to a relatively unimportant place. But some of the same feelings of reaction against romanticism and a desire for a new simplicity must also have motivated Paul Sacher when he established his Collegium Musicum in Basle in 1926: a chamber orchestra devoted to the exploration of the pre-classical repertory and to the presentation of new music.[25] As in Germany, the connection between the very new and the rather old was strong in Switzerland in the early years of the early music movement, a fact that explains, for example, Paul Hindemith's involvement with the music of the distant past.[26]

Whereas early music in Germany, Austria, and Switzerland was chiefly the province of academics and amateurs, Paris was the home of the first great virtuoso to specialize in the music of the seventeenth and eighteenth centuries, Wanda Landowska, who emigrated to the French capital from Poland (with several intervening years of study in Berlin) in 1900, and who soon established a glowing reputation for herself as a composer and pianist, and eventually as a harpsichordist. She was not alone in France in being interested in the music of the past: various scholars, such as Henry Expert, André Pirro, and Michel Brenet, had already begun to mine the great riches to be found

---

[24] Karl Vötterle's memoirs, *Haus unterm Stern. Über Entstehen, Zerstörung und Wiederaufbau des Bärenreiter-Werkes* (Kassel and Basle, 1963), offer a first-hand account of the musical side of the Wandervogel, the Singbewegung, and the German church music revival. On Peter Harlan and the relationship between English and German recorder players, see Edgar Hunt, *The Recorder and Its Music* (London, 1962; rev. and enlarged edn., London, 1977), 131–8. The periodicals *Der Blockflöten-Spiegel*, ed. Franz J. Giesbert (Celle, 1931–4), and *Die Zeitschrift für Hausmusik* (Kassel, 1934–49) offer a more detailed view of the early music movement in Germany in the 1930s.

[25] On Sacher in Basle, see *Alte und Neue Musik. Das Basler Kammerorchester . . . unter Leitung von Paul Sacher 1926–1951* (Zurich, 1952), and Samuel Borris, *Die grossen Orchester* (Hamburg, 1969), esp. pp. 301–10: 'Paul Sachers Orchester zur Pflege alter und neuer Musik'.

[26] On Hindemith's contact with early music in Germany, see Geoffrey Skelton, *Paul Hindemith: The Man Behind the Music. A Biography* (London, 1975), chap. 5: '1927–32: Music to Sing and Play', 85–102; and also Gerd Sannemüller, *Der 'Plöner Musiktag' von Paul Hindemith* (Neumünster, 1976).

in French libraries. And Charles Bordes, organist and choir-
master at the church of St Gervais in Paris had since 1892
devoted himself to the performance of sacred and secular
polyphony from the French and Italian Renaissance. As early as
1894, Bordes, along with Alexandre Guilmant and Vincent
d'Indy, founded the Schola Cantorum in Paris for the revival of
old church music.[27] (In England, their counterpart, Sir Richard
Terry, introduced English Renaissance music for the Latin rite
into the services of Westminster Cathedral from the time of his
appointment there as director of music in 1901.[28])

Like so many early musicians before the Second World
War—and indeed, most since—Landowska began her musical
training on a modern instrument, the piano, just as Arnold
Dolmetsch, for example, had studied the violin as a child, and
August Wenzinger the cello. Landowska even established her
first reputation in Paris as a performer on the piano, and only
gradually came to realize (against some opposition) that the
music in which she was most interested sounded better on the
harpsichord. She argued strongly that the harpsichord revealed
qualities in the music that modern instruments never can, and
she felt that she had to learn to play on original instruments and
to study old treatises if she were to do justice to the music.[29] She
certainly never pretended to perform baroque music exactly the
way performers in the seventeenth and eighteenth centuries
would have done. 'At no time in the course of my work', she
wrote, 'have I ever tried to reproduce exactly what the old
masters did. Instead, I study, I scrutinize, I love, and I recreate
. . . I am sure that what I am doing in regard to sonority,
registration, etc., is very far from the historical truth.'[30] Instead,
she based her decisions about how to play Bach, Handel,

---

[27] See Vincent d'Indy, *La Schola Cantorum* (Paris, 1927); Fernand Biron, *Le
Chant grégorien dans l'enseignement et les œuvres musicales de Vincent d'Indy*
(Ottawa, 1941); and Brother Philip Michael Dowd, 'Charles Bordes and the
Schola Cantorum of Paris', Ph.D. diss. (Catholic University of America,
1969).

[28] On Terry, see H. F. Andrews, *Westminster Retrospect: A Memoir of Sir
Richard Terry* (London, 1948).

[29] Landowska's views on music are given in her *Ancienne musique* (Paris,
1904), trans. William Aspenwall Bradley as *Music of the Past* (New York, 1924),
and in *Landowska On Music*, ed. Denise Restout assisted by Robert Hawkins
(New York, 1964).

[30] *Landowska On Music*, 355.

Scarlatti, or Mozart on her ideas about the essential character of the music, following presumably the spirit rather than the letter of the instructions in the old treatises she studied so assiduously, and translating them on to the large Pleyel harpsichord with sixteen-foot stop that she had built as an 'improvement' over the weaker instruments she found in museums. 'When I am working out a registration, for instance,' she explained,

I search for one that seems logical and beautiful to me, one that does justice to Bach's prosody by being punctuated in the right places. I am aware that the disposition of the registers in the harpsichords of Bach's time differed somewhat from those of my Pleyel. But little do I care if, to attain the proper effect, I use means that were not exactly those available to Bach.[31]

Landowska, in short, believed more strongly in her own personal understanding of the music and her commitment to it than in any more dispassionate quest for what the composers would have wanted or expected; and we have already seen that the early twentieth-century German academics and amateurs appear to have been more intent on rediscovering little-known music than in learning older techniques for playing it.

Of all the pioneers of early music active before the 1930s, then, it was Arnold Dolmetsch more than anyone else who was committed to the idea that performers should try to play music in the way its composers intended. He, more than anyone else, is the founding father of the 'cult of authenticity'. He is one of those seminal figures in the history of music who is as important for the enormous influence he had on later generations as for his own formidable achievements. Indeed, in considering Dolmetsch's place in the history of early music in the twentieth century, it is tempting to have recourse to the traditional concept of a past age of innocence when one extraordinary man appeared to be able to do everything. Dolmetsch built harpsichords, lutes, viols, and recorders which were exemplary for their time. He wrote a scholarly study of performance in the seventeenth and eighteenth centuries that was the first to take completely seriously the injunctions in the old treatises; it was the first modern book, therefore, to offer a detailed summary of such essential details of performance as phrasing, bowing,

[31] *Landowska On Music*, 356 (see also below, p. 148).

articulation, and ornamentation. And he himself played in concert a number of the instruments he collected and built well enough to earn the approbation of so discerning a critic as George Bernard Shaw.[32]

It is perhaps still fashionable to patronize a little Dolmetsch the polymath, or Dolmetsch the eccentric and inexpert performer, and to decry the activities of his cult following at Haslemere. But we should not forget the enormous influence Dolmetsch had on future generations. Along with Edgar Hunt and Walter Bergmann, he was the guiding spirit behind the recorder movement in England in the 1930s and later.[33] His students Richard Nicholson and Marco Pallis organized and ran for many years the English Consort of Viols and began the publishing activities that have made a substantial portion of the English consort repertory available in modern editions.[34] His student Diana Poulton has been responsible more than anyone else for encouraging the impressively high standards of lute playing, lute making and research on matters relating to the lute in England today. His student Robert Donington has been for many years a leading English scholar in the field of baroque performance practice, gathering together invaluable documentary evidence in his published studies.[35] It is no exaggeration to say that even today almost everyone involved in early music in England has been touched in some way by Dolmetsch, by his students, or by his students' students.

Whatever the level of his own performances, Dolmetsch reveals in his book on the interpretation of seventeenth- and eighteenth-century music a surprisingly up-to-date point of

[32] On Dolmetsch and his times, see Campbell, *Dolmetsch*, who includes a bibliography of studies about Dolmetsch, and gives information about his relationship with Shaw.

[33] For a first-hand account of the revival of the recorder in the twentieth century, see Hunt, *The Recorder and Its Music*, esp. chaps. 7–8, pp. 128–65. See also *The Consort: Journal of the Dolmetsch Foundation*, founded in 1930; and *The Recorder News: The Journal of the Society of Recorder Players*, begun in 1937 and continued after 1963 as *The Recorder and Music Magazine*.

[34] The English Consort of Viols has made numerous concert tours and recordings. Richard Nicholson has edited, among other things, John Jenkins, *Consort Music in Five Parts* (London, 1971), and, with Andrew Ashbee, John Jenkins, *Consort Music for Viols in Six Parts* (London, 1976).

[35] On Diana Poulton, see Suzanne Bloch, 'Saga of a Twentieth-Century Lute Pioneer', *Journal of the Lute Society of America*, 2 (1969), 37–43. On Donington, see Howard Mayer Brown, 'Donington', *The New Grove*, v. 552–3.

view.[36] Deeply devoted in the first place to the idea that a vast repertory of great music was waiting to be rediscovered and brought to life again, Dolmetsch urged performers to read, to learn and to take seriously what the writers of the time had to say about the details of performance, and then to use that information as the basis for an imaginative re-creation in performance of the notes on the page. To make this revival possible, Dolmetsch was convinced, musicians needed to have available old instruments or reliable copies of them. This attitude was not unrealistic since there were in England at the time collectors such as Canon Francis Galpin and others passionately interested in the history of instruments.[37] In learning how to build copies of old instruments Dolmetsch, more than anyone else of his time, faced the principal dilemma of all early instrument makers in the twentieth century: to what extent the best and musically most satisfactory instruments were those that copied most faithfully the originals. If many of Dolmetsch's instruments in fact fail by present standards to reflect the essential qualities of those built in the seventeenth and eighteenth centuries, it was nevertheless Dolmetsch who pointed the way for his successors. Many of his instruments, especially his harpsichords, are still very impressive by any standards.

For all their success and recognition, both Landowska and Dolmetsch remained somewhat isolated figures within the musical life of their times. They were individuals dedicated to ideals that were shared by few others. Since then, however, early music has gradually come to be accepted as a normal part of our concert life. The musicians most influential in introducing this repertory into our regular concert life can conveniently be divided into three chronological groups: those whose careers began in the 1930s, those who were active in the immediate post-war period, from 1945 onwards, and those active at the present time whose careers began about 1970. But in the post-

[36] Arnold Dolmetsch, *The Interpretation of the Music of the Seventeenth and Eighteenth Centuries* (London, 1915; 2nd edn. 1946; repr. with an introduction by R. Alec Harman, 1969).

[37] On Galpin, see F. Geoffrey Rendall, 'F. W. G. 1858–1945', *Galpin Society Journal*, 1 (1948), 3–8; and Stanley Godman, 'Francis William Galpin: Music Maker', *Galpin Society Journal*, 12 (1959), 8–16. The Galpin Society was formed in Britain in 1946 to commemorate and continue Galpin's work.

Dolmetsch period these influential figures must be further subdivided according to their activities, for scholars, instrument makers, and performers all have special interests and concerns, and no one since Dolmetsch has combined them all in one person.

The scholarly study of performance practice has made haste slowly, for by and large scholars have shown themselves to be surprisingly indifferent to the question of authenticity in performance. The area where the interests of scholars have overlapped most closely with those of performers has been in the realm of edition making (see Chapter 4). After the great scholarly editions had been established—the German *Denkmäler* and the new Bach edition (1851–99) as well as such series as Expert's collection of music from the French Renaissance (1894–1929), Fellowes's editions of the complete works of William Byrd (1937–50) and the music of the English madrigalists (1913–24), and *Tudor Church Music* (1922–29)—scholarly attention turned in the 1930s to the problem of the best way to prepare editions for performers. On the one hand, this was the era of the so-called *Urtext*, which offered refreshing contrast to those editions, not always made from the best sources, heavily annotated with recommendations by the great pianists (and other musicians) of the past.[38] On the other hand, scholars and performers debated the relative merits of a scholarly versus a so-called practical edition, in which for baroque music at least, the continuo parts were realized (albeit often in an unstylish fashion), ornamentation was sometimes written out, and detailed suggestions were given about phrasing and other details of performance. Especially in Germany, early music began to be published in small and relatively inexpensive editions, either separately or as part of a series such as *Hortus musicus*, *Nagels Musikarchiv*, or *Das Chorwerk*.[39] Editorial activity in England took a slightly different turn, for there the co-operation between academics and professional musicians has always been closer than elsewhere. Edward Dent, Professor of Music at Cambridge, was an

[38] On the concept 'Urtext', see Howard Mayer Brown, 'Editing', *The New Grove*, v. 842.

[39] For a list of such editions of early music, see 'Editions, historical,' *The New Grove*, v. 854–62, which does not differentiate between scholarly and so-called 'practical' editions.

important figure in convincing both his university students and the professional music world in London of the importance of good, scrupulously made editions, and he led the way in collaborating with conductors and opera producers.[40]

Instrument makers in the pre-war period concentrated largely on building harpsichords, recorders, and viols, and especially for the ever-expanding amateur market. While the general level of expertise grew higher, few makers yet realized the importance of studying original instruments in detail, and most were more than a little convinced that their mission was to build instruments that overcame some of the difficulties caused by the limited technologies of the past. John Challis's career can be taken as a case in point.[41] A student of Dolmetsch, Challis returned to America and devoted himself to making harpsichords that could withstand the extremes of the North American climate. His ideal was to create an instrument as stable in its tuning as a piano; it is not wholly unfair to claim that in his last years he began little by little to reinvent the piano. He was a superb craftsman, which is doubtless why William Dowd studied with him. After the Second World War, Dowd, along with his partner Frank Hubbard, opened a workshop in Boston, Mass. to build harpsichords that were significantly better than any others manufactured at the time. Hubbard's fine book on harpsichord building reflects a new stage of sophistication in the documentation of old instruments and the way they were built, a stage only now beginning to be reached by makers of instruments other than harpsichords.[42] For instrument builders, making faithful copies of individual old instruments represents an ideal analogous to the performer's goal of reproducing the composer's intentions. Both concepts have some of the same pitfalls. Quite aside from the technical expertise involved and the ambiguity of the evidence (for old instruments have changed over time, and some have been modified at a later date), makers (like performers) can never agree about precisely which details are essential to the success of an enterprise, or even whether the

[40] See Winton Dean, 'Edward J. Dent: A Centenary Tribute', *Music and Letters*, 57 (1976, 353–61; and Philip Radcliffe, *E. J. Dent: A Centenary Memoir* (London, 1977–8).

[41] See 'John Challis: Portrait of a Builder', *The Harpsichord*, 2 (1969), 14 ff.

[42] Frank Hubbard, *Three Centuries of Harpsichord Making* (Cambridge, Mass., 1965).

aim of exact copying is justifiable if it inhibits a necessary sense of creativity on the part of the maker or leads him to ignore significant qualities in the material with which he is working. It is in any case never possible to copy exactly, for there are simply too many variables to account for, and certain materials (such as quills from the feathers of now extinct ravens) are impossible to obtain.

By the 1930s some musicians who were not dedicated solely to the revival of early music became interested in some repertories from before 1750. The recordings of the Boyd Neel Orchestra, for example, those by Nadia Boulanger of Monteverdi's madrigals (with her remarkable continuo playing on the piano) and of extracts from Rameau operas, and those by Adolf Busch of the Brandenburg Concertos (among other works), reflect an indifference to the ideal of authenticity, to say the least, but nevertheless represent a significant stage in the acceptance of 'early music' as a part of normal concert life.[43] More important, these recordings offer sensitive and highly musical performances that were revelations to intelligent music-lovers of the time. They offered listeners some acknowledgement that early music was to be taken seriously. Although they make no attempt to be authentic, they nevertheless make clear that to play early music, performers need to approach the works differently from those of the standard concert repertory. Also in the 1930s, Curt Sachs organized the series of recordings called *Anthologie sonore*, illustrating the entire history of western music and reflecting the general standards of proficiency of that time as well as very diverse attitudes towards the question of authenticity.[44]

Performers from the 1930s onwards have been extraordinarily open to the idea that they should learn both the spirit and the letter of older techniques of performance. Some, like Ralph

[43] On Boyd Neel, see R. Wimbush, 'Boyd Neel', *Gramophone*, 1 (1972), 178 ff.; on Adolf Busch, see Robert Philip, 'Adolf Busch', *The New Grove*, iii. 498–9; and on Nadia Boulanger, see Alan Kendall, *The Tender Tyrant: Nadia Boulanger* (London, 1976), and Léonie Rosenstiel, *Nadia Boulanger: A Life in Music* (New York, 1982)

[44] For a more general assessment of Sachs's contribution to musicology, including his involvement in the preparation of the recordings, see Erich Hertzmann, 'Curt Sachs: A Memorial Address', *Journal of the American Musicological Society*, 11 (1958), 1–5.

Kirkpatrick, a student of Landowska and the first American virtuoso on the harpsichord, did extensive scholarly work. His editions of Bach's *Goldberg Variations* and the sonatas of Domenico Scarlatti reveal a thorough command of early writings on performance, and represent a new stage in the history of the idea of authenticity, for he was one of the first to incorporate into a printed edition extensive informed commentary about original performance techniques.[45] Certainly he was more concerned to modify his playing technique according to the old writers than his teacher, the rather more passionate and impressionistic Landowska. Safford Cape, the organizer and conductor of the Pro Musica Antiqua of Brussels, the first group to tour extensively with a repertory of medieval and Renaissance music, must also have attempted to achieve 'authentic' performances, although, like so many performers, he did not express himself in print on the subject. He asked his father-in-law, the distinguished musicologist Charles van den Borren, to serve as musicological adviser, and his group cultivated a light, clear, transparent singing style and a quiet, introverted manner of presentation that contrasted sharply with contemporary manners of performance.

Perhaps the most important event in the history of early music in the 1930s, however, was the founding of the Schola Cantorum in Basle in 1933 by a group of musicians including August Wenzinger, distinguished virtuoso on the viola da gamba, and already the author of a tutor for the instrument. For the first time, a formal curriculum was established for training young musicians in older techniques.[46] The establishment of the Schola Cantorum, which has maintained its eminence to the present day, marked another important stage in the history of

[45] Ralph Kirkpatrick (ed.), *The 'Goldberg' Variations* (New York, 1938); Kirkpatrick, *Domenico Scarlatti* (Princeton and London, 1953); Scarlatti, *Sixty Sonatas*, ed. Kirkpatrick (New York, 1953); and Scarlatti, *Complete Keyboard Works in Facsimile*, ed. Kirkpatrick, 18 vols. (New York, 1972). On Kirkpatrick's early years and his lessons with Landowska (about which he was not always enthusiastic), see Ralph Kirkpatrick, *Early Years*, with an epilogue by Frederick Hammond (New York, 1985).

[46] See 'Wenzinger', *Schweizer Musiker Lexikon* (Zurich, 1964), 402–3, and also A. Fantanzeller, 'Barockmusik in Basel: Besuch bei August Wenzinger', *Westermanns Monatshefte*, 107 (1966), 15 ff. On the Schola Cantorum and its relationship with the other conservatories in Basle, see Hans Oesch, *Die Musikakademie der Stadt Basel* (Basle, 1967).

the early music movement, for its existence offered official
recognition of the fact that early music was a legitimate branch
of study, and it offered a forum to explore such questions as
those about authenticity. Moreover, Wenzinger, quite aside
from his role in the establishment of the Schola and his
achievement as the first modern virtuoso on the viola da gamba,
has continued throughout his entire career to lead in the effort to
play early music in authentic ways. In 1955 he directed an
important recording of Monteverdi's *Orfeo* with a Hamburg
Collegium Musicum and the Capella Coloniensis, which he
directed in the mid-1950s was probably one of the first modern
orchestras to be modelled on eighteenth-century practices.

During the 1930s, then, a greater number of musicians than
ever before became interested in the problems of performing
early music, and they did much to establish early music as a
normal part of the general musical life of the times. Most of
them had an open, eager, and perhaps slightly naïve attitude
towards questions of authenticity, and expressed themselves
interested in learning as much as they could about the way
musicians in the past had played and sung. This activity,
temporarily halted during the war years, picked up again
quickly in the immediate post-war period, and especially in
England, America, and the Netherlands. In England, musicians
at universities and colleges, the organizers of the newly formed
Third Programme of the BBC, church musicians, and amateurs
all supplemented an increasingly active professional musical life
(especially on London's South Bank after 1951) to promote
early music, and the quest for authenticity. At universities, the
example set by Dent of combining the preparation of good
editions with stylish performance continued in such students of
his as Anthony Lewis, whose idea it was to found the series
Musica Britannica and who, as well as being influential in the
early days of the Third Programme, also organized at the
University of Birmingham a notable series of revivals of Handel
operas, and made many pioneering recordings for the Oiseau-
Lyre label.[47] At Cambridge, Boris Ord, conductor of the King's
College Chapel Choir, inspired several generations of young
musicians, some of whom subsequently made careers in early

---

[47] See Thurston Dart, 'A Background for *Musica Britannica*', *Music 1952*, ed.
Alec Robertson (Harmondsworth, 1952), 24 ff.

music.[48] At Oxford Jack Westrup had presented as early as 1925 the first complete staged performance in modern times of Monteverdi's *Orfeo*, a performance which signalled the beginning in Britain of the great interest in baroque opera in general and Monteverdi's music in particular.[49]

The importance of the Third Programme in encouraging early music (as well as all kinds of other music) can scarcely be exaggerated. Under Anthony Lewis's direction and with the co-operation of such scholars as Denis Stevens and Basil Lam, broadcasts offered a dazzling variety of early music. Although many English musicians in this field even today react strongly against what they see as the serious limitations of the English church music tradition, the truth is that sacred music of the sixteenth and seventeenth centuries is better cultivated in Britain than in any other country; the training the various choral foundations provide explains more than anything else the extraordinarily high standards of ensemble singing in Britain today, since many collegiate choral scholars and boy singers go on to take up professional singing careers. In the post-war period London's active musical life gave early music ever greater room. The first great counter-tenor of modern times, Alfred Deller, for example, made his début in 1943 at one of the important series of concerts of early music directed by Michael Tippett at Morley College. Julian Bream, basing his technique on that for the guitar and never obsessed with questions of authenticity, established himself as a virtuoso on the lute, bringing its repertory for the first time in the twentieth century to large audiences. George Malcolm's revolutionary choral sound made Westminster Cathedral once again a place of pilgrimage for many interested in early music.

Of all the British musicians of the post-war period, Thurston Dart best represents the ideal prototype, typical of his countrymen in the way he combined scholarly and practical interests, and yet extraordinary for his energy, the diversity of his interests, and for his vision. As editor, expert performer on the

---

[48] See Philip Radcliffe, *Bernard (Boris) Ord: A Memoir* (Cambridge, 1962)

[49] For an assessment of Westrup's contribution to musicology and his influence on the revival of baroque opera, see Peter Dennison, 'Westrup', *The New Grove*, xx. 376–7, and the brief preface to *Essays on Opera and English Music in Honour of Sir Jack Westrup*, ed. F. W. Sternfeld, Nigel Fortune and Edward Olleson (Oxford, 1975), pp. ix–x.

clavichord, organ, and harpsichord, conductor of the Philo-
musica, and educator—in short, as a polymath and catalyst—
Dart came closer than anyone else in later times to filling the
role played earlier by Arnold Dolmetsch. Dart was a scholar
unafraid to offer his imaginative hypotheses on a number of
subjects for critical examination, a conductor unafraid to test
out his sometimes radical ideas about authenticity in performance, and an educator intent on the reform of an educational
system he found stifling. His influential book, *The Interpretation
of Music*, offers an amalgam typical in the post-war period of
practical advice for making compromises and genuine concern
for historical authenticity.[50]

But the decisive event in the popularization of early music in
Britain was the emergence in the late 1960s of David Munrow
and his Early Music Consort of London. Munrow combined
personal vitality with a desire to communicate with a large
audience. As I wrote at the time of his death, 'The special
quality that set David Munrow apart, or so it seems to me, was
a rare combination of abundant musical talent, the energy and
skill to organize and lead other people, and an uncanny ability,
given only to a few great teachers, to convince large numbers of
people that what was important and attractive to him should
also be attractive and important to them.'[51] Less overtly
popularizing, though still influential through their concerts and
many recordings was the group Musica Reservata, directed by
Michael Morrow, which challenged the audience's conception
of the sound of early music by cultivating a harsh vocal quality
based on Morrow's firm ideas of authenticity; it was perhaps to
counteract the view of the distant past as an era when sweet,
gentle Pre-Raphaelite sounds prevailed.

There was much less activity in the United States than in
Britain during this period. Much of it centred around two men:
Paul Hindemith and Noah Greenberg. Hindemith organized at
Yale a Collegium Musicum modelled on the German academic
pattern and using some of the old instruments that are a part of
the collection of the Metropolitan Museum in New York. If
Hindemith's concerts did not reach much beyond New Haven,
their influence did, for his infectious enthusiasm and energy
inspired such students as Joseph Iadone, the lutenist, and others,

---

[50] Thurston Dart, *The Interpretation of Music* (London, 1954; 4th edn. 1967).
[51] *Early Music*, 4 (1976), 288.

who in turn trained several generations of students intent on careers in early music.[52] By far the greatest excitement about early music in America during the post-war years, however, came from Noah Greenberg, whose New York Pro Musica offered a new vision of early music both to already committed devotees and to new, eager, large audiences. The brilliance, polish, and professionalism of the Pro Musica's concerts were something hitherto unknown in early music circles in America; the rise of the Pro Musica seemed to carry early music from the realm of dilettantes into that of real music. Greenberg believed wholeheartedly in the idea that he should learn as much as he could about how the music he programmed was originally performed; he was committed to the idea of authenticity. If some of his recorded performances now seem over-orchestrated and sung in a style more appropriate to the opera-house than the early music concert-hall, the explanation lies in changes in taste, changes in our notions of what sorts of compromises are acceptable, and, of course, changes in the amount and kind of information he had available. His ideals were the same as those of the present generation of performers of early music, even though the musical results were so markedly different.

Radically different in sound and style from any other performers of early music before them, the Studio der frühen Musik in Munich, organized in 1959 by yet another American, Thomas Binkley, approached medieval music, like most performers, with a healthy respect for the concept of authenticity. Concentrating much of their attention on the repertory of medieval monophonic song that had largely been neglected by performers, Binkley, the virtuoso singer Andrea von Ramm (who has in recent years established an independent career) and the other members of the Studio took what might be called an ethno-musicological approach to performance practice, rather than relying solely on written documentation from medieval Europe.[53] Since westerners have no first-hand experience of

---

[52] On Hindemith in America, see Skelton, *Hindemith*, 206–8.

[53] After some years of apprenticeship at the University of Illinois with George Hunter (one of the most influential figures in the revival of early music in America), Binkley organized the Studio der frühen Musik in Munich especially to perform the music of the Middle Ages, both secular and sacred, and eventually directed the medieval programme of the Schola Cantorum in Basle. Most recently, he has established an early music programme at Indiana University, the largest and most ambitious such programme in America.

how monophonic art music is handled in a living tradition, we
can learn—they seem to have argued—from studying monophonic traditions in other cultures. As a result they scored some
of the music they played for highly colourful ensembles of
instruments, they explored techniques for improvising accom-
paniments, interludes, and even rudimentary counterpoint that
went far beyond what was justified on the basis of the cryptic
remarks about performance in most medieval writings on
music, and they borrowed practices from north African and
middle Eastern musicians. The validity of their approach seems
under particularly strong attack at present, as medievalists
appear more and more to favour austere, even unaccompanied
performance of much of the monophonic repertories. Whatever
the final verdict may be about the way the Studio arranged
music, however, we should not forget that single-handedly the
group brought back to life a repertory of music most people
thought was unrevivable, and, more important, they proposed
a completely new approach to the performance of early music,
whose intellectual foundations have yet to be fully explored,
and whose usefulness to performers has by no means yet been
exhausted.

Munich, while it provided a home for Binkley and the
Studio, became for a time the centre of the medieval avant-
garde, but the cities of Amsterdam, Rotterdam, and the Hague
began to attract in the 1960s the followers of a much more
austere and traditional approach to the performance of early
music, and yet one that was equally radical in some of its
manifestations. The importance of the Netherlands (and to a
lesser extent Belgium) to the early music movement can be
attributed in the first place to the activities there of a number of
virtuosos distinguished for the elegance of their playing, and
especially Gustav Leonhardt on the harpsichord, Frans Brüggen
on flute and recorder, and the three brothers of the Kuijken
family on violin, viola da gamba, and flute. These men recruited
a number of superb instrumentalists to perform with them, and
began to collaborate in larger productions. Leonhardt formed
his own consort, performing a wide repertory of baroque
music, and later Kuijken began to direct a baroque orchestra, La
Petite Bande, which made some outstanding recordings of
Handel, Corelli, and Rameau. Not least, they also assisted in the

distinguished early music programme set up at the Conservatory in the Hague. Their style of playing, characterized by careful attention to detail, is sometimes criticized for its exaggerated mannerisms, and especially for its dependence on the effect of messa di voce (swelling and dying down on single notes) which, it is argued, has a tendency to destroy the listeners' sense of melodic line. But their manner of playing has been carefully developed from intensive study of what older writers on music had to say. The contrast between the way members of the Netherlands school and others play is therefore especially illuminating for the evidence it gives that musical results can differ widely even when two people base their performing style on the same assumptions, and even on the same treatises for their information.[54]

Early music activity blossomed in the post-war period in England, America, and the Netherlands, but it was slower to revive (or begin) in other countries. In France and Italy, for example, there have been no early music groups of international fame until the past decade. Austria, seldom open to new musical ideas, nevertheless produced the violinist Eduard Melkus and René Clemencic and his consort. But the most significant activity there has been the pioneering work by the enormously successful and influential group Concentus Musicus, founded back in the 1950s by the cellist Nikolaus Harnoncourt, which is still very active today. The first post-war German early music groups to achieve international fame began to appear only in the mid-1950s, when the Capella Antiqua München was organized as a student group, conducted by Konrad Ruhland.[55] The character of its membership—mostly Roman Catholic laymen—reveals itself in their sober, straightforward singing

[54] See, for example, the recordings of French viol music of the seventeenth and eighteenth centuries made by Wieland Kuijken and those made by John Hsu. The two performers produce quite different results even though they base their playing style on exactly the same historical evidence.

[55] The proceedings of a conference on the idea of early music, held in Kassel in 1967, and published as *Alte Musik in unserer Zeit. Referate und Diskussionen der Kasseler Tagung 1967*, Musikalische Zeitfragen. Eine Schriftenreihe, ed. Walter Wiora, vol. 13 (Kassel and Basle, 1968) makes fascinating reading in that it reveals so clearly how different the orientation of English and American scholars has been from that of German musicologists towards questions of authenticity, performance practice, and early music in general.

style, often doubled not by the colourful instrumental combinations of a Noah Greenberg, but rather with the sackbuts and cornetti characteristic of northern European chapel choirs in the sixteenth century. Their emphasis on sacred music identifies them, too, as carrying on in the pious Christian tradition that characterized some of the early music activity in Germany in the first third of the present century. Another German ensemble active in the 1960s was the Collegium Aureum, an eighteenth-century-style orchestra made up of regular professional performers but never very seriously devoted to the ideals of authenticity; it was founded in 1964 primarily to make recordings.

For the period since 1970, it would be foolhardy to offer more than a very summary view of the principal trends in early music performance, as so much continues to happen. (Nicholas Kenyon's introduction provides some more detailed information).[56] I can do no more than to sketch in outline what seem to me to have been the most important developments—the increasing acceptance of early music as a normal part of our concert life, the increasing specialization of performing groups, and a near obsession with questions of authenticity that has led in various directions, including the preparation of this volume of essays.

When J. M. Thomson founded the journal *Early Music* in England in 1973 the 'early music movement' finally had a forum of its own to air its views. The journal's phenomenal success suggests that having such a forum was an idea whose time had come. But an even greater indication of the new acceptance of early music has been the incorporation of a number of early music groups into the regular tour schedules of the major concert managers, and the great success of many of these groups on record. Groups such as the Academy of Ancient Music directed by Christopher Hogwood, the Consort of Musicke led by Anthony Rooley, the English Concert directed by Trevor Pinnock, and the continental groups directed by Leonhardt,

---

[56] For an impression of early music activities in the present decade, see Joel Cohen and Herb Snitzer, *Reprise. The Extraordinary Revival of Early Music* (Boston and Toronto, 1985). Due to be published at the same time as this book is Harry Haskell, *The Early Music Revival: a History* (Thames and Hudson, London).

Harnoncourt, Brüggen, and Kuijken, make it clear that early music has at last become a part of the official musical establishment.

At the other extreme, in recent years a number of smaller groups have been formed whose goals are much more specialized than those of earlier twentieth-century ensembles. Sequentia, for example, performs primarily medieval monophonic song; Organum, conducted by Marcel Pères, chant and early polyphony; Gothic Voices and the Medieval Ensemble of London secular music of the late Middle Ages; Musica Antiqua of Cologne baroque chamber music, and so on. Moreover, the quest for authenticity has now invaded the regular concert repertory and concert-goers in New York and London especially are increasingly offered 'authentic' performances of music by Mozart and Beethoven, even in such 'establishment' series as Lincoln Center's 'Mostly Mozart'. To some extent, of course, it can be argued that such specialization is necessary as the amount of knowledge increases, and our perceptions of particular repertories grow more and more refined, but it is also true that performers can feel greater freedom within a style if they concentrate their energies in this way. And there can be little doubt that individual groups have found it necessary to limit their repertories as audiences, critics, and fellow musicians have demanded ever greater attention to the minutiae of authenticity.

It is important to realize that this all-embracing concern for authenticity, a perfectly natural and inevitable result of fifty years of involvement with the subject, is relatively new. Discussion, often heated, as to the nature and purpose of authentic performance styles, has led among other things to a special issue of *Early Music,* and to an equally natural reaction on the part of some musicians against the idea of authenticity, or, as they would say, against a mindless obsession with authenticity.[57] Their feelings can be attributed in part to a legitimate concern

---

[57] Richard Taruskin, Daniel Leech-Wilkinson, Nicholas Temperley, and Robert Winter, 'The Limits of Authenticity: A Discussion', *Early Music,* 12 (1984), 3–25. See also Taruskin, 'The Musicologist and the Performer', in *Musicology in the 1980s: Methods, Goals, Opportunities,* ed. D. Kern Holoman and Claude V. Palisca (New York, 1982), 101–17; and Laurence Dreyfus, 'Early Music Defended Against its Devotees: A Theory of Historical Performance in the Twentieth Century', *Musical Quarterly,* 69 (1983), 297–322.

that questions of authenticity have begun to take precedence over more important questions about the best way to bring great music to life in performance, and partly to hurt feelings on the part of those musicians criticized on the grounds that they are inauthentic.

It is only in the past decade, then, that questions about authenticity have been raised in such detail that we are forced to ask: is the quest for authenticity resulting in the dead hand of scholarship forcing performers into corners and quelling their creativity? Or is it itself an act of freedom, freeing the conservatory-trained student to think for himself about questions of style and history and helping him to present the music in the best light possible? Is the point of playing music in the way the composer intended it (which is an ultimately impossible goal) to intimidate the performer and force him to change his playing style in ways he cannot easily accept? Or is it rather to help the performer to introduce audiences to new repertories and to new ways of playing that can enlighten us not only about the particular repertories in question but also about the nature of all music?

Surely the answer to the question of how and why we should be concerned about the composer's intentions will change depending on whether we are scholars, instrument makers, or performers. In the past, instrument makers have often worked at the leading edge of research and have pushed both performers and scholars into thinking in new ways about a number of things. Although some of them would surely disagree, a consensus does in fact exist that we will need to go on copying faithfully particular old instruments for a long time to come. They still have much to teach us, and the practical research involved in copying the essential features of an instrument (and, more important, of deciding which the essential features are) has hardly yet begun, in spite of the spate of activity during the past fifty years.

Scholars of performance practice and editors, it seems to me, ought also to be committed to the ideal (whether it is realistic or not) that they are engaged in the positivistic task of discovering *wie es eigentlich gewesen,*, 'how it really was'. But on the other hand, they should have a complex and sophisticated attitude towards the idea of commitment. To a good scholar, no question can ever be closed. All our most cherished notions should always remain open for discussion, debate, and correction. The editor who imposes his own solution to a difficult problem in an edition without helping the reader to find out on what basis his decision was made and what the alternative possibilities are may get high marks for personal commitment, but should be severely criticized for obscuring the difference between what can be known for certain (very little) and what is more or less fanciful reconstruction.

The luxury of alternative possibilities and endless debate is clearly not one that can be enjoyed by a performer, who needs to know what he must do at a particular performance, and who also seems to need the psychological protection of actually believing in what he is doing. Personal commitment is a necessary virtue for performers (who ought not to play music in a particular style unless they are in sympathy with it), but it may be a luxury to which scholars ought not to aspire. Intelligent performers, of course, will inform themselves about the possibilities open to them, and the playing of the most intelligent will almost certainly these days, be 'historically informed'.

But the whole purpose of playing early music authentically is for the sake of the music and not for the sake of the performance. Dolmetsch certainly understood that, and so have the best of the musicians mentioned here, although in the last decade we have sometimes lost sight of that simple idea. I would be reluctant to criticize severely a performance purely on the grounds that it was not authentic. But this is a reluctance not shared by everyone, and such widespread criticisms of 'inauthentic' performance have brought their own backlash of controversy. This is, I suspect, one of the reasons why the present volume of essays was commissioned. Many have objected to those critics who, failing to be stirred by a particular performance, gave as a reason the fact that it was 'not authentic'. But the critics should probably have said that they objected to the performance because the interpretation of the music—whether done for reasons of authenticity or not—seemed to destroy some essential features of the work. Very few performances stand or fall just on the question of whether or not they are authentic. We should take care not to confuse historical with aesthetic questions, for the latter are often simply questions of personal taste. But they often involve, too, matters of propriety, decorum, and imagination. The test of a good performance more often than not is surely whether or not the music was projected with vitality and musical imagination, or whether or not the performers have in fact brought the music to life. The relation between that process and the rediscovery of past instruments and past playing techniques is a controversial area.

The fact that a performance is a creative reconstruction of the notes on the page, new each time, surely explains a point made in the advertising brochure of a recent Paul Fromm Concert at the University of Chicago. Ralph Shapey returned in the middle of his year's leave of absence to conduct the concert, and the advertisements described him as a person well known in Chicago for his authentic performances of new music. Presumably the anonymous writer of the blurb did not mean that Shapey normally uses instruments current in Chicago in the 1980s, tuned to pitches in current use in Chicago in the 1980s, and in ensembles accurately reflecting common practice in Chicago in the 1980s. Instead he meant, I think, that Shapey's performances are expertly played and sung, genuinely committed, and artistically convincing, and that, it seems to me, is the sense in which we should all use the word 'authentic'.

3
TRADITION, ANXIETY, AND THE CURRENT MUSICAL SCENE

ROBERT P. MORGAN

The title that first occurred to me in thinking about an essay on current attitudes towards early music and its performance was 'The Age of Authenticity', suggested, I suspect, by unconscious association with a poem I have long admired, W. H. Auden's 'The Age of Anxiety'. Although I discarded it, the fact that it came spontaneously does suggest the particular direction of my approach to the subject. For what interests me about authenticity, or more precisely about the authenticity movement in musical performance, is not so much whether it is a good thing: whether it should be lauded or censored, or as most seem to hold, accepted with moderation, accompanied by a strong dose of common sense. My concern is rather with the movement as a widespread cultural phenomenon that reflects our current way of thinking about music and musical history. Concern for historical authenticity represents an unmistakable symptom of the present situation of our musical culture, a situation characterized by an extraordinary degree of insecurity, uncertainty, and self-doubt—in a word, by anxiety. The current rage for authenticity is inseparably linked to this condition and is fully comprehensible, I believe, only when viewed within the larger context that has spawned it.

There is little doubt that the authenticity question has acquired the status of a major cultural phenomenon. Although interest in authentic performance has been with us for some time, and is tied to strands of western thought stretching back several centuries, the concern for authenticity as presently encountered is an essentially modern development that has taken root only since the early years of the twentieth century. Moreover, its importance has increased dramatically until, within the past two or three decades, it has emerged as one of the central musical issues of our time. It is debated not only in journals of performance and in specialized musical periodicals, but also in magazines and newspapers intended for the general reader.

Why this sudden concern for authenticity? What is its historical significance? These are very large questions, ultimately touching upon matters that encompass our entire cultural environment. But they are worth addressing, however tentative and provisional the answers may be, for they impinge upon matters that are of the utmost significance for the contemporary state of our art.

A good place to begin is with the concept of musical tradition, since questions of authenticity in performance—as opposed, say, to questions of accuracy—arise primarily (though not exclusively) in connection with works of the past. Since we find ourselves at one end of a long and unbroken line of western thought that has been characterized by its pronounced historical orientation, a line that can be traced back at least to the eighteenth century, we are apt to assume that our way of viewing the past today is, though certainly broader and more detailed, not appreciably different from that of our ancestors. Yet there has been a radical shift during the present century in attitudes towards music pre-dating our own period; and as a consequence, there has been a fundamental transformation in the way we relate to musical tradition.

The older sense of tradition—one is tempted to call it the 'traditional' one—comprehends the past as a steady, chronologically ordered succession leading directly up to the present (and ultimately beyond it to the future). It locates the present at the end of a continuum that stretches straight backwards. One's view of the past resembles that of someone walking down a long corridor, whose length is constantly extended as the walker moves steadily forward into the future, the past at his back. The walker—the musician—always faces forward; and since he never looks back, what he knows of the past, of what lies behind him, is limited to what he picks up on the way, to what has 'come down' to him (or rather with him) as part of an *enduring* tradition. His knowledge of the past is thus saturated with—we might say contaminated with—current conceptions. Moreover, the further something lies in the past, the dimmer it appears to be, unless, of course, it has managed to survive as an active ingredient in the developing tradition.

Within this framework one is not inclined to think about the past in a conscious way at all; one does not think of it primarily as the *past*, but as part of a living—and thus constantly changing—musical culture. The past, to the extent that it prevails at all, is not isolated from the present but forms part of it; and the musician carries whatever past he possesses within himself as part of a total and undivided musical consciousness. The way he thinks about older music, including the question of how it should be performed, is thus inseparably tied to assumptions embodied in the music of his own time. Although his relationship to the past will necessarily be limited, it will be extremely intimate and profoundly personal.

It takes little reflection to realize how drastically our own relationship to the past has changed. The past no longer forms a continuous corridor; it has become a field of instantaneous possibilities. The contemporary musician, rather than finding himself in a neatly ordered, linear hallway of tradition, resides somewhere in the centre of a very large mansion, a complex, ill-defined edifice with seemingly innumerable rooms, each of which contains some particular storehouse of historical knowledge. Moreover, the architecture of this building is of a fundamentally new sort. The rooms are not connected by hallways through which one passes in order to move from one chamber to the next; all rooms are immediately accessible to one another. Thus chronologically more distant cultures may be just as available as those temporally closer at hand—in many cases more so. The musician, sitting somewhere in the middle, can go instantaneously to any room he wants, with no regard for distance. He simply enters the room of his choice, turns on the light, makes whatever use of the particular cultural goods he wants, then turns out the light, shuts the door, and goes home again.[1]

Indeed, the spatial character of this mansion is sufficiently peculiar to render the architectural metaphor problematic, despite a certain consistency of the analogy with a corridor. A better analogy might be drawn with a computer, within whose memory bank the past is stored. All locations within the

---

[1] We shall see, however, that one of the particularities of this house is that the owner does not really seem to have a room of his own; so just where and what 'home' is becomes a pressing question.

memory are equally accessible (and thus equally present) to the musician, who sits at the console limited only by the amount of currently stored information. It makes little difference where anything is housed, since there is no necessary connection, logical or chronological, among the various locations. All are equally available to the central terminal. One simply calls up whatever bit of past one wants, moving from one past to another, and back and forth from past to present, with complete freedom and ease. As a result, the very distinction between past and present tends to be obscured, and such concepts as chronological time and cultural distance become extremely vague at best.

This change in thinking about the past is discernible in various aspects of twentieth-century music. One striking demonstration of the distinction can be found in the conceptions of history shown by Schoenberg and Stravinsky. These two composers are often said to represent the two dominant and most clearly defined compositional positions of the first half of the century;[2] their views on the relationship of their own music to that of the past, like so many aspects of their work, prove to be diametrically opposed.

Schoenberg, of course, holds the traditional view, but in a form whose very extremity shows that it is reaching a critical, and perhaps even terminal stage. He understood his own development as a logical and necessary continuation of the dominant compositional tendencies that had (in his view) consistently shaped the mainstream of serious western music.[3] This explains Schoenberg's discomfort at being considered a revolutionary—a composer in some way fundamentally separated from the past. In his own eyes, the course he followed offered the only possible realization of the musical implications inherent in the work of his greatest predecessors. Schoenberg believed his music to be progressive, certainly, but not in its

---

[2] This view has been most deeply and persuasively argued by Theodor W. Adorno, in his *Philosophy of Modern Music*, trans. Anne G. Mitchell and Wesley V. Bloomster (New York, 1973).

[3] Cf. Christian Martin Schmidt, 'Über Schönbergs Geschichtsbewusstsein', in *Über das musikalische Geschichtsbewusstsein*, ed. Rudolf Stephan, *Veröffentlichungen des Instituts für neue Musik und Musikerziehung Darmstadt*, 13 (Mainz, 1973).

basic aesthetic (or even technical) assumptions, fundamentally different from the music of the past.

This conception of the past is revealed with unmistakable clarity in a few quotations taken almost at random from Schoenberg's writings: [4]

It is seldom realized that there is a link between the technique of forerunners and that of an innovator and that no new technique in the arts is created that has not had its roots in the past. And it is seldom realized that these works in which an innovator prepares—consciously or subconsciously—for the action that will distinguish him from his surroundings furnish ready information about the justification of an author's turn toward new regions. (p. 76)

I am convinced that eventually people will recognize how immediately this 'something new' is linked to the loftiest models that have been granted to us. I venture to credit myself with having written truly new music which, being based on tradition, is destined to become tradition. (p. 174)

This was not a natural development; it was not evolution, but man-made revolution. (p. 409)

I was never a *revolutionary*. (p. 137)

It seems—if this is not wishful thinking—that some progress had already been made in this direction, some progress in the direction toward an unrestricted musical language which was inaugurated by Brahms the Progressive. (p. 441)

The method of composing with twelve tones grew out of a necessity. (p. 216)

It seemed inadequate to force a movement into the Procrustean bed of a tonality without supporting it by harmonic progressions that pertain to it. This dilemma was my concern, and it should have occupied the minds of all my contemporaries also. (p. 86)

The most decisive steps forward occurred in the Two Songs, Op. 12, [5] and the Three Piano Pieces, Op. 11. (p. 110)

While composing for me had been a pleasure, now it became a duty. I knew I had to fulfill a task: I had to express what was necessary to be expressed and I knew that I had the duty of developing my ideas for the sake of progress in music, whether I liked it or not. (p. 53)

---

[4] *Style and Idea*, ed. Leonard Stein, trans. Leo Black (New York, 1975). All page references in the text are to this volume.

[5] Schoenberg must actually mean the Two Songs, Op. 14, as is pointed out by Leonard Stein, editor of *Style and Idea* (ibid., 517).

I was not destined to continue in the manner of *Transfigured Night* or *Gurrelieder* or even *Pelleas and Melisande*. The Supreme Commander has ordered me on a harder road. (p. 109)

Certain telling words and phrases in these quotations appear again and again in Schoenberg's writings: 'destined', 'necessity', 'duty', 'the decisive step', and of course 'progress'. Schoenberg sees himself as an innocent, even as an unwilling agent of historical necessity—a composer who, having submitted to destiny, is carried willy-nilly upon the currents of progressive compositional thought in a direction he cannot personally control. This is perhaps most pointedly expressed in a well-known anecdote from Schoenberg's First World War days, recounted in one of his articles: 'In the army, a superior officer once said to me: "So you are this notorious Schoenberg, then." "Beg to report, sir, yes," I replied. "Nobody wanted to be, someone had to be, so I let it be me."' (p. 104)

Always implicit in Schoenberg's remarks is the belief that music history is linear in nature—that one compositional development leads logically and inexorably to the next, producing the progressive growth of an ever more varied, complex, and differentiated musical language. 'It would be most annoying if [music] did not aim to say the most important things in the most concentrated manner in every fraction of . . . time. This is why, when composers have acquired the technique of filling one direction with content to the utmost capacity, they must do the same in the next direction, and finally in all the directions in which music expands.' To which is added: 'Such progress can occur only step-wise.' (p. 116)

In light of these views, it is interesting that Schoenberg himself occasionally 'regressed' historically in his later years, returning to a more conservative and tonally orientated language. Yet an explanation once offered for this may be the composer's single most telling statement regarding his conception of the past. In a letter written in 1947 to René Leibowitz, Schoenberg remarks on the Variations on a Recitative for Organ, Op. 48, a tonal work dating from 1941: 'Almost every composer in a new style has a longing to go back to the old style (in Beethoven, fugues). The harmony in the Organ Variations fills out the gap between my Kammersymphonie and the 'dissonant' music.'[6] Schoenberg sees the Variations as supplying a sort of missing link, resolving what had apparently become in his mind a historical inconsistency, a lacuna in his own evolution. Similarly, when writing to Pablo Casals on his 'free arrangement' of a concerto by G. M. Monn, he remarks that his 'main concern' was to replace its sequences and filler passages 'with true substance' and to rid it in general of 'the principal deficiencies of the Handel style', and concludes: 'I think I've succeeded in making the whole thing approximate, say, to Haydn's style.'[7] With Schoenberg's assistance, Monn is brought into the 'true' tradition.

Since Stravinsky was almost as obsessed with the past as Schoenberg—indeed in some ways perhaps more so—many of his comments on tradition seem not dissimilar, as in the following quotation from the *Poetics of Music*:[8]

A real tradition is not the relic of a past that is irretrievably gone; it is a living force that animates and informs the present . . . Far from implying the repetition of what has been, tradition presupposes the reality of what endures. It appears as an heirloom, a heritage that one receives on condition of making it bear fruit before passing it on to one's descendants . . . Tradition thus assures the continuity of creation. (p. 57)

Yet these words, so immanently 'traditional' in character, are followed immediately by a revealing disclaimer: 'This sense of tradition which is a natural need must not be confused with the desire which the composer feels to affirm the kinship he finds across the centuries with some master of the past.' (p. 57) Here one sees that Stravinsky is enough of a 'traditionalist' to distinguish his own compositional practices of the post-*Sacré* years from those embodying a more 'normal' relationship to earlier music. Yet note how his new attitude towards the past colours even his most specifically historical observations:

The artist imposes a culture upon himself and ends by imposing it

[6] *Arnold Schoenberg Letters*, ed. Erwin Stein, trans. Eithne Wilkins and Ernst Kaiser (New York, 1965), 248.
[7] Ibid. 171.
[8] Igor Stravinsky, *Poetics of Music*, trans. Arthur Knoedel and Ingolf Dahl (Cambridge, Mass., 1947). All references in the text are to this edition.

upon others. That is how tradition becomes established. Tradition is entirely different from habit, even from an excellent habit, since habit is by definition an unconscious acquisition and tends to become mechanical, whereas tradition results from a conscious and deliberate acceptance. (pp. 56–7)

Or on the use of 'old Russo-Italian' models in his opera *Mavra*:

This sympathy [for the musical characteristics of these models] guided me quite naturally along the path of a tradition that seemed to be lost at the moment when the attention of musical circles was turned entirely towards the music drama . . . But I wanted to renew the style of these dialogues-in-music whose voices had been reviled and drowned out by the clang and clatter of the music drama. So a hundred years had to pass before the freshness of the Russo-Italian tradition could again be appreciated, a tradition that continued to live apart from the main stream of the present, and in which circulated a salubrious air, well adapted to delivering us from the miasmic vapors of the music drama, the inflated arrogance of which could not conceal its vacuity. (pp. 58–9)

And writing in his autobiography on *Oedipus Rex*:

The more deeply I went into the matter the more I was confronted by the problem of style . . . Just as Latin, no longer being a language in everyday use, imposed a certain style on me, so the language of the music itself imposed a certain convention which would be able to keep it within strict bounds and prevent it from overstepping them and wandering into byways, in accordance with those whims of the author which are often so perilous. I had subjected myself to this restraint when I selected a form of language bearing the tradition of ages . . . [I]n borrowing a form already established and consecrated, the creative artist is not in the least restricting the manifestation of his personality. On the contrary, it is more detached and stands out better when it moves within the definite limits of convention. This it was that induced me to use the anodyne and impersonal formulas of a remote period and to apply them largely in my opera-oratorio . . . [9]

Considerably later in his life, Stravinsky returns to the question of tradition in one of his 'conversations' with Robert Craft:

In fact, the true tradition-making work may not resemble the past at all, and especially not the immediate past, which is the only one most

[9] Igor Stravinsky, *An Autobiography* (New York, 1936), 131–2.

people are able to hear. Tradition is generic; it is not simply 'handed down,' fathers to sons, but undergoes a life process: it is born, grows, matures, declines, and is reborn, perhaps. These stages of growth and regrowth are always in contradiction to the stages of another concept or interpretation: true tradition lives in the contradiction. *Notre héritage n'est précédé d'aucun testament* [Our heritage was left to us by no will].[10]

Just how different this position is from Schoenberg's becomes evident when one considers the key words. As opposed to Schoenberg's 'necessity', 'progress', 'next steps', etc., Stravinsky speaks of a tradition that is 'apart from the main stream of the present', that 'results from a conscious and deliberate acceptance', that 'the artist imposes . . . upon himself', and that makes available 'the anodyne and impersonal formulas of a remote period'. Here there is no necessity, but a calculated choice. With Stravinsky, one cannot speak of *the* tradition at all, but only of *a* tradition (as in fact he does in one of the above quotations). One chooses the tradition one wants, or even creates a unique tradition for one's own personal requirements. The past is not forced upon the composer, handed down by decree (or 'testament'); he shapes it himself. And the particular past that he chooses will be 'always in contradiction' to one shaped by another. Moreover, 'true tradition lives in the contradiction'.

As is to be expected, the differences in the historical views of Schoenberg and Stravinsky are clearly mirrored in their music. Schoenberg proceeds steadily from one work to the next, following a stylistic course that appears to be aimed in a definite direction. Stravinsky, on the other hand, seems almost to adopt a new manner with each new work, leaping back and forth through history as if by whim, taking his model now from Haydn, now from Machaut, now Tchaikovsky, now Webern, now Handel; or else he adopts some purely 'synthetic' style (as in the first movement of the *Symphony of Psalms*) that reverberates equally with historical associations.[11]

---

[10] Igor Stravinsky and Robert Craft, *Memories and Commentaries* (London, 1960), 126–7. The French quotation is from René Char's *Feuillets d'Hypnos* (Paris, 1946).

[11] There is of course consistency in Stravinsky's use of diverse models: one is aware of his own voice, which filters through the historical masks with unmistakable clarity. (In this connection, see Edward T. Cone's two seminal

It is indicative of the revolutionary nature of Stravinsky's conception of music history that, despite the countless composers he influenced during his own lifetime, the influence was limited almost exclusively to technical, or purely compositional, matters. Until more recently, Stravinsky's view of tradition remained largely his own property. Now, however, it appears that in this respect Stravinsky was—to borrow a traditional metaphor—ahead of his time; his conception of the past has become the dominant one.

Compositional developments of the past quarter century or so have radically redefined the very meanings of such words as 'tradition', 'style', and 'culture' in ways that bring them solidly into the Stravinsky orbit. Composers adopt and discard musical styles at will, not only from work to work but within single compositions. Moreover, they carry Stravinksy's historical inclinations considerably further than he did. They do not limit themselves to the repertory of western concert music, but extend their grasp to music of other cultures, popular music, folk music, jazz, etc., moving freely back and forth across cultural boundaries as well as temporal ones.

The variety evident in current compositional fashions is reflected throughout contemporary musical life in general. One need only sample the offerings of the radio stations in a major American city, or look over a week's concert schedule, to realize the extraordinary breadth of offerings—astonishing by reference to any previous yardstick. There is new music, old music, *very* old music, art music, folk music, pop music, country music, eastern music, western music, to say nothing of the various sub-types found within each category.

But there is one point about a musical culture of this sort, capable of supporting such a wide range of activity, which requires emphasis. Such variety is possible precisely because, and only because, we have no well-defined sense of the musical present. This, in my view, is the most critical factor in

articles: 'The Uses of Convention: Stravinsky and his Models', *Musical Quarterly*, 48 (1962), 287–99; and 'Stravinsky: The Progress of a Method', *Perspectives of New Music*, 1 (1962), 18–26.) Nevertheless, this does not detract from the fundamentally new historical orientation implicit in Stravinsky's music (although even here one can find precedents—e.g., in Satie, whom Stravinsky himself acknowledges in his autobiography).

Stravinsky's new attitude towards history. Only when the current moment loses an essential character and personality of its own, and thus loses its ability to cast its own peculiar colouration on the past, is one able to look upon the past with such detachment and objectivity. And when one *is* able to do so, the concept of culture, at least as previously understood, becomes extremely shaky. One might even say that we no longer have a culture of our own at all. By way of compensation, we attempt to assimilate everyone else's, including the fragmentary remains of our own, creating in the process a sort of all-world, all-time cultural bazaar where one traffics freely. Our sense of the musical present, and thereby of our our own musical selves, is fatally threatened, dissolving into a patchwork of disconnected fragments snatched from here, there, and everywhere.

The current fashion for authenticity in performance—defining that for the moment as the desire to resurrect, to the extent possible, works of the past in their original state—directly reflects this new orientation towards musical history. The idea of historical 'purity' as presently understood would have occurred to few (indeed would have been virtually unthinkable) in an age that viewed the present as an unbroken extension of the past. Any age, with a well-defined musical culture of its own, and consequently with a clear (and necessarily restricted) idea of the types of music and musical performance adequate to its own situation would find an 'authentic' approach to past music incredible. In musical societies with a strong sense of self-identity, where basic aesthetic and technical assumptions are taken for granted, music is played according to the dictates of that society. The only 'authentic' music from the past will be music that has survived as a vital part of a living tradition—literally as part of the *present*—and the only authentic way of performing it will be according to the requirements of current custom.

Consider an example from the not-so-distant past: Bach performances of the later nineteenth century, when Bach's music was comprehended as part of a vibrant and continuing heritage and thus adjusted to conform to the musical conventions of the day. The keyboard music, for example, was played on the piano, complete with legato articulation, sustaining pedal, a full and continuous dynamic spectrum, and octave doublings. Compositional 'corrections' were made: accidentals altered, bars or groups of bars omitted, or entirely new bars added. Free arrangements, transcriptions, and even paraphrases were composed, transforming the originals into what were in essence entirely new pieces.

From our own vantage point, such liberties may strike us as unforgivable perversions; yet we should recall that they were deemed acceptable precisely because Bach's music persisted as part of a flourishing tradition, unbroken and in constant transformation—renewing itself through new ideas and developments. Bach was altered in order to protect the currency of his music and to preserve his place within the tradition. Reasons then offered in justification of such practices make this apparent. Philipp Spitta, the principal Bach biographer of the nineteenth century (and a major figure in the development of musicology), went so far as to assert that the pianoforte actually 'floated in the mind of Bach' as an ideal instrument: 'No instrument but one which should combine the volume of tone of the organ with the expressive quality of the clavichord, in due proportion, could be capable of reproducing the image which dwelt in the master's imagination when he composed for the clavier. Every one sees at once that the modern pianoforte is in fact just such an instrument.'[12] Bach is seen as so integrally tied to the tradition that he is not only able to influence future musical developments but can exploit the properties of instruments not yet invented.

We, on the other hand, having lost this more personal and involved relationship with the past, interact with it in a more detached and objective way. We no longer 'bring it up to date', for we have no clear idea of what 'up to date' means. Ironically, however, as our understanding of the present becomes increasingly obscure, our view of the past appears to clarify. We believe that we can see it 'as it really was', to borrow the famous phrase of Ranke's rather than as transformed and distorted through our own cultural filters.

This difference can be brought out through an analogy with language that, although it should not be stretched too far, is

---

[12] Philipp Spitta, *Johann Sebastian Bach*, trans. Clara Bell and J. A. Fuller-Maitland, 2 vols. (New York, 1951), ii. 44.

useful and illuminating. It is frequently noted that an encompassing distinction separating twentieth-century music from earlier music, cutting across all stylistic and geographical categories, is the absence of a shared musical language capable of providing a common framework for individual stylistic divergences. In linguistic terms, we have no native language; and as a consequence, we are forced to borrow foreign ones. But these latter, because they are not our own, have no permanent attachment to us and can be exchanged at will. This means that we can no longer deal with the music of the past in our own terms. The necessary terms, to say nothing of a grammar to connect them, are simply not there. Deprived of a means of translation, we must try to speak the music in the original.

This leaves us, however, with a difficult problem. Since we speak the music of the past as a foreign tongue, we are no longer able to bring to its performance the kind of personal inflection and idiosyncratic intonation that one habitually draws upon in employing the vernacular. And the problem is further complicated by the fact that the musical languages of the past are not only foreign, but are for the most part dead. There are no native speakers left, which means that we have no way even to observe how the language is authoritatively spoken. All we can do is study the sources, musical and otherwise, that happen to have come down to us, attempting to guess what the language actually sounded like in a remote past to which we now have, at best, marginal access. We are thus forced to reconstruct the music purely in terms of a documented practice that, since it is no longer living, is apt to be perceived as frozen in a state of perpetual perfection, untouched by the passage of time.

Playing music of the past today is thus a little like speaking Latin, a language that is perhaps understood by many but whose use is necessarily limited to special circumstances. What is fundamentally different, however, is that our pluralistic musical culture offers us no native language as a basis for comprehension—no 'basic English' with which to define meanings and thus no mechanism for translation into our own terms.

(An amusing article in the *New York Times Magazine* is enlightening in this connection. Entitled 'Latin Dead? Veni, Vidi, Vici', it tells of a Father Reginald Foster of Milwaukee, who, as one of the Vatican's top Latin experts, dedicates himself to keeping the language up to date. He seeks out—or rather invents—Latin equivalents for essential current terms: e.g., 'microchip' (*assula minutula electrica*), 'fast food' (*victus acceleratus*), and 'rock and roll' (*musica titubantium*). Yet as the author of the article observes, 'the first sign that a language is dying is its inability to adapt to the times'. Father Foster thus tries to save Latin by keeping it current, adopting an attitude not unlike that of nineteenth-century Bach performers. The problem today is that we have no basis for determining which terms need definition, to say nothing of how they should be defined.[13])

Given the impossibility of finding any definitive means of interpreting early music on our own terms, one understands the appeal—or, in the view of some, the moral imperative—of treating this music as irrevocably cut off from the present, hermetically sealed from the contamination of anachronistic impurities. Thus the tendency to handle these musical languages as fixed and inviolable entities, impervious to time and historical process. Rather than trying to revive them, to give them new life through an infusion of new ideas, lending them the sort of richness and flexibility characteristic of a living tradition, we bring them back as fossils, emblems from a lost world that we may greatly admire (indeed, perhaps infinitely prefer to our own) but in which we can never reside as natives. Older music thus comes to resemble the mechanical bird of 'hammered gold' in Yeats's 'Sailing to Byzantium'; captured in a state of timeless purity, it sings eternally on its 'golden bough', beautiful but remote.

An ironic result of this attitude towards early music is that it precludes the recreation of what is arguably the most authentic component in its original performances: the immediate, un-reflected, and 'natural' delivery of a native speaker. Those particular ways of inflecting, bending, or even distorting music that are so characteristic of vernacular renderings will necessar-ily be missing. There is really no way to re-establish that fundamentally inimitable psychological and physiological rela-tionship of the performer to a language he has not learned but absorbed unconsciously, so that it is encoded as a fundamental determinant of his very way of thinking, hearing, and speaking.

[13] E. J. Dionne, Jr., 'On Language', *The New York Times Magazine* (20 July 1986), 8–10.

We can pretend to speak the languages of the past as our own, but we cannot in fact do so.

In this basic sense there is simply no way to re-create a truly authentic performance of earlier music. This does not mean that we should abandon efforts to understand the notation of this music as best we can, to consider certain physical factors that may have influenced the original performances (types of instrument, sizes of performance space, etc.), or to study the historical and cultural environment within which early music was conceived.[14] But we cannot re-create the 'aura' of the original (to borrow Walter Benjamin's useful term), no matter how hard we try.

Perhaps even more critical in this regard than original performance inflections is the deeper context in which the works were originally experienced—their status as integral components of a larger cultural environment that has disappeared and is fundamentally irrecoverable. To mention only the most obvious, yet basic point: early music was not intended to be performed in concert. Indeed, if we take the notion of context at all seriously, we are left with the painful realization that *any* concert performance of this music constitutes a basic perversion of its original intentions. The authentic function of the music—its *raison d'être*—is lost to us and cannot be reconstituted. As soon as we place these works in a museum, we wrench them out of their own frame and utterly transform their original meaning.

It is worth remembering, however, that only by doing so are we able to invest this music with any meaning for ourselves. Even in the case of the 'purest' performance, then, we are left with the unavoidable fact that we have used the music in a new way to suit our own purposes. We have made it 'relevant'— have appropriated it for that all-encompassing cultural exchange I mentioned previously—by converting it into concert music, thereby destroying its own functional basis. We have incorporated it into the modern institution called 'art', where musical

---

[14] There has recently been some interesting and suggestive work in this last area. See, e.g., Leo Treitler, 'History, Criticism, and Beethoven's Ninth Symphony', *Nineteenth-Century Music*, 3 (1980), 193–210; and Gary Tomlinson, 'The Web of Culture: A Context for Musicology', *Nineteenth-Century Music*, 7 (1984), 350–62.

compositions, along with other art works, are relegated to an autonomous realm of experience.[15]

It should also be added that the early music movement in general, as well as the authenticity movement in particular, is thereby a faithful reflection of the current stage of our thinking about art: it is itself, in other words, an entirely 'authentic' manifestation of our age. As such it reveals numerous parallels with other tendencies in present-day music and art that help define the special character of contemporary culture.

There are several such interdisciplinary connections. Beginning with the state of present-day musical composition, the absence of a prevailing school or aesthetic that can claim widespread (much less universal) validity can be seen as an equally necessary consequence of the breakdown of cultural self-identity I discussed previously. Deprived of an indigenous language that is truly their, or their public's, own, composers try out and discard new styles and techniques with remarkable alacrity.

Similarly, the extraordinarily fragmentary nature of much contemporary music, evident, for example, in the widespread use of quotation and in the tendency towards pastiche, betrays the absence of a common core. Though anticipated by Stravinsky (the inevitable concomitant of his historical views) and by still earlier forerunners such as Ives and Satie, only recently has the trend reached epidemic proportions. In composers as disparate as Luciano Berio, Bernd Alois Zimmermann, Lukas Foss, Peter Maxwell Davies, and George Rochberg, we hear bits and pieces of previous music, which have been torn from their original contexts and then reassembled into new, collage-like configurations. Deprived of their original meaning, which was dependent upon a total structural context, these fragments are bestowed with a new meaning in which the pretence of totality and integration is largely abandoned. A purely synthetic context is created where no 'natural' one exists.

This applies equally to compositions containing actual quotations and to those more freely constituted reconstructions (so characteristic of today's music) that rely upon general stylistic evocations rather than literal citation. It is remarkable how often

[15] Cf. Peter Bürger, *Theory of the Avant-Garde* (Minneapolis, 1984), esp. pp. 20–27.

one hears music today that intentionally conjures up the spirit of the past—and of at least one, but possibly several, former composers. Admittedly, the music of most composers has no doubt always sounded like that of others, but surely never before have the associations been linked to such temporally distant styles.

Another feature of current compositional practice relevant to these considerations is the use of elaborate pre-compositional systems. This is probably most readily evident in composers such as Milton Babbitt, but it is also found in other, very different types, such as John Cage and Steve Reich. Faced with the prospect of composing without a conferred compositional style, these composers resort to pre-formed schemata to help generate compositional events. For present considerations it is unimportant whether these schemata comprise complex serial relationships, as in Babbitt, or relatively simple transformational processes, as in Reich, or are the products of chance operations, as in Cage. What matters is that, much as in quotation, the actual musical result is not a relatively unmediated statement, a direct expression. It has been passed through an abstract structural filter; or, more precisely, it has been largely *formed* by this filter. Such systems respond to the linguistic crisis of which I have spoken: they provide a surrogate for a missing grammar. But at best they offer external grammars for the internal ones that operate in native languages. They must be worked out individually, in advance of each composition; and like the languages themselves, they can be exchanged at will. Though the aesthetic intent and compositional product obviously differ widely in the case of the three composers I have mentioned, all share something fundamentally common, a characteristically modern mode of operation that makes all three such 'authentic' representatives of our time.

What is so striking in these figures, and in so many other contemporary composers, is the relative absence of the immediacy that has informed most western music up to the twentieth century—although this immediacy has been present with markedly decreasing force over the past 150 years or so. This lack, which naturally affects the listener as much as the composer, is closely tied to our fascination with more distant repertories (a fascination that would otherwise be very difficult to comprehend) and to the particular problems we encounter in performing them. There is throughout contemporary musical life what might be described as a particular type of linguistic inadequacy, an inability to speak in our own terms and thus a need for external props of one kind or another—whether they be quotations, compositional systems, or documentary evidence.

This may explain why so much modern art is concerned expressly with matters of language. A self-reflexive stance is evident in contemporary music but it is perhaps even more characteristic of literature, where it may lead, as in a writer such as Samuel Beckett, to an attempt to communicate the very impossibility of communication or, as in Joyce, to the erection of elaborate structures incorporating highly differentiated levels of verbal expression. It may also explain the large number of twentieth-century writers who have avoided their native languages in favour of a foreign one: Conrad, Nabokov, Beckett, and others.[16] (Contemporary musicians might even have the advantage here, as they have *only* foreign languages at their disposal.)

Contemporary painting provides a final example. There are of course some obvious correspondences to tendencies I have been discussing in music: fragmentation, collage, and pastiche (all of which were firmly established in painting before they appeared in music). But here is a more recent development, namely the kind of 'hyperrealism' found in such artists as Chuck Close and Philip Pearlstein. One of the most significant features of this brand of realism is the almost total absence of atmosphere, of what might be called individual context. All details are rendered with a sort of absolute distinctness, thereby acquiring a degree of 'purity' inconceivable in the realm of actual visual experience. Everything is equally in focus. The image is viewed as if through a vacuum, with none of the visual distortion created by actual atmospheric conditions. If the Impressionists (in search of another type of 'hyperrealism') took delight in viewing the world through the distorting influence of various types of vision-transforming screens (rain, mist, fog, or fading light), today's superrealists contemplate the object 'as it

---

[16] Cf. the title essay in George Steiner, *Extraterritorial*, (New York, 1971).

really is', untouched by any disturbing influences of a temporary, transitory nature. One of the things that makes these paintings seem so strange and disturbing is that their pure, rarefied focus is normally imposed upon an ordinary, 'unartistic' subject, for example, a woman lying casually on a bed, seemingly unposed, or an expressionless face in extreme close-up. (This is yet another way contemporary artists have found to give ordinary material a new and more distanced meaning.)

Are these painters in fact presenting reality 'as it really is'? Pearlstein clearly thinks so, remarking on his work: 'I have been involved in exploring the problems of painting perceptually rather than conceptually: to paint only that which meets my eye, in as unpreconceived a manner as possible: to distort nothing, for the sake of expressivity, 'correct' anatomical proportions or style.'[17] Yet the world Pearlstein depicts is in fact one that could never be directly experienced. The strong sense of 'presence' accorded the objects, a result of the artist's uncompromisingly neutral attitude, is achieved at the expense of any possible sense of presence from the viewer's perspective.

It is not hard to understand the attraction of Pearlstein's brand of realism, or of the kind of hands-off compositional processing basic to the music of a Babbitt, Reich, or Cage. They offer the promise of, if not a simpler world, at least a more ordered and regimented one, free of the muddled uncertainties of the present day. There is no doubt that many of us, driven by feelings of dissatisfaction for the present, search for ways of escaping into a more structured existence. Our search for 'authentic reconstructions' in houses and furniture stems, I suspect, from desires similar to those fostering the early music movement. We attempt to protect the past from a chaotic present, preserving it as a time-frozen environment. Nostalgia, as everyone knows, is the order of the day, and the early music movement is but one of its countless signs.

Yet the movement also reflects a seemingly opposed, though equally characteristic, feature of contemporary life: the desire for novelty. Nostalgia and novelty, however, turn out to be the reverse sides of a single coin; we also look for the new when we are unhappy with what we have. The failure of a single, vital

[17] Exhibition catalogue, *Contemporary American Painting and Sculpture 1969* (Urbana, 1969), 142.

artistic movement to capture the collective imagination of our age encourages a constant search for unexplored possibilities. Since what we have is by nature ephemeral, unable to sustain any sort of extended development, we keep searching for something else.

On the one hand, early music is a symptom of this malady, as it provides concert music with a novel repertory. (And the more authentic the performance, the more novel—the more unlike 'regular' music—the result will be.[18]) But at the same time, it offers a sort of cure as well: the claim to an ancient heritage, which lends it an air of stability and continuity in marked contrast to the kaleidoscopic stylistic transformations that inform new music. Although they offer very distinct varieties of relief for the attendant woes of the current musical scene, the old and new music movements prove to be inseparably linked, tied to the same musical causes. Both carry the implication that western musical history as we have known it is over, having itself receded into history. Today we find ourselves 'beyond history', able to transcend temporal and stylistic boundaries in a single leap. We have made the past coextensive with the present, thus eliminating any meaningful distinction between the two.

Although this process is by no means complete, one can observe on an almost day-by-day basis the continuous shrinking of the past as a personal legacy, even as it expands in an archival sense. In his entry on 'Performing practice' in *The New Grove*, Howard Mayer Brown points out that the 'very continuity of tradition poses particular problems for those committed to the view that music is best served by performances that reproduce as exactly as possible the conditions and conventions current when it was written'. Thus he notes that the study of performance practice in music since 1750 is 'fundamentally different' from that of earlier music in that there is no '"lost tradition" separating the modern performer from the music of Haydn, Mozart and their successors comparable with that which separates him from Machaut, or even from Monteverdi'.[19]

---

[18] For an interesting discussion of this and other aspects of the early music movement see Laurence Dreyfus, 'Early Music Defended against its Devotees: A Theory of Historical Performance in the Twentieth Century', *Musical Quarterly*, 64 (1983), 297–322.

[19] *The New Grove*, xiv. 388.

Yet, significantly, Mayer Brown, writing in 1980, sets his cut-off date at 1750. He no longer feels justified to include Bach and Handel, for example, as part of our 'continuing tradition', whereas as recently as fifty years or so ago it would have been unthinkable not to do so. The late Baroque has apparently ceased to be 'ours'. But the shrinking has not stopped there; it encroaches more and more upon the present. The authenticity movement is now in the process of appropriating the music of Haydn, Mozart, and Beethoven, and it is beginning to establish a foothold in the early Romantic period as well. More recently, attempts have been made to resurrect late nineteenth-century interpretative mannerisms for the performance of Brahms.[20]

The extent of the contemporary music historian's reformulation of the concept of tradition is illustrated by the revised version of Mayer Brown's article appearing in *The New Grove Dictionary of Musical Instruments* (London, 1984), for which Robert Winter contributed a new section on performance practice after 1750, replacing Mayer Brown's original (see also Nicholas Kenyon's Introduction). Winter states that the problems of performing music from this period are in fact not substantially different from those associated with earlier music: ' . . . neither the assumption of an unbroken performing history nor the corollary of an unbroken performing tradition stands up.' Winter bases this view, however, solely on the fact that the performing tradition has *changed* over the course of time. But the way Mozart was played in the earlier nineteenth century (to say nothing of today) was already quite different from the way Mozart himself played. This does not mean that a performing tradition did not exist, but simply that it did not remain unchanged. For Winter the only 'true' tradition is apparently one fixed in time, preserved in its original innocence—an odd point of view for a historian of western music, whose tradition has always been characterized by gradual transformation.

And it continues. 'Authentic' revivals of the American musicals *No, No, Nanette* and *On Your Toes* were recently presented in New York; and the National Institute for Music Theater, aided by grants from the National Endowment for the

---

[20] See Jon Finson, 'Performing Practice in the Late Nineteenth Century, with Special Reference to the Music of Brahms', *Musical Quarterly*, 70 (1984), 457–75.

Arts and the American Express Company (a conjunction that also says something about the peculiarities of the current artistic situation), has started to compile a catalogue of 'authentic' performance materials used in Broadway musicals during the first half of the twentieth century. But the most remarkable example of this trend that has come to my attention is offered by the cabaret singer/pianist Michael Feinstein, whose record album *Pure Gershwin* attempts a re-creation of Gershwin's popular songs in their original form. 'In the 50 years since George Gershwin died,' Mr Feinstein remarks, 'his music has been distorted in all kinds of insidious ways that are losing track of his original authentic sound, which was so vibrant. Each new year takes us farther away from it. New editions of his music are being published while orchestrations are lost, and different versions of songs are being published that purport to be the original but aren't.' This from, of all things, a cabaret singer—a type *traditionally* committed to extremely personal, even blatantly idiosyncratic, stylizations.[21] Apparently it is no longer Mabel Mercer's or Bobby Short's Gershwin we want, it is some sort of reincarnation of Gershwin himself.

All this suggests that the past is slowly slipping away from us. It is no longer ours to interpret as we wish, transforming it for our own purposes, but ours only to reconstruct as faithfully as possible. That is because we *have* no purposes of our own, or at least are so unsure of the validity of those that we do have as to render them purposeless. So we take a back seat, assuming the role of an impartial observer who, just along for the ride, takes things as they are given, 'as they really were', rather than as we might want them.

The authenticity movement, as well as other manifestations of the contemporary music and art scene I have mentioned, are reflections of what might be described as a cultural identity crisis. Indeed, viewed in the broadest context, the movement can be understood as part of a more general crisis of identity characterizing modernity as a whole. It betrays both the self-consciousness and the sense of personal inadequacy endemic in an ever more complex and puzzling world.

Although we think of this crisis, naturally enough, as peculiar

---

[21] Stephen Holden, 'Cabaret's Bright Young Star', *The New York Times Magazine* (29 January 1986).

to our current state, it has actually been with us for some time. The idea of the divided self, or of a lost self, can be traced back over an extended period of western thought, from Eliot's 'dissociation of sensibility', to Nietzsche's 'defiance of oneself', to Hegel's 'disintegrated consciousness', to Rousseau's loss of the 'sentiment of being'. (Eliot locates the roots of his 'dissociation' as early as the middle of the seventeenth century.) Its most significant symptom is a difficulty in 'being oneself', of being true to one's inner nature, in the face of the strictures of an increasingly institutionalized society. Dissatisfaction with ourselves is thus intimately linked with, and dependent upon, dissatisfaction with the present.

One of the major documents in this line of thought concerning divided consciousness is Diderot's *Rameau's Nephew*. Although written in the latter half of the eighteenth century, and thus hardly contemporary in chronological terms, it is an ideal text for present purposes as it touches upon many of the matters discussed. First of all, it concerns a musician, and, moreover, one who is nameless—or rather, carries only the name of a famous ancestor. In place of the classical Everyman, the nephew is a modern No-man, a faceless someone who assumes whatever identity circumstances may dictate.

Diderot's book, framed as an extended conversation between the author himself and this nameless Rameau, is a remarkably modern work characterized by constant shifts in topic, point of view, and literary style. The conversation revolves around the opposed views of the two characters regarding the proper nature of human conduct. Diderot defends traditional truths and the current order, the conventions and proprieties of eighteenth-century society (of what he at one point even calls 'the universal order of things'), and the need for consistency, honour, and sincerity in thought and action. Rameau, the unscrupulous opportunist, is willing do whatever necessary—to play any role—to find favour with those in a position to help him.

The dialogue of *Rameau's Nephew* is periodically punctuated by moments when the nephew begins to act out what he is saying. At times this involves illustrating the roles he adopts to exploit the weaknesses of the wealthy; but at others, since much of the conversation concerns music, it means actually mimicking musical performances. These intermittent pantomimes reach

their culmination in an extended musical outburst which forms
the climax for the entire dialogue. It is an extraordinary passage
that bears at least partial quoting:

> He sang thirty tunes on top of each other and all mixed up: Italian,
> French, tragic, comic, of all sorts and descriptions, sometimes in a bass
> voice going down to the infernal regions, and sometimes bursting
> himself in a falsetto voice he would split the heavens asunder, taking
> off the walk, deportment and gestures of the different singing parts: in
> turn raging, pacified, imperious, scornful. Here we have a young girl
> weeping, and he mimes all her simpering ways, there a priest, king,
> tyrant, threatening, commanding, flying into a rage, or a slave
> obeying. He relents, wails, complains, laughs, never losing sight of
> tone, proportion, meaning of words and character of music. . . . But
> you would have gone off into roars of laughter at the way he mimicked
> the various instruments. With cheeks puffed out and a hoarse, dark
> tone he did the horns and bassoons, a bright, nasal tone for the oboes,
> quickening his voice with incredible agility for the stringed instru-
> ments to which he tried to get the closest approximation; he whistled
> the recorders and cooed the flutes, shouting, singing and throwing
> himself about like a mad thing: a one-man show featuring dancers,
> male and female, singers of both sexes, a whole orchestra, a complete
> opera-house, dividing himself into twenty different stage parts, tearing
> up and down, stopping, like one possessed, with flashing eyes and
> foaming mouth.

This text gives almost surrealistic expression to the identity
crisis of which I have spoken. Rameau's nephew, the nameless
musician deprived of a musical self of his own, adopts the roles
of others—singers, dancers, instrumentalists, even instruments
themselves. There is something laudable in his virtuoso
performance, but also something disturbing: and it reflects our
current musical plight in a remarkably cogent way. Like the
nephew, the modern musician, with no music of his own, looks
elsewhere for sustenance, taking on the styles, manners, and
conventions of others as if to make them his own. One
significant difference, however, is that Rameau restricts himself
to music of his own time; he may be faceless, but the music of
his age is not. Thus the historical dimension of the loss of self-
identity is not yet clearly evident in Diderot, although it is
strongly suggested in the constant presence of the elder
Rameau, whose famous name forms a sort of threatening

leitmotiv heard throughout the dialogue. The authentic Rameau, the embodiment of a hallowed and envied past, hangs over the dialogue like a pall.

I have closed with this relatively ancient text because it reveals that the problems we are dealing with have been developing for some time, though their current historical and world-cultural ramifications are uniquely our own. The authenticity movement can thus be viewed as one manifestation of a central problem in the evolution of western thought over the past two or three centuries. As such it represents, once more, an entirely 'authentic' phenomenon in its own right, a valid response to a past that has become psychologically remote at the same time that it has become more readily accessible.

The transmissibility of the past, as Hannah Arendt once remarked, 'has been replaced by its citability'.[22] And one way of citing is to do so as faithfully as possible. In this light, efforts to achieve historical authenticity in musical performance are not only comprehensible but entirely defensible. But they must not acquire a monopoly on the performance of older repertories. The so-called authentic way to perform early music is only one of many ways, any of which may be an equally authentic expression of present musical circumstances. The authenticity movement, in other words, is itself historically conditioned, and thus comprehensible only in light of the particular course that western thought, and western music, have followed since the Renaissance. There are many ways of citing, some of which are arguably even more representative of the modern temper— for example, ways that incorporate distortion, stylization, and radical transformation. These too offer authentic modes of dealing with historical material, as their current ubiquity in other musical contexts makes clear.

The tendency of the authenticity movement, inevitably (and no matter how much its practitioners may protest), is to place older music in a museum. Museums, we should recall, are essentially a modern invention; and although they certainly play an important role in culture today, they can provide only one dimension of a total artistic experience. We should learn to deal

[22] In her introduction to Walter Benjamin's *Illuminations*, trans. Harry Zohn (New York, 1968), 38.

with the music of the past not only for what it once was but for what it can be today, in our own cultural context, however uncertain that is. Otherwise it will necessarily be confined to a marginal existence.

4

TEXT, CONTEXT, AND THE EARLY MUSIC EDITOR

PHILIP BRETT

For Joseph Kerman, teacher, colleague and friend

'Editing is a mug's game.' That was how a noted American musicologist put it to me one day in a characteristically offhand aside. I saw what he meant. Since the time when the twentieth century's critical thrust replaced the nineteenth century's philological one in most of the humanities, editing has been regarded in some academic circles as a marginal activity, requiring ingenuity and patience but rarely engaging the full force of the intellect. In this view editing is an occupation for the not-so-smart, whose only chance of overcoming the stigma is to go spiralling off into the arcane world of scientific bibliography where critically or theoretically inclined colleagues do not care to follow. A late developer among the humanities, musical scholarship provides one of the last strongholds of respectability for the editor. But the fortress is at present under siege and its advocates, though mighty, are on the defensive.[1] Musical editing may not surrender entirely, but it will surely no longer dominate the field as it once did.

Editors are scarcely better regarded in the musical world outside universities. Owing to the platitudes about the relation of musicology to performance that have grown up in the walled garden of early music, performers naturally tend to think of editors as their servants, or as mascots who are useful in upholding the credentials of the enterprise—so long as they make no trouble. They can soon be viewed as pedantic or 'unrealistic' when they do not support the conclusions reached by the performer, who nowadays increasingly acts as his own editor. The way things are going in the early music world today, the editor may in any case soon be superannuated. The

---

[1] On the attack is Joseph Kerman, *Contemplating Music: Challenges to Musicology* (Cambridge, Mass., 1985), 48–9 *et passim* (published in England as *Musicology*); for a reply see Margaret Bent, 'Fact and Value in Contemporary Scholarship', *Musical Times*, 127 (1986), 85–8.

search for authenticity, though slow to get started, now appears ready to stop at nothing. And indeed, if it remains committed to the ideal of re-creating the musical performance in its original terms then it will not stop at the present situation. Already there are several vocal groups who sing fifteenth- and sixteenth-century music from original parts; no self-respecting lutenist plays from anything but tablature; and there must be many string players who have mastered the French violin clef. As one writer put it a good twelve years ago, 'I would not hesitate to say that a mere pianist who can play from the original score of *Parthenia Inviolata*, for example, has penetrated further into the Jacobean musical world than someone who plays from a transcription on a Ruckers-type virginal, with the proper bass accompaniment.'[2] One can imagine not so far down the road a state of affairs in which original performing materials, whatever their difficulty, will be as common as original instruments. Mistakes will of course be aspects of authenticity, and poor readings the sacrifices made to a sense of original context. In this scenario the editor will be lucky to find employment running the copying machine and brewing the herbal tea.

Portraits as gloomy as these prompt one to think further about the role of the editor in music today, and a useful way of doing that is to examine the assumptions and principles with which editors have operated in the past. Accounts of musical editing tend to proceed from a conviction that a solution can or must be found to the problems encountered: they are mostly instruction manuals of one kind or another.[3] Hence the part played by editing and editions in our musical culture is rarely approached in a spirit of historical exploration. The need to produce rather than reflect is of course understandable when one considers the lack until recently of modern editions of what would be considered basic texts in other fields. The period since

[2] Joscelyn Godwin, 'Playing from Original Notation', *Early Music*, 2 (1974), 15.

[3] See, for a distinguished example, Howard Mayer Brown's article on 'Editing' in *The New Grove*, v. 839–48; also *Editionsrichtlinien musikalischer Denkmäler und Gesamtausgaben*, ed. Georg von Dadelsen (Kassel, 1967); *Musikalische Edition im Wandel des historischen Bewusstseins*, ed. T. G. Georgiades (Kassel, 1971); Arthur Mendel, 'The Purposes and Desirable Characteristics of Text-Critical Editions' in Edward Olleson (ed.), *Modern Musical Scholarship* (Stockfield-Boston-Henly-London, 1978) 14–27; and John Caldwell, *Editing Early Music* (Early Music Series, 5) (Oxford, 1985).

the Second World War, as Kerman allows, has seen the publication in score for the first time of Haydn symphonies, lesser works of Beethoven, major works of Dufay, Josquin, and Lasso, and '*practically the whole corpus of music* by important secondary figures of the Renaissance and Baroque eras'.[4] To this day there is no complete edition of Ockeghem, and some of the standard editions of the major composers (a notorious case is Monteverdi) are far from being either critical or even musical. Yet historical perspective is needed, for we are not likely to find an explanation of the editing phenomenon, and a way out of its present dilemma, in its various methods but rather in the history of the development of those methods and of the attitudes and assumptions that lie behind their application.

The earliest editions of historical music were made either by those brave antiquarians of the eighteenth century such as Martini, Burney, and Hawkins, who needed examples for their histories of music, or by musicians such as William Boyce and Samuel Arnold, who wished to preserve some tradition, which in their case was the musical repertory of the English cathedral.[5] We need not linger over them except to remark that they already exhibit the two principal motives—exploration and preservation—which have typified the early music movement and, as some would argue, still provide the tension on which it thrives today.

Though some of the many anthologies and collections that followed in the first part of the nineteenth century are respectful in their attitude to the text, 'editorial criteria did not, properly speaking, exist during this early period', to quote the judicious words of *The New Grove*.[6] The *Œuvres complètes* of Mozart, Haydn, Clementi, and Dussek published in Leipzig by Gottfried Christoph Härtel (1763–1827) were none of them complete.[7] They are important, however, as forerunners to Breitkopf and

[4] *Contemplating Music*, 49.

[5] William Boyce (ed.), *Cathedral Music*, 3 vols. (London, 1760–73); Samuel Arnold (ed.), *Cathedral Music*, 4 vols. (London, 1790). They are not unimportant as sources: Boyce's collection contains, for example, Morley's Funeral Sentences ('I am the resurrection and the life'), a substantial work which does not survive in pre-Restoration sources.

[6] Sydney Robinson Charles, 'Editions, historical', v. 849. The bibliography covers all the major collections.

[7] Mozart, 17 vols., 1798–1806; Haydn, 12 vols., 1800–43; Clementi, 13 vols., 1803–19, Dušek, 12 vols., 1813–17, repr. 1967 as *Collected Works*. Härtel

Härtel's remarkable series of collected works begun in the 1850s and 1860s under Härtel's sons Raymond (1810–88) and Hermann (1807–75). It was with these editions, devoted (in order of inception) to Bach, Handel, Palestrina, and Beethoven, that the nineteenth century's philological enthusiasm manifested itself in music.[8] This was the first serious and systematic attempt to establish the works of musical authors in a canonic way: the editions of Mendelssohn, Mozart, Chopin, Schumann, and others that quickly followed indicate its success.[9] It had the incidental effect, one might say, of canonizing the German tradition to which these composers belonged either in fact or by adoption.[10] Indeed, a second wave of philological energy produced national collections such as the *Denkmäler deutscher Tonkunst* and the *Denkmäler der Tonkunst in Bayern*, monuments of the past on which modern Germany, finally achieving statehood, could stake out its cultural heritage.[11] Perhaps the whole endeavour can be understood, along with the various methods of structural analysis, such as those of Riemann, Réti, and Schenker, as an outgrowth of the organicist movement of the nineteenth century: if individual works are entities in which

took over the Leipzig firm made successful by the typographical inventions and good business sense of Johann Gottlob Immanuel Breitkopf (1719–94) shortly after the latter's death.

[8] J. S. Bach, *Werke*, ed. Bach-Gesellschaft, 61 vols. in 47 Jg., 1851–1926; repr. 1968; G. F. Handel, *Werke*, ed. F. W. Chrysander, Deutsche Händelgesellschaft (93 vols. 1–48, 50–94), 1859–1903; repr. 1965, suppls. 1–6, 1888–1902; G. P. da Palestrina, *Werke*, ed. F. X. Haberl and others, 33 vols., 1862–1907; Ludwig van Beethoven, *Werke: Vollständige kritisch durchgesehene überall berechtigte Ausgabe*, 25 ser., 1862–90.

[9] Felix Mendelssohn, *Werke: Kritisch durchgesehene Ausgabe*, ed. J. Rietz, 19 ser. 1874–80; repr. 1967–70; Wolfgang Amadeus Mozart, *Werke: Kritisch durchgesehene Gesammtausgabe*, ed. L. von Köchel and others, 24 vols., Revisionsbericht, 1877–1905; Frederic Chopin, *Werke: Erste Kritische durchgesehene Gesammtausgabe*, ed. W. Bargiel, J. Brahms, A. Franchomme, F. Liszt, C. Reinecke, and E. Rudorff, 14 vols., Suppl., Revisionsberichte, 1878–1902; Robert Schumann, *Werke*, ed. Clara Schumann and others, 14 ser., 1880–93; repr. 1967; Franz Schubert, *Werke: Kritisch durchgesehene Gesammtausgabe*, ed. E. Mandyczewski, J. Brahms and others, 21 ser., Revisionsbericht, 1884–97; repr. 1965–9; Heinrich Schütz, *Sämmtliche Werke*, ed. Philipp Spitta and others, 18 vols., 1885–1927; repr. 1968–73.

[10] It is true that collected editions of the works of Purcell and Grétry were also initiated during this era (in 1878 and 1884 respectively), but the latter was nevertheless part of the enormous Breitkopf enterprise and, unlike the editions mentioned above, neither was completed within a half-century.

[11] See *The New Grove*, 'Editions, historical'.

all the parts relate to the whole, then it becomes more tempting to view the composer's total output in similar terms and to codify and canonize it accordingly.[12]

It was of course in Germany that the greatest progress was made earlier in the nineteenth century in the techniques of palaeography and textual criticism, particularly with regard to biblical and classical texts. The method of restoring a text from multiple sources by constructing a *stemma*—a summary analysis of their line(s) of descent gained from collating them—is still associated with the name of Karl Lachmann (1793–1851), whose edition of the New Testament (1831) overcame the almost divine sanction attributed to the then received text. Similar techniques were used by the monks of Solesmes in their work of restoring the plainchant—though the Vatican chant books published after Pope Pius X's *Motu proprio* of 1903, which hallowed their efforts, reflect a compromise between their 'archaeological' point of view and the more traditional one of incorporating later readings. Otherwise, musical editors seem at this stage to have been innocent of the Lachmann method, though they began to use the word 'critical' to describe their efforts. They aimed at a text that would reflect the composer's intentions, of course, but their ways of going about it were circumscribed by the lack of agreed standards and methods, by the desire for completion, and also, in some cases, by a certain arrogance. Karl Friedrich Chrysander, for instance, had access to the Handel autographs in the collection of the British royal family, but he preferred to base his work on the (non-autograph) conducting scores which he had in his own possession.

The methods of evaluating the sources and achieving a text have not, however, been a matter of overriding concern to musical editors, at least not until comparatively recent times. Far more important has been the question of how the edition presents its information. In a performance art such as music, in which notational symbols are shorthand for living musical gestures, it is understandable that the essence of an edition has often been understood to reside not in the authenticity or otherwise of the symbols it contains but in the manner in which

[12] For a wider discussion of canon, see Joseph Kerman, 'A Few Canonic Variations', *Critical Inquiry*, 10 (1983–4), 107–25.

they are presented to the performer. It seems realistic, then, first to examine that part of the history of musical editing which concerns the changing relation between the editor and the user of the edition.

The monumental editions of the works of earlier composers made during the nineteenth century are commonly thought to belong exclusively to the library as repositories or monuments claiming the same status as other codified texts. More important from a modern perspective, perhaps, is the concern for tradition exhibited in their notation and the suggestion their appearance gives of an open relation between editor and user allowing for a number of possibilities. Consider for a moment the layout of Breitkopf's Palestrina edition. Unlike its sources, it is in score with regular bar-lines, a format unusual (but not unknown) in the Renaissance.[13] The preservation of original note values reminds us that *alla breve*, as reflected in the *stile antico* of the eighteenth century, was considered an appropriate notation not in need of revision. Brahms, after all, was still using it (e.g. in the *German Requiem*), and with a similar historical sense of propriety. A clear pointer to a concern for practical issues in the first nine volumes, however, is the concession over clefs. Later on, when Haberl took over, the edition would reproduce every part in its original clef, to the discomfort of even the most intrepid score readers.[14] But in the earlier volumes the remoter clefs are exchanged for the soprano (C1), alto (C3), tenor (C4), and bass (F4) clefs familiar to German choral singers of the day (and to later composers such as Schoenberg who still used them). Practicality, then, was not alien to the original concerns of the editors. It took its place in the tangle of interests behind

[13] See Edward Lowinsky, 'Early Scores in Manuscript', *Journal of the American Musicological Society*, 13 (1960), 126–73.
[14] The transcriptions of Theodor de Witt (1823–55) were used for vols. 1–4, edited respectively by J. N. Rauch (1–3) and Franz Espagne (4). Vols. 5–8 were transcribed and edited by Espagne (1828–78) and vol. 9, by Franz Commer (1813–87). Haberl was responsible for the remainder of the series, and his main principle, 'so genau als möglich die Originalien wiederzugeben', resulted in various other small changes, such as the use of italic for the underlay of text indicated by the iterative sign 'ij' in the original prints, and a slightly different (and very precise) system of handling accidentals (see vol. 10, p. vii). The same methods are reflected in Orlando di Lasso, *Sämmtliche Werke*, ed. F. X. Haberl and A. Sandberger, 21 vols. (incomplete) (Leipzig, 1894–1927).

the edition—including the desire for the reform of church music (a movement in which Haberl and other Regensburg musicians played a considerable part) as well as the romantic ideal of recapturing and codifying the past.

If the origins of modern musicology lie nevertheless chiefly in German romantic historicism, then as Richard Taruskin points out, 'musicological ideals of performance style owe as much if not more to the modernist aesthetic that rose to dominance out of the ashes of the first world war'.[15] About that time, accordingly, early music editions began to change and their aims to diverge. The confusion already incipient in the nineteenth century between the needs on the one hand of the performer and on the other of the scholar became more acute, because modernism, in reacting against the living, unreflective, musical tradition, also called into question the nature and degree of the 'element of restoration' which, as Dahlhaus has suggested, essentially distinguishes 'early music' from that tradition.[16] This led to a paradoxical situation. Performers seeking a cooler, less personal style of interpretation in accordance with the modernist aesthetic increasingly sought scores free of extraneous expressive and interpretative markings. Scholars on the other hand, wishing to encourage or even to demand a more historical approach to performance, began to see the edition as a means of indoctrination rather than as simply a repository of the text.

The needs of the performer, then, fuelled by the model of musicology as science and performance as reproduction, led by way of the removal of performance history to the ideal of a text as clean and pure as driven snow—to the ideal, in a word, of

---

[15] 'The Musicologist and the Performer', in D. Kern Holoman and Claude V. Palisca (eds.), *Musicology in the 1980s: Methods, Goals, Opportunities*, (New York, 1982), 107. The essay also appeared as 'On Letting the Music Speak for Itself: Some Reflections on Musicology and Performance', *Journal of Musicology*, 1 (1982), 338–49.

[16] Carl Dahlhaus, *Foundations of Music History*, trans. J. B. Robinson (Cambridge, 1983), 67–8. According to his view, Bach's St Matthew Passion was 'early music' from its revival in 1829, but after more than 150 years Beethoven's symphonies are still part of the tradition. It remains to be seen whether the current recordings of the latter, and other classical works, by early music orchestras mark the 'self-destruction of the historical performance movement' (Kerman, *Contemplating Music*, 214) or the undermining of the tradition itself.

Urtext. Editions so advertised, however, always seemed less interested in reaching an 'original text' than in stripping an accepted one of accretions. The *Urtext* label was indeed principally associated with keyboard music, in which the usurpation of the role of editor by the solo virtuoso had become extreme in the late nineteenth and early twentieth centuries.[17] It is very much alive today in the elegantly printed but often woefully unexplained editions published by Henle.[18] Scholars, of course, have never had much use for it.[19] Their chief objection may be stated in the words of Walter Emery (whose sceptical little book is still the best introduction to editing for the general musician):

there is no such thing as an 'original text' of any piece of old music, unless either there is only one source, or all the sources give identical readings. . . . When there really is an identifiable original (such as a unique MS), it is often manifestly wrong; in which case it cannot be printed as it stands, or in other words, it has to be edited.[20]

Lamenting the 'Cult of the *Urtext*', he pointed out that

its devotees . . . do not realize that an 'original text' represents, as a rule, not what the composer wrote, but an editor's theory about what the composer meant to write; and they forget that although the editor's theory may be right, there may be a great difference between the notes the composer meant to write and those he meant to be played.[21]

---

[17] Nicholas Kenyon reminds me of a classic instance of the performer-editor's whimsical disregard of a text—the extra bar containing a thumping final low octave B flat which Czerny added to the B flat prelude in his edition of Book 1 of the *Well-Tempered Clavier*. For a good discussion of nineteenth-century 'virtuoso editing' in another repertory, see Robin Stowell, 'Bach's Violin Sonatas and Partitas' (Building a Music Library, 5), *Musical Times*, 128 (1987), 250–6.

[18] Günter Henle (1899–1979) is an interesting figure, an ex-diplomat, steel manufacturer, and amateur musician who turned to music publishing after the Second World War. 'It was clear to me from the beginning that the purpose of publishing *Urtexts* must be to present music lovers with the works of our masters in as unadulterated a form as is humanly possible', he writes in his autobiography, *Weggenosse des Jahrhunderts*, trans. Annette Jacobsohn as *Three Spheres: A Life in Politics, Business and Music* (Chicago, 1971), 238. See also his article, 'Über die Herausgabe von Urtexten', *Musica*, 8 (1954), 377–80.

[19] An attempt to render the term acceptable despite its difficulties was undertaken for Henle by Georg Feder and Hubert Unverricht in 'Urtext und Urtextausgaben', *Musikforschung*, 12 (1959), 432–54.

[20] Walter Emery, *Editions and Musicians* (London, 1957), 9. His examples, taken from the works of Bach, are telling.

[21] Ibid. 39.

The distinction between written note and intended sound is what ultimately made the editorial non-intervention implied by *Urtext* deeply unsatisfactory for most scholars (and particularly scholar-performers). With greater emphasis being placed upon the realization of early music in a style differing ever more sharply from that associated with the romantic tradition, the text could not simply be left to speak for itself to the performer. In some circles, accordingly, the notation in which early music was presented began more and more to reflect a concern for what Arnold Dolmetsch and Thurston Dart called 'interpretation'.[22] As Dart put it in his widely-read manual, 'first of all we need to know the exact symbols the composer used; then we must find out what these signified at the time they were written; and lastly we must express our conclusions in terms of our own age'.[23] The method, then, was similar in essence to the one Busoni, Petri, and other virtuoso performer-editors employed, but the priorities and aims were strikingly different.

Support for this method came also from the context in which early music flourished. The reconstruction of the art music of past ages was not so very different in aim from the recapture of folk-song. In England at least, early music—especially of the Tudor variety—went hand in hand with folk-song in a not very heavily disguised programme to purify national culture. As David Josephson's fascinating analysis of Percy Grainger's differences with Cecil Sharp and Ralph Vaughan Williams indicates, it is a moot point whether at this stage the ennobling qualities of folk-song and early music were more or less important than their authenticity.[24] Most notable for our purposes is the fact that the music was in both cases 'digested'

---

[22] Arnold Dolmetsch, *The Interpretation of Music of the Seventeenth and Eighteenth Centuries* (London, 1915; 2nd edn. 1946; repr. 1969); Thurston Dart, *The Interpretation of Music* (London, 1954; 4th edn. 1967). Kerman draws attention to the confusion caused by Dart's appropriating, for historically informed (or 'stylish') performance, a term generally used to denote the way performers bring their own musical personality to bear on works in the standard repertory—'the mischievous implication . . . was that interpretation is a normative matter, not an individual one', *Contemplating Music*, 191.

[23] Dart, *Interpretation*, 13–14.

[24] David Josephson, 'The Case for Percy Grainger, Edwardian Musician, on His Centenary', in Edmond Strainchamps, Maria R. Maniates, and Christopher Hatch (eds.), *Music and Civilization: Essays in Honor of Paul Henry Lang* (New York, 1984), 355–60.

by an intermediary, the editor, who made it suitable for modern consumption.

In one substantial tradition, then, musical editing became from the 1920s onward increasingly prescriptive rather than descriptive (to use Josephson's terms). On the grounds that performers would be misled about tempo by the symbols chosen by early composers, note values were halved, then quartered—though to my knowledge no one took up Dart's challenge to re-edit the late piano sonatas to eliminate 'Beethoven's own rather oddly chosen note-values (27/32 and so on)'.[25] In order to rescue performers from the 'tyranny of the bar-line' various methods were devised in editions of fifteenth- and sixteenth-century music for getting rid of it and of highlighting the rhythmic patterns as discerned by the editor.[26] Suggested ornamentation and realized continuo parts began to be a more regular feature of scholarly editions of music of the seventeenth and eighteenth centuries. And so I could go on— the areas in which editors exercised interpretative discretion are numerous. If the most professional editorial precepts were followed their interventions were distinguished from the marks that derived from the composer or from the 'original'. Several grey areas developed, however, where an ambiguity in the use of symbols or an unwillingness to clutter the text with explanation made it very hard to discover the exact nature of the editorial action.[27] In various ways, both overt and covert, an

[25] *Interpretation* , 22.

[26] There is a good discussion of the *Mensurstrich* and other bar-line alternatives in Caldwell, *Editing Early Music* (Oxford, 1985), 48–9; Hans Albrecht's article on 'Editionstechnik' in *MGG* (iii. 1125–6) gives three examples, including one, edited by Otto Gombosi, in which each part is barred differently, a method advocated recently by Karl Kohn in 'The Renotation of Polyphonic Music', *Musical Quarterly*, 67 (1981), 29–49. For a recent compromise, entailing bar-lines drawn through the stave lines when a tie will not result and small ticks either side it when one would, see the editions of the London publisher Mapa Mundi.

[27] At various points in the variation Masses on the 'Western Wind' tune by John Taverner and John Shepherd (e.g. the Osanna at the end of the Benedictus) there are variations in triple metre indicated by a proportional sign. In my edition of the former (London, 1962) and Nicholas Sandon's of the latter (*Early English Church Music*, 18 (London, 1976), 60–84) the note values, normally quartered, are reduced by eight in these places. We both interpreted the proportion as *tripla*. I later became convinced that the intended proportion was *sesquialtera*, which completely changes the musical effect. A rapid 'drive to the cadence' becomes instead a stately broadening out. My attempt to give an

interpretative element became very much part of the text as the editor conceived it and the reader/performer received it. Whether conscious of it or not, the editor became a pre-interpreter, part of the chain of creativity that led from the composer to the realized work.

A good example of an editor who covered in one lifetime the principal phases of editing—from the antiquarian to the descriptive to the prescriptive—is E. H. Fellowes (1870–1951), an English clergyman who has few rivals as the most indefatig-able musical editor of this century. The very title of his first edition, *The English Madrigal School*, smacks of Victorian nationalistic ideals.[28] And his attitudes towards his texts were characteristic of that era. On the one hand he would silently bowdlerize such indelicate expressions as 'From Virgin's Womb' (which became 'From Virgin Pure'), and on the other he would rely so heavily on what he found in the British Museum and be so impatient for completion that he would not balk at making up a part missing from a London manuscript instead of taking the train to Oxford where the concordant source, well known to him, lay in the Bodleian.[29]

As *The English Madrigal School* was nearing completion, Fellowes joined a group of editors (including Sir Richard Terry, and Sylvia Townsend Warner, better known for her stories in *The New Yorker*), in producing a national collection entitled *Tudor Church Music*.[30] This was a purely 'descriptive' edition designed for the library shelf. It differed from the earlier monuments of sixteenth-century polyphony, such as the Pales-trina and Lasso editions, in an evolutionary rather than radical

indication of this change of heart in a reprint was undermined by the unfortunate choice of note reduction, which vividly urges the performer to adopt a faster tempo. In his edition, Sandon forgot to signal the change in reduction ratio, leaving the user unable to reconstruct the notation of the sources at all.

[28] 36 vols. (London 1913–24).

[29] See *The English Madrigal School*, vol. 15 (London, 1920), 135–6; and 'As Caesar wept' (the viola I part), in *The Collected Vocal Works of William Byrd*, vol. 15 (London, 1948), 74–6.

[30] *Tudor Church Music*, ed. P. C. Buck, E. H. Fellowes, A. Ramsbotham, S. Townsend Warner, 10 vols. (London, 1922–9); appendix and supplementary notes by Fellowes (London, 1948). R. R. Terry, whose work at Westminster Cathedral prompted the Carnegie Trust's interest in financing the venture, was included in the original editorial committee, from which he later resigned.

way. Modern choral clefs were adopted, and the ones in the early sources were not even noted after the first volume. There was a system of irregular barring. The edition was also marked by its own beautiful music typeface which accurately suggested the influence on the Tudor enthusiasm of William Morris and the Arts and Crafts movement. In the view of many it rendered the music invisible when held at any distance from the eyes, and this became a standard excuse for the reduction of note values in later British editions.[31]

One of the edition's more interesting features was its adoption of the method used in editions in other disciplines (and also in Bischoff's well-known editions of Bach's keyboard music) of listing variants and textual comments at the foot of the page on which they occur. Equally open in its implication about the relation of the edition to its users is its statement of purpose: 'And our aim will be attained when we have presented in all faithfulness that which we know to exist, leaving to others to make use of it, whether for the study of early musical structure, or for the writing of musical history, or for "public or private exercise".'[32] This was the traditional attitude of the *Gesamtausgabe* or *Denkmälerausgabe*. Fellowes went along with it in this context for reasons best known to himself—his autobiography is silent on the question, though clear on how much performance of the music mattered to him in general.[33] He promptly domesticated this alien territory by making practical editions of as many as sixty-one pieces from the contents of *Tudor Church Music*, mostly those works that could be sung in the Anglican services.[34]

Concessions had been made to the performer in *The English*

---

[31] See Dart, *Interpretation*, 22.

[32] vol. i, p. x.

[33] *Memoirs of an Amateur Musician* (London, 1946), especially 'Musicology and Research', 119–38. (The title of the book is ironic: despite Elgar's efforts Fellowes was not allowed—because of his being in Holy Orders—to join the Incorporated Society of Musicians, Britain's professional organization for musicians.) More typical of his attitude than the preface to *Tudor Church Music* is the pamphlet he published in 1924, *The English Madrigal: A Guide to its Practical Use*, which consists of the commendably extensive editorial preface to *The English Madrigal School* (printed only in vol. i), a chapter entitled 'Some Further Points about Madrigal Singing', an index to the series, and a list of identified poems set as madrigals.

[34] *Tudor Church Music* (Octavo series) (London, 1921–37).

Madrigal School, not the least being its octavo format. (Most memorable of its devices is the ubiquitous accent used—ambiguously—to denote irregular rhythms rather than dynamic effects.) But it did not incorporate either transposition or diminished note values. These came later, in various church music editions and principally in *The Collected Vocal Works of William Byrd*, begun in 1937 and completed in 1950 with three volumes of the keyboard music unblushingly adapted for the pianoforte. These scores put a narrow concept of practicality ahead of every other consideration. In Byrd's *Gradualia*, for example, where the first twenty-five numbers of the first book provide music for the Propers of all the Marian Masses of the Roman rite (both on feast days and Saturdays) in an abbreviated system derived from contemporary Graduals, Fellowes, a staunch Protestant, ignored the liturgical background and therefore failed to understand the actual constitution of several pieces.[35] In addition, his transpositions interfered with the perception of a set of Propers as a single musical unit—the Christmas music is printed in as many as four different keys.

Whatever his failings, Fellowes exemplifies the influence of the interpreting editor, for his programme was highly success-ful. With allies such as Steuart Wilson, founder of the English Singers, T. B. Lawrence, conductor of the Fleet Street Choir, and Boris Ord, director of the Cambridge University Madrigal Society and organist of King's College, he saw during his lifetime both madrigals and Tudor church music become part of the national tradition and the style of performance he favoured firmly entrenched. Similar efforts, some equally successful, are characteristic of European editors; *Das Chorwerk* is an example of a comparable thrust in German music of the period. When Fellowes died, his spiritual heir was Thurston Dart, the professional harpsichordist and scholar who was the moving force behind the national edition, *Musica Britannica*, which he co-founded in 1953, and who became a director of the firm, Stainer & Bell, which had published much of Fellowes's work. Dart was the representative of a new generation instrumental in introducing more professional standards into the editing of early

[35] As, to be fair, did everyone else until the appearance of James L. Jackman's 'Liturgical Aspects of Byrd's *Gradualia*', *Musical Quarterly*, 49 (1963), 17–37.

music (see Chapter 2). But if Fellowes's attitude to the user of his editions was slightly avuncular, Dart's became positively paternal. He was fond of what one might call the legislative future tense: 'performers will want to follow such and such an editorial direction' was a common expression of his prefaces, and there was always a certain 'told-to-the-children' attitude behind his pronouncements.[36] It is an attitude common in early music circles still. A recent book, almost paraphrasing Dart, who seems rather mild by comparison, announces that 'the edition *will* provide the performer with a clear modern equivalent of the obscure, incomplete and archaically written sources' (my italics), and is heavily prescriptive throughout.[37]

The firm entrenchment of prescriptive (or to be kinder, interpretative) methods emerges from the dialogue between even the most sane and enlightened of editors. In his recent book on editing John Caldwell gives the following advice about the beaming of groups of quavers and semiquavers in order to 'guard against over-interpretation': 'it is best to stick to standard patternings, limiting the cross-beam to simple subdivisions of the bar (e.g. 𝅘𝅥𝅯𝅘𝅥𝅯𝅘𝅥𝅯 𝅘𝅥𝅯𝅘𝅥𝅯𝅘𝅥𝅯 rather than 𝅘𝅥𝅯𝅘𝅥𝅯𝅘𝅥𝅯 𝅘𝅥𝅯𝅘𝅥𝅯𝅘𝅥𝅯𝅘𝅥𝅯)'.[38] 'But', writes Richard Taruskin in his review of the book, 'the "standard patterning" is itself an interpretation, and an especially insidious one, since it wears the sheep's clothing of accepted (and for Renaissance music, irrelevant and anachronistic) convention', and he goes on to talk about the performer's unconscious inclination to 'squeeze' the tie.[39] What is interesting here is the temporary loss by both sides in the debate of a sense of the superiority in this regard of the early sources themselves—even though Taruskin himself has taken the lead in publishing performing editions in original notation.[40] More

---

[36] This was more evident in his popular series, such as *Invitation to Madrigals* and *Invitation to Medieval Music* (both published by Stainer & Bell), than in his *Musica Britannica* volumes, needless to say. For a similar tone from another scholar during the same period see Alfred Dürr, 'Wissenschaftliche Neuausgaben und die Praxis', *Musik und Kirche*, 29 (1959), 77–82.

[37] David Wulstan, *Tudor Music* (London and Melbourne, 1985), 178.

[38] *Editing Early Music*, 25.

[39] *Notes*, 42 (1986), 779.

[40] Ogni Sorte Editions, Miami, Florida, have published several works edited by Taruskin in which a score edited according to current conventions, with reduced note values and bar-lines, is accompanied by separate parts in original notation, including ligatures, clefs, etc.

important than the sources' not being in score or lacking bar-lines is the fact that their notation never calls for the 'beaming' that implies a rhythmic interpretation. They embody in themselves an ambiguous presentation of the relation between the notes and the 'stroke' (as Morley translates 'tactus') or any other quasi-metrical element, such as *modus*. (It is rarely pointed out, though worth noticing, that rests were not syncopated against the tactus in the best notational practices of the sixteenth century.) The contemporary performer was therefore forced into a decision over the claims of the *arsis* and *thesis* of the tactus and the expressive quality of the rhythmic profile of the phrase. I assume that there was a decision—the emphasis on synco-pation in both music and theory indicates as much—and that the decision was made on more informed grounds than exist today. It may equally have been internalized to the point of seeming instinctive. We shall not recapture it exactly; but there seems no intrinsic reason why modern performers should have their predecessors' predicament entirely removed by an intermediary.

Even in the climate of what many regard as over-respect for the composer's intentions, then, the possibility of getting out of such embattled positions simply by preserving as much as possible of the composer's own notation within the context of the modern score is rarely entertained. Naturally, editors have had a vested interest in maintaining that earlier notational systems are conceptually different—like languages that need translating rather than dialects that require a broader vocabulary and better ear. Those who sailed against the prevailing wind, however, often ended up with an unexpected advantage. As Richard Langham Smith pointed out in discussing the peculiar-ities of François Couperin's notation in his review of a recent revision of Paul Brunold's edition of *Leçons de Ténèbres, Élévations et Motets Divers*:

Quite possibly, such notational niceties were not understood by the original editors. All the more praiseworthy, therefore, that so many details were retained, for it has ensured the longevity of the edition beside many others which have become obsolete as we have learned more about performance practices.[41]

A way out of the prescriptive method that allows the

---

[41] *Early Music*, 14 (1986), 284.

educative function to remain intact is to accompany a 'clean' text with copious annotation.[42] The common complaint of editors that no performer reads prefatory matter or commentary is not a good reason for omitting either. It can be met to some extent by flagging important matters in footnotes on the music page where they are most relevant and most hard to ignore. Yet the lack of interpretative, critical, historical, or even textual essays in editions is a constant complaint, and one that shows musicology in an unflattering light.[43] Perhaps it is true, as Joseph Kerman avers, that the uncertainty surrounding performance practice alienates positivistically trained scholars, who 'given the choice between preparing an edition of Josquin's Masses and determining how they were sung . . . will opt instinctively for the former undertaking'.[44] When more than cursory attention is given to performance in an edition, the tone adopted is sometimes unhelpfully dogmatic. It is true that no performance can itself be ambiguous or indecisive, but it is the performer, not the editor, who needs to turn knowledge into action in order to communicate with conviction; and what the performer needs from the editor is surely an open discussion of the possibilities and a measured judgement as to which courses of action are preferable.

The question might be asked of editors today exactly who is this 'performer' for whom they make their editions 'practical'. Judging by the proliferation of early music recordings, the success of early music festivals, and the currency of early music journals, today's performer tends to have a rather sophisticated notion of the imaginative re-creation of early music along historical lines, and is ready to embrace as 'practical' anything that helps to bring the original performing situation into closer focus. One conductor may take Taruskin's ideal of Renaissance rhythm as a model. With the notation of the original sources to hand, another may adopt quite a different approach, which,

---

[42] The idea is endorsed, in different terms of course, by Ludwig Finscher in 'Gesamtausgabe—Urtext—Musikalische Praxis' in Martin Bente (ed.), *Musik—Edition—Interpretation: Gedenkschrift Günter Henle* (Munich, 1980), 193–8.

[43] See, for instance, the review of Italian madrigal editions by Anthony Newcomb in *The Journal of the American Musicological Society*, 39 (1986), 395–408.

[44] Kerman, *Contemplating Music*, 189.

done with equal conviction, may well turn out to be equally 'authentic' (to borrow Taruskin's sense of that awkward word for a moment). Neither needs spoon-feeding unless one feels that those who are treated like children will remain like children, allowing the editor to assert a parental role. The child of Fellowes's era, however, has become at the very least an adolescent who needs challenging. Undoubtedly the acknowledgement on the part of editors that performers are collaborators to be persuaded and reasoned with rather than subjects to be legislated for would involve a rewriting of the 'interface' of current editions that is too radical for some people in both camps. But as the personalization of the computer has shown, 'user-friendly' (as opposed to 'well-documented') turns out to imply a certain tyranny, and—to pursue the metaphor—early music performers were always hackers at heart.

So far I have addressed chiefly the question of presentation, that part of the edition which principally determines the relationship between the editor and the user. Upon this area debate always seems to have fastened, incidentally revealing one of the reasons for the curiously uncomfortable nature of the relation between scholar and performer (even when, as in the case of Dart, they are embodied in the same person). Of even greater importance is the relation of the editor to the source or sources of the work or works under consideration. The degree of penetration into the various problems the sources pose, and the discrimination with which they are treated, are the criteria that ultimately determine the quality of the editor's work. However beautifully or thoughtfully an edition is presented, it is seriously flawed if the relationship of the sources has been misinterpreted, or if poor decisions have been made about the evidence they present.

Once again a sense of history is important for a consideration of the issues and assumptions involved. The same nineteenth-century legacy that gave us collections of works and a sense of the unity and authority of text also provided a means of achieving a text that would satisfy the demands of the programme. Though musical scholarship has only comparatively recently begun to make direct reference to the method of textual criticism developed primarily for biblical and classical texts, to a greater or lesser extent it has been influenced by it all along. Margaret Bent has provided a good summary of recension and the other features of the Lachmann method in an essay that both relates it to a class of musical sources and argues strongly for the ideal, eclectic text it is designed to produce:

> *Recensio* is the reconstruction from the surviving copy or copies of the earliest recoverable version of what is transmitted. It is achieved largely by accumulating and sifting the evidence provided by variant readings and errors. If there is a single witness, it must be deciphered. If there are several, their relationship to each other must be established. If the tradition is 'closed' (i.e. with no source being copied from more that one exemplar), a *stemma* may be drawn up. In an 'open' tradition, *contaminatio* has taken place through promiscuous copying: . . . Any sources that are totally dependent on others should be eliminated from consideration (*eliminatio*). Then the lost version from which the survivors ultimately descend should be reconstructed as far as the evidence permits. The text thus achieved, whether deriving from one source or several, is examined for correctness and plausibility (*examinatio*), and subjected where necessary to *emendatio* by conjecture.[45]

It will be sufficient to note that the words 'contamination' and 'promiscuous' carry in ordinary contexts sufficient moral opprobrium (and are so related to the nineteenth-century's linking of abnormality with disease) to suggest an ideological framework. The unity and purity of text were to be assured by a method designed to produce them. Furthermore, the principle of authorial intention was reinforced by the method of emending texts according to the way they were discerned to fall into an ancestral series. The method did not go unchallenged. Most notable among the revisionists was the French medievalist, Joseph Bédier (1864–1938). He observed that most stemmata turned out to be bipartite, and since he could not believe that this seemingly objective phenomenon accurately reflected the way texts were transmitted he concluded it must occur

---

[45] 'Some Criteria for Establishing Relationships between Sources of Late-Medieval Polyphony' in Iain Fenlon (ed.), *Music in Medieval and Early Modern Europe* (Cambridge, 1981), 295–6. The description is based on the classic and largely abstract formulation of Paul Maas in *Textual Criticism*, trans. Barbara Flower (Oxford, 1958), but the article is also informed by the less austere approach of G. B. Pasquali as reflected in the best modern handbook on the subject, Martin L. West's *Textual Criticism and Editorial Technique* (Stuttgart, 1973).

principally in the minds of textual critics. This led him to seek on purely pragmatic grounds the 'best text' among the extant documents and to edit it.[46] One casualty of his scepticism was of course the concept of honouring the author's intentions. But for Bédier the Lachmann method had overestimated its powers of being able to reach a lost original. It was better to admit the limits of one's knowledge and respect the integrity of the text that *had* survived.

The 'best text' method has recently found increasing acceptance among musicologists. As Howard Mayer Brown puts it in his article on editing in *The New Grove*, 'most modern editors agree that it is better to base a new edition on one good source than to publish a conflation resembling nothing that existed at or soon after the period of the work itself'.[47] Yet this proposition naturally provokes some disagreement. Margaret Bent, arguing the traditional Lachmannian view in powerful terms, invokes (among other things) the 'respect . . . owed to the original intentions of the composer'.[48] For Richard Taruskin, attacking the 'best text' method from a different direction, its adoption by modern musicologists is yet another symptom of their craven fear of exercising critical judgement. Connecting it with the current vogue for editions of single extant sources, he sees it as 'tacitly raising what are, after all, mere redactions to the status of authentic texts' and giving them spurious authority.[49] There is in addition an unfortunate tendency among best-text or single-source editors to augment their unavoidable ideological biases with what one might label, to coin a term, 'codicocentricity'. The pressing need Edward Lowinsky seems to have felt to assert the superiority of *all* the readings in his 'Medici Codex' over and above those in concordant sources is perhaps merely a tiresome feature of an otherwise exemplary edition, yet it illustrates a special kind of danger for the editor.[50]

---

[46] See his article 'La tradition manuscrite du *Lai de l'ombre*', *Romania*, 54 (1928), 161–96, 321–56.

[47] v. 840.

[48] 'Some Criteria', 311–16.

[49] 'The Limits of Authenticity: A Discussion', *Early Music*, 12 (1984), 4; see also *Notes*, 42 (1986), 776–7.

[50] *The Medici Codex of 1518*, ed. Edward E. Lowinsky (Monuments of Renaissance Music, 3–5) (Chicago and London, 1968); see the textual commentary in part three of the first of these volumes.

For, needless to say, the degree to which either conflation or 'best-text' methods will result in a good edition depends far less on either than on the editor's ability to identify and deal with the individual textual problems that all sources contain.

When Housman came to write his famous diatribe against those who applied the rules of the method too rigidly and those, like Bédier, who ultimately rejected its excesses, he described it thus: 'Textual criticism . . . is the science of discovering error in texts and the art of removing it'.[51] And indeed, 'in practice it was *emendatio* that continued to bulk larger than *recensio*', as E. J. Kenney points out in his useful and humane book: '*Recensio* may be shirked; *emendatio* cannot be. That is to say, the editor must print something, and what he prints is determined by the choices made at the stage of *emendatio*.'[52] If the first crisis of the editor is to decide, when choosing readings, between the 'controlled eclecticism'[53] of the Lachmann method and a pragmatic 'best-text' approach along Bédier's lines, the second is to decide what to emend and how. The subjectivity of editors and their need for judgement and intuition have rarely been contradicted when considering this process. If a tendency can be discerned, it is towards excessive emendation rather than the reverse. As Kenney sagely observes, 'It has always seemed to most people a more distinguished intellectual feat to correct a text by altering it than to explain it as it stands.'[54] The extremes of the 'conservative' and 'radical' categories into which all editors seem to fall may be illustrated by editions of Schoenberg's *A Survivor from Warsaw*. The editors of the *Sämtliche Werke: Chorwerke II*, Josef Rufer and Christian Martin Schmidt, holding the autograph in exaggerated respect, reproduce patent

[51] 'The Application of Thought to Textual Criticism', *Proceedings of the Classical Association*, 18 (1921); reprinted in Ronald Gottesman and Scott Bennett (eds.), *Art and Error* (Bloomington, Indiana, 1970), 2.
[52] *The Classical Text: Aspects of Editing in the Age of the Printed Book* (Berkeley, 1974), 112. Kenney's book contains a very useful history and critique of the Method in chaps. 5 and 6 (pp. 105–51). An extensive bibliography of other works on the topic is given by Stanley Boorman in 'Limitations and Extensions of Filiation Technique', in Iain Fenlon (ed.), *Music in Medieval and Early Modern Europe*, 319–46.
[53] The expression is Philip Gaskell's and is his description of the process of converting a 'copy-text' (see below) into a critical text; see *From Writer to Reader* (Oxford, 1978), 4.
[54] *The Classical Text*, 114.

errors. Jacques-Louis Monod, in his revision of the first edition, tends to rewrite extensively whenever the music does not follow the logic of the serial method. Schoenberg, however, was mistrustful of a mechanical approach to his method, and 'learned to treat his "mistakes" with respect as the product of intuition'. In both these cases, as in many others, the problem is the rigid application of a rule of thumb, as Oliver Neighbour concludes in the review from which I quote.[55] But it is also a mistake to believe that the sort of radical approach that Taruskin, for example, seems to urge must necessarily result in solutions that owe more to the editor's overt or covert prejudices than to a historical reading. Kenney again places the emphasis correctly in describing textual criticism as 'the art and science of balancing historical probabilities'. Referring to a typical Housman outburst on 'scholars who have neither enough intellect nor enough literature' to decide between two variant readings in Propertius, he comments:

The problem that he was posing was not of a purely literary order. The critic has to decide, not which of these variants is 'better', but which of them Propertius, living when he did, being the sort of poet he was, and practising a particular genre, is more likely to have written. That the answer in this case leaps to the eye tends to obscure the fact that it is not the taste of the critic but his understanding of Propertius' taste on which the decision turns. Of course the two things are intimately connected, but they are not identical.[56]

A brief account of how the Lachmann method was put to work on British and American literature will reveal further complications that apply to music. Its inheritors in the English-speaking world were the New Bibliographers, who worked first and foremost in the Shakespearean field where the problems were in some ways analogous to those encountered by the founding fathers, but in others (for instance the preponderance of bibliographical over scribal contexts and of 'monogenous' stemmatic patterns over 'polygenous' ones) quite different. The variable orthography in English texts of the period (most notably) led W. W. Greg to draw a distinction between 'substantive' and 'accidental' (i.e. indifferent) readings

[55] *Music and Letters*, 57 (1976), 443–6.
[56] *The Classical Text*, 146.

and to formulate what he called 'the English theory of "copy-text"' whereby the editor would choose 'whatever extant text may be supposed to represent most nearly what the author wrote and to follow it with the least possible alteration' in the matter of the so-called accidentals. Greg was, however, at pains to dissociate himself from the 'fallacy of the "best text"'. As he wrote, 'the choice between substantive readings belongs to the general theory of textual criticism and lies altogether beyond the narrow principle of copy-text'.[57] Greg's theory has (at least indirectly) influenced musical editors in the English-speaking world, where there has been some confusion about the essential difference between the concept of 'copy-text', useful as it is in a musical situation fraught with indifferent variants, and the theory of 'best text'.

Greg stood firmly behind the eclectic choice of text, and his influence on subsequent bibliographers, most notably Fredson Bowers and his followers, was considerable. When the technique Greg and others had developed was applied to more recent literature, in which not only authors' manuscripts, but also drafts, sketches, and corrected proofs all provided a different dimension to the textual critic's problems, a new theory had to be worked out. Bowers, following the great tradition, regarded what happened during the publishing-house and printing stages in the same light as the corruptions introduced into earlier works by scribes or typesetters. In his theory, an author's manuscript represents his final intentions, and is therefore chosen as copy-text, with the usual eclectic approach taken to the formation of the final text.[58]

---

[57] This is from Greg's classic article, 'The Rationale of Copy-Text', *Studies in Bibliography*, 3 (1950–1), 19–36; reprinted in *The Collected Papers of Sir Walter W. Greg*, ed. J. C. Maxwell (Oxford, 1966), 374–91, and in Ronald Gottesman and Scott Bennett (eds.), *Art and Error* (Bloomington, Indiana, 1970).

[58] The Bowers position is defended in a series of magisterial articles by G. Thomas Tanselle in *Studies in Bibliography* over the last fifteen years. Musical editors have been less prone to theorize along such lines; for a few examples, dealing with the editing of later musical texts, see Georg von Dadelsen, 'Die "Fassung letzter Hand" in der Musik', *Acta Musicologica*, 33 (1961), 1–19, Eva Badura-Skoda, 'Textual Problems in Masterpieces of the 18th and 19th Centuries', *Musical Quarterly*, 51 (1965), 301–17, and Robert Pascall, 'Brahms and the Definitive Text' in Robert Pascall (ed.), *Brahms: Biographical, Documentary and Analytical Studies* (Cambridge, 1983), 59–75.

His view has recently come in for considerable criticism.[59] If problems first emerged in connection with editions of modern authors, they were intensified when controversy began to break out in the very field in which the most sophisticated work had been done—Shakespearean studies. The relation between the earlier Quarto and the later Folio texts of a play provide an instructive example:

> For if scholars were misguided in their assessments of the two original printed texts of *King Lear*—if, for example, these are not two *relatively corrupted* texts of a pure (but now lost) original, but two *relatively reliable* texts of two different versions of the play (as we now think)— then our general methods for dealing with such texts is called into serious question.[60]

The discerning of 'versions', such as is common for instance in Handel research, and the articulation of a theory based on them, is one answer to this predicament, but it is an answer that leaves us largely within the system we have inherited. What if the very nature of our perception of the production of texts, as McGann suggests, is 'desocialized'? If it can be shown that 'the literary work is always produced under institutional conditions . . . and their impact on the author's work in the literary production is by no means always an alien or contaminating influence', then how much more should we be on our guard against romantic ideology in approaching a composer's work, which depends absolutely and over and over again on institutional co-operation for its realization.[61]

A recording of the Mozart Requiem in an edition by C. R. F. Maunder furnishes an extreme example of the degree to which the early music movement is still in the grip of this ideology.[62] Doubts about the amount of this work actually composed by Mozart have been public debate since the 1825–6 controversy

---

[59] See Jerome J. McGann, *A Critique of Modern Textual Criticism* (Chicago, 1983), where the recent disruptions of the literary bibliographical world are sympathetically discussed.

[60] Ibid. 4.   [61] Ibid. 103.

[62] The Academy of Ancient Music directed by Christopher Hogwood, Oiseau-Lyre 411712–20H, 1983, with sleeve-note by C. R. F. Maunder from which the quotations in this paragraph are taken. Since this chapter was written, Maunder has published his detailed findings in his book *Mozart's Requiem: On Preparing a New Edition* (Oxford, 1988).

between Gottfried Weber and Maximilian Stadler summarized by Blume in an article aptly entitled 'Requiem but no Peace'.[63] Maunder believes that the way to find out is to examine the music itself 'to see whether its craftmanship measures up to Mozart's rigorous standards'. His test shows him 'that there is no genuine Mozart in the Lacrimosa completion, the Sanctus, Osanna and Benedictus'. The next step is the unargued assumption that only genuine Mozart will do, and the operation becomes a search-and-destroy mission against Süssmayr. Those movements must go, and 'like the C minor Mass K427, the work must remain a torso'. In other words, the peculiar nature of the work as an historical entity is to be discounted. Even Mozart's intention to have the Requiem completed is to be ignored. The issue is simply 'authentic material', the pure form of *Urtext*.

This attitude to texts is of course not confined to music. In a radical article based on earlier work, Stephen Orgel examines the notion of an 'authentic' Shakespeare.[64] His arguments are applicable to a number of musical situations, since he starts from the position that plays were written not for publication but for performance. He shows that 'Shakespeare habitually began with more than he needed, that his scripts offered the company a range of possibilities, and the process of production was a collaborative process of selection as well as of realization and interpretation'. The acting text, in other words, was different not only from the printed text but also from the author's script.

The fluidity of the written text, the divergence between published and performing texts are, then, historically authentic, if not historically determined. And the claim of textual authenticity as a function of the author's hand – the folio's claim to preserve 'the true original copies' – becomes an issue only when the plays are printed, and are then claimed to be authors' plays, not actors' plays.

The enormous industry that has gone into 'establishing' the Shakespearean text, as a consequence, only serves to falsify the nature of the historical entity, and instead reveals more about us

---

[63] *Musical Quarterly*, 47 (1961), 147–69.
[64] 'The Authentic Shakespeare', *Representations* 21 (Winter 1988), 1–25. One can see the process he outlines at work in Stoppard's *Travesties* as described by Philip Gaskell, who addresses (without resolving) the questions of authorial intention and the work in Example 12 of *From Writer to Reader*, 245–62.

and our needs: 'What we want is not the authentic play, with its unstable, infinitely revisable script, but an authentic Shakespeare, to whom every generation's version of a classic drama may be ascribed.'

The danger of misrepresenting the historical fact by superimposing a later sense of what constitutes both text and work, as in the case of Shakespeare, emerges from an essay by Reinhard Strohm on the similar context of the *opera seria*. 'What is to us the "work", he writes, 'was 250 years ago only the "production",' and that was dominated to such an extent by singers that, as reconstruction, 'a revival of an *opera seria* today should really concentrate less on what Handel or Hasse wrote than on what Senesino or Farinelli did with the chief role'. And if we had a Senesino, 'it might not matter so much that some of his arias were by Harnoncourt and not Handel. In fact they could even be by Penderecki.'[65] Similar problems attend the historical reconstruction of Italian opera of the nineteenth century. There is nothing wrong with our wanting an authentic Shakespeare, Handel, or Verdi, of course, or with our creating 'works' out of 'productions', so long as we realize what we are doing. The editor, as historical critic, ought to be in a good position to show us that, because the choice of what to make into a 'text' can only proceed from a rather thorough understanding of the historical context and its implications.

The effect of the theatre in the cases mentioned above adds considerably to the destabilizing effect of performance in general. Are all musical texts therefore unstable? As it happens, my own editorial experience has centred on the work of Shakespeare's contemporary, William Byrd. It is hard to believe that any greater contrast could exist. Seizing the opportunity offered by the royal grant of a monopoly over music printing in 1575, Byrd seems in middle age to have organized the publication of most of his vocal compositions in a deliberate and definitive manner. As collation of all the copies of each edition of his prints has proceeded in the course of producing *The Byrd Edition*, it has become increasingly apparent that the composer controlled the whole printing process to a degree unusual

---

[65] 'Towards an understanding of the *opera seria*', in *Essays on Handel and Italian Opera* (Cambridge, 1985), 94–8.

among Elizabethan authors in general. Corrections made by lifting pieces of type out of the forme during the course of a press run, or by sticking small 'cancel slips' over the offending notes on the finished sheets, reflect a concern for the most minute details, including punctuation and word underlay. In an age of variable orthography even the spelling of the English texts is consistent in indicating certain patterns of syllabification. These unusual features led me and my fellow editors to abandon the procedure of Fellowes, who would unhesitatingly modernize punctuation; for Byrd, as for the early medieval reader of whom Leo Treitler writes in his article on the origin of music-writing, 'punctuation signs were indications for the performance of a text', and they become an important part of the edition.[66] We also parted company with Fellowes in emending the underlay of the prints. He would feel so confident of his sense of the idiom that he would often introduce the up-beat pattern that is prominent in the manuscript choirbooks of the Anglican church in the period immediately following Byrd's death, but rare in these printed sources. Fellowes's procedure was not in itself wrong, merely his approach to and interpretation of the evidence.[67] For here is a composer to whom the printed text mattered. How much it mattered to him can be judged by his publishing several collections of Roman Catholic liturgical music, a very risky action in the political climate of the time. The performance of these works, if that were the chief aim

---

[66] 'Reading and Singing: On the Genesis of Occidental Music-Writing', *Early Music History*, 4 (1984), 141.

[67] Craig Monson, who had the unenviable task of editing Byrd's Anglican church music, much of which survives only in these posthumous sources, took a position similarly 'radical' but quite the opposite of Fellowes. He frequently changed choirbook underlay patterns such as

|Ho^m–ly^m Ghost$^{m·}$ the^c|^c Com^{cs}–fort^m|–er^m to
|Ho^m–ly^m Ghost$^{m·}$ the^c|Com^{ccs} –fort^m|–er^m

according to the principles observed in the prints and confirmed in the copies of the few Anglican anthems that do survive in Elizabethan and Jacobean as well as Caroline manuscripts (^{m} = minim, ^{c} =crotchet, $^{m·}$ = dotted minim and so on). See *The Byrd Edition*, vols. 10a, 10b, and 11. His work illustrates the limits of the 'best text' approach (none of these texts is good), and the need for the modern editor to be critical of the early scribe. Monson was reconstructing the text along lines that Housman himself might have approved; his procedure, based on the weighing of historical probabilities, clearly relies less on theory, however, than on common sense in dealing with sources exceptionally distant from the composer's influence.

of him and his fellow Catholics, could easily have been promoted by circulating manuscript copies among the households of the recusant or sympathizing nobility. To print them was to make a special statement about their importance and the authority of their texts; and it places equally special obligations upon the editor.

Can we conclude from these two cases, a playwright and musician living in the same town at the same time, that no easy generalizations will help their editors? As Kenney says, 'each case is special. Every textual problem imposes its own terms of reference and demands to be approached on its own individual premisses.'[68] Theory is instrumental, as we have seen, in articulating certain recurring patterns in the endeavour of editing, and in providing (especially in the Greg-Bowers–Tanselle system) a framework within which to place each new problem. Yet it often does little to help us out of real editorial difficulties—it is, as one wag suggests, 'often just practice with the hard bits left out'.[69] It may also keep us from simply doing good work in a straightforward way.

One theoretical concept, however, will continually worry the textual critic who looks beyond the immediate problems of creating an edition. Casual mention has been made throughout this essay of the composer's intention, a term that is frequently invoked among musicians and scholars, sometimes as though it were a sort of talisman. Yet the issue of authorial intention is not an easy one. The musician may not, perhaps, be too concerned that the various forms of 'immanent criticism' in the twentieth century have dispensed with it—the New Critics with their so-called intentional fallacy and the post-structuralists with Barthes' rallying cry on their lips, 'The birth of the reader must be at the cost of the death of the Author'.[70] We have our own

---

[68] *The Classical Text*, 138.

[69] John M. Robson, review of McGann, *A Critique*, in *Library*, 6th series, 7 (1985), 359.

[70] W. K. Wimsatt, Jr, and M. C. Beardsley, 'The Intentional Fallacy', *The Sewanee Review*, 54 (1946), 468–88. Roland Barthes, 'The Death of the Author', in *Image—Music—Text*, trans. Stephen Heath (New York, 1977), 148. I derive the expression 'immanent criticism' from Jerome J. McGann; see his 'Introduction: A Point of Reference' in *Historical Studies and Literary Criticism*, ed. Jerome J. McGann (Madison, 1985).

form of immanent criticism in music, after all, which we call, a bit oddly, analysis, and though it has not gone so far as to kill the composer, it is strongly convinced about the irrelevance of anything extrinsic to the text. The problem with authorial intention for the editor as historical critic, once one grants the certain degree of ethical imperative it entails, is that it is too narrow a concept to adopt as a base of operations. Almost every work has implications beyond what its composer can consciously have intended; and often other people determine much of what transforms a composer's text or idea into what we conceive of as a work.[71] How then do we salvage the concept of the composer's intention as a guiding principle?

One of the chief difficulties with authorial intention is that it can denote a variety of things, and that different intentions can occur at different times or even exist at the same time in conflict. Peter Shillingsburg has recently attempted to articulate a level of intention that is of use to editors: 'an intention to record on paper, or in some other medium, a specific sequence of words and punctuation according to an acceptable or feasible grammar or relevant linguistic convention.' Only three things, he believes (perhaps with excessive optimism), stand in the way of the recovery of this 'intention to *do*': 'scribal errors, "Freudian slips", and shorthand elisions'.[72] With some adjustment for music, this reduced meaning of intention will help—so long as we remember Tanselle's warning when dealing with multiple versions that 'many writers have different intentions at different times', and that 'no one critical text can reflect these multiple intentions simultaneously'.[73] With this limitation upon the extent of intention the musical editor can then deal separately

[71] Richard Taruskin has provided sufficient examples in performing contexts; see Chapter 6. Each reader will no doubt be able to add others. I have drawn attention to what seems to me an interesting case of a dichotomy between intention (as reflected in the composer's performance) and underlying meaning in 'Character and Caricature in "Albert Herring"', *Musical Times*, 127 (1986), 545–7.

[72] *Scholarly Editing in the Computer Age* (Athens, Georgia, and London, 1986), 36; see also James McLaverty, 'The Concept of Authorial Intention in Textual Criticism', *Library*, 6th series, 6 (1984), 121–38, where the literary text is compared to a musical score (p. 127). Both these are reviewed by Tanselle in 'Historicism and Critical Editing', *Studies in Bibliography*, 39 (1986), 1–46.

[73] G. Thomas Tanselle, 'Recent Editorial Discussion and the Central Questions of Editing', *Studies in Bibliography*, 34 (1981), 62. Shillingsburg's practical suggestions about the apparatus of editions may be found helpful.

with the question of the composer's (and contemporary audience's) expectations, those important and often undocumented facets of the work as originally performed.

Shillingsburg and Tanselle are traditionalists who seek to shore up the editorial enterprise in the face of destabilizing influences of all kinds. However carefully they define and limit the standard expressions and terms that have challenged editors, they remain within the tradition that we have known. They would probably argue that some definition of authorial intention could be of use even in approaching those situations in which other critics see a succession of symbols deriving from no single authority and making neither a text nor a work in the sense that we normally assume. But if the 'work' is not recoverable, because it is not a work, or because any attempt to fix it as a text results in anachronism, or worse, why edit it at all? The reason we might ask that question seriously is that we tend still to feel that editing consists of the application of objective procedures to produce a definitive text. But editing is principally a critical act; moreover it is one (like musical analysis) that begins from critically based assumptions and perceptions that usually go unacknowledged. If these assumptions were to be openly stated, if we began to recognize and allow for legitimate differences in editorial orientation, and if we ceased to use the word 'definitive' in relation to *any* edited text, then much of the polemics surrounding editing might subside. At least, that is the hope of Shillingsburg in proposing four editorial orientations, the historical, the aesthetic, the authorial, and the sociological on the basis of where the textual critic locates authority.[74] Clearly these categories need the discussion he gives them for their distinctions to be fully appreciated. Yet in essence they can be reduced to the historical and the critical, the two that lie at the heart of the difficulty faced by editors—by musical scholars in general—in all facets of their work. And those whose orientation is historical tend to prefer diplomatic transcription, which is a form, after all, of 'not editing'.

When texts are subjected to the techniques of recension, the effect is often disturbing. F. A. Wolf, on setting out to discover

[74] *Scholarly Editing in the Computer Age*, 18–30 *et passim.*

the true form of the *Iliad*, was chagrined to reach the conclusion that it had neither a form nor an author, and the story has parallels from that day to this. It is not surprising, then, to find a discussion of filiation in early music (by one of its most earnest proponents) concluding that its use will remain for some time in the realm of discovering local and scribal habits, and gloomily dismissing the pursuit of a text as 'seeking the chimera, and . . . essentially irrelevant'.[75] Then as now, the irony of historicism is that the techniques it uses to recover and restore works of art often tend to render them unusable. First, recension may have a splintering effect on the text, and second, contextualizing the work may lead to its being totally submerged and absorbed by its surroundings, and therefore to its losing whatever trans-historical significance might otherwise be claimed for it. The answers to this dilemma have historically taken various forms. *Geistesgeschichte*, for instance, gave value to art by taking an idealized view that discerned permanent value in an atemporal-ity at the heart of history. New Criticism resisted all contextualization by seeking through interpretation permanent truths that give legitimacy not merely to works of art but to the whole enterprise of cultural understanding. In textual criticism an idealized method was developed, as we have seen, to neutralize the effect of the new techniques by discerning an originality as it were submerged in the contexts of scribalisms, an originality it sought to reconstitute and call a text. This effort has constantly been under fire from 'conservative' editors, not because of their inordinate faith in documents, but because of their scepticism, expressed in the quotation at the beginning of this paragraph, that the documents can be made to yield originality. And we can be sure that new waves of scepticism will threaten to engulf the editing enterprise as different critical or theoretical currents sweep towards the shores of musicology. But as Lee Patterson asks, 'If we are to reconstruct a usable past, what are the enabling assumptions upon which that work is to depend? If the idealist premises that have underwritten textual criticism are to be dismissed, what is to take their place?'[76] There are at present no answers to those questions.

---

[75] Stanley Boorman, 'The Uses of Filiation in Early Music', *Text*, 1 (1981), 168.

[76] 'The Logic of Textual Criticism and the Way of Genius: the Kane-Donaldson *Piers Plowman* in Historical Perspective', in *Textual Criticism and*

In the end, then, we reach the same crucial issue in editing as in other branches of scholarly engagement with works of art. It is the question that Dahlhaus and Treitler have wrestled with, and it is one that will remain with us in various forms. Are works of art significant in their own terms in some trans-historical way, or can they be approached only as products of their context? Can we project them in the idealized form of a truly critical edition or must they be preserved only as they occur in a single historical record at a time? As a musician I shall always give my assent to the first of each of those propositions. And as a pragmatist who resists theorizing I shall continue to try to have it both ways by demanding that context be explored in order to turn up evidence that will enhance and change the understanding of works of art, while resisting those contextual elements that threaten their complete submersion and the implied destruction of their modern relevance. I can cheerfully spend energy helping to propose a different understanding of Handel's methods in the oratorios based on their relation to contemporary English stage drama in the hope that it will ultimately affect the way those works are perceived and performed; and yet I resist the implications of the conclusion to Iain Fenlon's study of Monteverdi's *Orfeo* that 'the work was no more than an ephemeral entertainment for courtiers', and I find my critical sensibilities offended by Andrew Parrott's changing the order of movements, and interpolating other pieces, in the same composer's *Vespers* of 1610 on the basis of a normalizing theory about contemporary liturgical practice that does not take into account the evident special nature of that work and its publication.[77] Musical scholarship has traditionally embodied a strong vein of aggression of this sort against works, of course, particularly ones that have held the imagination of more than

Literary Interpretation, ed. Jerome J. McGann (Chicago and London, 1985), 90. In this paragraph I have paraphrased various points from this excellent essay, which begins by examining and demolishing the traditional distinction in textual criticism between 'internal' and 'external' evidence, and goes on to examine the history of textual criticism in an unusually interesting way.

[77] Philip Brett and George Haggerty, 'Handel and the Sentimental: the Case of "Athalia"', *Music and Letters*, 68 (1987), 112–27. Iain Fenlon, 'The Mantuan "Orfeo" ' in John Whenham (ed.), *Claudio Monteverdi: Orfeo*, Cambridge Opera Handbooks (Cambridge, 1986), 19. Claudio Monteverdi, *Vespro della Beata Vergine (1610)*, Taverner Consort, Taverner Choir, Taverner Players, dir. Andrew Parrott, EMI CDS 747078–8, 1984.

the small early music audience. It is perhaps understandable as a reaction against the opposite tendency to adopt what one might call a 'masterworks mentality'; but it is an unattractive feature of our discipline that reflects insecurity and fear more than strength, as I once ventured to suggest.[78]

The chief characteristic of the early music movement, however, has been a liberating thrust. Like several other 'musics' in our culture (as Robert Morgan, taking the opposite point of view, shows in Chapter 3) its effect has been to disrupt the authoritarian cultural phenomenon enshrined in the phrase 'classical music'. As 'early music' goes about undermining the validity of the established institutions of 'classical music', it creates its own problems of course, not least of which is the danger of new orthodoxies, but at least it has given us a sense of *difference*, a sense that by exercising our imaginations we may, instead of reinforcing our own sense of ourselves by assimilating works unthinkingly to our mode of performing and perceiving, learn to know what something different might mean and how we might ultimately delight in it. And yet the difficulty with incorporating historical context in a performance art such as music is that, once understood, it is difficult to know what to do with it. We cannot reconstruct it exactly or in all its ramifications, because bound up with its understanding is the acknowledgement of our own difference. And that acknowledgement entails a recognition of our own contemporary need. 'Our delight in comparisons, in distance, in dissimilarity', as Brecht once pointed out when urging the development of a historical sense in the theatre, 'is at the same time a delight in what is close and proper to ourselves.'[79] And this delight is embodied in turn in a quality that most befits the editor and musical historian, but which is least susceptible of discussion or even expression: a strong intuitive feeling for the music itself. When that is reflected without self-consciousness in all our various activities, then the early music movement will have achieved maturity, and authenticity will no longer be an issue.

---

[78] 'Facing the Music', *Early Music*, 10 (1982), 347–50.
[79] Appendix to 'A Short Organum for the Theatre', in *Brecht on Theatre: The Development of an Aesthetic*, trans. and ed. John Willett (New York and London, 1964; repr. 1978), 276.

5

THE HISTORIAN, THE PERFORMER, AND AUTHENTIC MEANING IN MUSIC

GARY TOMLINSON

The phrase 'authentic meaning' in my title seems to me to characterize the shared goal of music historians and historical performers more precisely than the usual 'authenticity'. It is what we seek to understand in any attempt at musical authenticity. Our interest in creating the authentic sounds of music can be justified only by our belief that they lead us closer to its authentic meanings. But what is the nature of these meanings? Is historically informed performance the most effective way to illuminate them? This chapter offers answers to both questions.

The authentic meaning of a musical work is not the meaning that its creators and first audience invested in it. It is instead the meaning that we, in the course of interpretative historical acts of various sorts, come to believe its creators and audience invested in it. The first formulation—let us simplify it to state that the authentic meaning of a work is the meaning its creator invested in it—this formulation faces the historian or historical performer with daunting obstacles, since both participate in an intellectual world that has relinquished the comforting notion that we can know with objective certainty any complex historical situation. Locating authenticity in the creators' original intent poses a question that we no longer believe we can answer: what was that intent? Authentic meaning becomes an inscrutable cipher closed away in a time that no longer exists, an unsolvable enigma standing between us and fruitful historical enquiry.

In recent years this enigma of original intent has weighed more and more heavily on the historical performance movement. For the leaders of this movement have found it difficult, even in today's post-objectivist historical climate, to cast off the notion that they seek a single, true, certain authenticity.[1] The

---

[1] On the objectivist premises of the historical performance movement see Laurence Dreyfus, 'Early Music Defended against its Devotees: A Theory of Historical Performance in the Twentieth Century', *Musical Quarterly*, 69 (1983), 297–322; esp. p. 299.

vexing elusiveness of such unambiguous truth has engendered a
sense of crisis in historical performance and a pessimism evident
in many writings on the subject. Both are apparent, for
example, in Michael Morrow's *cri de cœur* published ten years
ago under the title 'Musical Performance and Authenticity'.[2]
Here Morrow maintained with impassioned *naïveté* that
'authenticity can only mean the real thing'; historical performers, unable to attain this thing, are no more than boring 'cultural
parasites'. Such pessimism reappears, in the guise of *Schaden-
freude*, in Nicholas Temperley's statement on authenticity in
Early Music.[3] A detractor of much historical performance,
Temperley rejects the notion, central to one customary defence
of authentic performance, that 'the mode of performance that
suited the composer is necessarily the best for all time'. 'In the
end,' he concludes, 'historical authenticity is a false criterion for
musical performance.' And the pessimism is evident as well in
the chapters here by Howard Mayer Brown and Robert
Morgan. Neither writer can shake completely the idea that we
attempt in detached, objective fashion to perform the music 'as
it really was'. That phrase, with all its Rankean resonance,
appears in both articles; it leads Morgan to view the historical
performance movement as a symptom of modernist *malaise*, of
cultural escapism and 'identity crisis'.

Paradoxically, growing uncertainty about achieving an absolute historical authenticity in performance has stimulated a new
optimism in some writers on the subject, most notably Richard
Taruskin[4] and Will Crutchfield. Both dismiss the evocation of
the composer's intent as the goal of historical performance and
locate authenticity instead in the performer. Crutchfield writes
(Chapter 1): 'the authenticity of a performance is to be
understood in terms of the sources of the performance; and
these lie within the person who is performing.' Here authenticity has been redefined, its meaning shifted from some kind of
historical knowledge to a presentist self-awareness achieved by
the performer in communion with the music performed.

[2] *Early Music*, 6 (1978), 233–46.
[3] In 'The Limits of Authenticity: A Discussion', *Early Music*, 12 (1984), 3–
25; Temperley's contribution is on pp. 16–20.
[4] Richard Taruskin, 'On Letting the Music Speak for Itself: Some
Reflections on Musicology and Performance', *Journal of Musicology*, 1 (1982),
338–49.

Crutchfield's optimism is fair enough; but it has been won only at the expense of history. We need not deny the performer the right to self-expression, however, in order to realize that this right is not the only (or even the richest) source of authentic meanings. Crutchfield's wholesale subsuming of the composer, the musical text, and its myriad meanings under the performer brings to mind a remark made by a fan of Riccardo Muti and quoted not long ago in the Philadelphia press: 'When he conducts,' the fan enthused, 'I hear *him* in the music, even more than the original score.'

For his part, Taruskin has dispatched the composer's intent by sounding a rallying cry of yesterday's literary criticism—the intentional fallacy, the idea that knowledge of the expressive aims of past artists is irrelevant to our understanding of their works, and the search for it pointless. This leads Taruskin to circumscribe narrowly the role of historical research in the pursuit of authenticity and to seek it instead, like Crutchfield, in the performer's own imaginative conviction. But the outcry against the exploration of past intentions only arose in a different historiographical climate than ours, at a time when such exploring was most often equated with a positivistic hunt for specific biographical 'causes'. Having exorcised the demon of such positivism, we must rid ourselves also of the desperate measures once invoked to combat it; the intentional fallacy is one of these. What Taruskin calls 'the familiar epistemological impediments to learning what the composer's intentions were'[5] are impediments only to a by-now outmoded historical theory. The notion that a search for historical intent is basic to any construction of authentic meanings is, in light of other historiographical strategies, no fallacy. At any rate it deserves a fresher airing than Taruskin gives it.[6]

The second formulation offered above—that the authentic meaning of a work is the meaning we come to believe in the course of our historical interpretations its creators invested in it—yields fresh ideas by side-stepping the snare of objectivism. It highlights our own role in *constructing* authentic meanings and frees us from the presupposition that a single, true meaning is waiting out there to be found. I do not offer it primarily to

---

[5] 'On Letting the Music Speak for Itself', 340.
[6] See also Taruskin's contribution to 'The Limits of Authenticity', 3–12.

relieve performers of the burdens of objectivist history—as an Agnus Dei, so to speak, for the beleaguered devotees of early music. For unlike Taruskin and Crutchfield, who delimit the role of historical research in authentic performance, I would instead circumscribe the function of performance itself in making authentic meanings. I offer my proposition and its implications, then, as Credo rather than Agnus—as an optimistic creed for the music historian and his or her practice. The creed is a post-positivist approach to the discovery of historical intent. It rests on two fundamental tenets, the first an axiom about the nature of meaning, the second a metaphor for the transaction by which the historian conceives of the past.

The axiom is straightforward enough; it has been a fundamental premiss in the human sciences—fields such as linguistics, sociology, interpretive anthropology, and history—since the end of the nineteenth century. It holds that meanings arise from the connections of one signifying act to others. Meaning, that is, does not inhere in individual signs but instead is determined by their interactions with other signs. Together congeries of such signs, groups of signifying acts, make up contexts in which individual signs or acts gain significance. Without context there is no meaning; individual acts do not signify; isolated signs are mute. Meaning is contextual, and—the first corollary follows immediately—the meaning of any one act deepens as we broaden and enrich the context in which we perceive it.

Understanding, to state a second corollary, consists in our accommodation of signs new to us into familiar contexts. This is a reciprocal process: at the same time as a new sign derives meaning from its context it alters more or less markedly the context itself and the meanings it offers. The philosopher Michael Oakeshott long ago characterized this reciprocity: 'A new discovery cannot be appeased by being fitted into an old world, but only by being allowed to transform the whole of that world; and the character of a new discovery is not given and fixed, but is determined by its place in the world . . . as a whole.'[7] Some other corollaries arising from this view of meaning, and their musical and historical implications, will be explored below.

[7] Michael Oakeshott, *Experience and Its Modes* (Cambridge, 1933), 98–9.

My metaphor for doing history also is ostensibly straight-forward.[8] It pictures history as a *conversation* between the historian and the agents in the past he or she studies. This metaphor of conversation is a fundamental one in the hermen-eutic theories of Hans-Georg Gadamer and in some earlier theories of interpretation as well.[9] I borrow it instead from the cultural anthropologist Clifford Geertz, who proposes it as the aim of all cultural interpretation. In ethnographic research, Geertz says,

We are not . . . seeking either to become natives . . . or to mimic them . . . . We are seeking, in a widened sense of the term in which it encompasses very much more than talk, to converse with them, a matter a great deal more difficult, and not only with strangers, than is commonly recognized . . . . Looked at in this way, the aim of anthropology is the enlargement of the universe of human discourse.[10]

For Geertz the idea of conversation is not, strictly speaking, metaphorical. The agents that the anthropologist studies are after all alive and capable of talking; the conversation is real, however halting the resulting communication might be. Trans-ferred to history, however, the notion of conversation grows more metaphorical. The historian's agents are typically not alive to talk with him, and his conversation with them is not real conversation at all. Rather it is a colloquy in which the historian

---

[8] Since a suspicion of metaphorical thought in rational endeavours has lingered from Aristotle's time to our own, the legitimacy of such thought may perhaps be worth briefly affirming. Linguists such as George Lakoff and Mark Johnson (*Metaphors We Live By*, Chicago, 1980) have argued convincingly that metaphors are more than poetic ornament; they are forceful ways of shaping our conceptions of the world. Our choice and use of metaphors carry deep implications and even injunctions for our thoughts and actions. Historical change and the historian's act in understanding it have often been conceived in metaphorical ways. Examples are the Hegelian view of history as organism, the Marxist view of history as mechanism, and various characterizations of the historian's methods as hermeneutic circle, story-telling, epistemological archaeology, and manifestation of myth. For discussion of many of these metaphors see Hayden White, 'Interpretation in History', *New Literary History*, 4 (1973), 281–314; for an explanation of 'epistemological archaeology' see Michel Foucault, *The Order of Things* (New York, 1973), preface.

[9] In hermeneutic theory the conversation usually occurs between the interpreter and the text interpreted. For Gadamer's view of this conversation see Hans-Georg Gadamer, *Truth and Method* (New York, 1985), 330–3, 345–51; also David Couzens Hoy, *The Critical Circle: Literature, History, and Philosoph-ical Hermeneutics* (Berkeley, 1978), 65–8.

[10] Clifford Geertz, *The Interpretation of Cultures* (New York, 1973), 13–14.

examines, ponders, and questions his subjects and then, through
an act of historical imagination reminiscent of R. G. Collingwood, supplies responses from them.

The responses he supplies are those that are most meaningful
in the context of significant acts he has conceived around his
subjects. Like all other understanding, historical understanding
is only as deep as its context is 'thick'—broad, richly varied, and
internally consistent. It is only authentic in so far as the historian
is able to construct a coherent context that he imagines to have
been available to his subjects and relevant to their modes of
thought. As Collingwood put it in a classic formulation: for the
historian 'the past is what he carefully and critically thinks it to
be . . . the only mistake he (can make) is the philosophical
mistake of arranging in the past what is actually all present
experience'.[11] From this we might derive a general rule:
authenticity in historical thought is a product of the historian's
ability to dissociate two meaningful contexts that he himself has
created: his own and his subjects'.[12]

A number of implications follow from my metaphor. The
historian's conversation, just like the anthropologist's, aims to
widen our understanding of human concerns, beliefs, actions,
and so on by juxtaposing our culture with some inkling of
another. The conversation is, in other words, an attempt to
broaden our own humanity by confronting the foreignness of
other modes of thought and action. History, like Geertz's
anthropology, has as its goal 'the enlargement of the universe of
human discourse'.

[11] R. G. Collingwood, *The Idea of History* (Oxford, 1982), 155.

[12] This is not to deny the inevitable merging of these contexts, Gadamer's
'fusion of horizons' of interpreter and text, observer and observed (see *Truth
and Method*, 269–74; also Hoy, *The Critical Circle*, 95–8); I am not attempting to
restore the innocent, objective observer of classical hermeneutics. But our
confidence in the authenticity of our historical constructions seems to me to
rest in part on our cognizance of their otherness, their difference, their novelty
in relation to the state of our understanding before it was informed by them.
Gadamer puts the two-phase dialectic of historical understanding, distinguishing and then merging differing horizons, thus: ' . . . it is part of the
hermeneutic approach to project an historical horizon that is different from the
horizon of the present. Historical consciousness is aware of its own otherness
and hence distinguishes the horizon of tradition from its own. On the other
hand, it is itself . . . only something laid over a continuing tradition, and hence
it immediately recombines what it has distinguished in order, in the unity of
the historical horizon that it thus acquires, to become again one with itself'
(*Truth and Method*, 273).

This is the foremost aim of the histories of the various arts as well. We study, or should study works of art as records of human aspiration, achievement, and meaning in contexts different from our own. We should cherish them for what they tell us about the diverse creative acts that gave rise to them. When instead we view them ahistorically—as aesthetic objects uprooted from some context that we believe engendered them and transplanted into our own cultural humus—then we forfeit the possibility of conversing meaningfully with their creators. With easy but all-too-familiar meanings we talk mainly among ourselves, reflected in the work, and not with the work's creators shining *through* it. The work is a mirror rather than a magnifying lens, so to speak. And by regarding it as a mirror we give up or at least drastically limit our ability to broaden our world of discourse.

Such forfeiture occurs all too often in modern writings about art—in many formalist discussions of visual works of art, for example, and in much music analysis as well. It arises also in musical performance from the resistance of many performers to the broadening influence of music history, though it should be said that this resistance is at times an understandable response to the restrictive ways in which some historians conceive of their discipline. And such forfeiture seems to me the inevitable result of the positions of Taruskin, Crutchfield, and others who arrogate to the performer the achievement of authenticity. For few performers—Taruskin himself is a happy exception—are equipped by temperament or training to construct rich, historical contexts of meaning around the works they perform.

This returns us to the question of meaning, to the axiom that the meaning of an individual act or sign arises from its participation in a context. What constitutes a single sign or act? The answer must be a flexible one, for it is obvious that what might look from one perspective like a single unit of meaning can from another be seen to consist of many smaller significant units. Beethoven's *œuvre* as a whole is, on a very broad level, a unified if complex sign, taking its meaning from whatever context of musical and extra-musical events we structure around it. The *Waldstein* Sonata is another sign, still complex, and the first movement of that sonata yet another. We can follow this process of magnification down to the smallest

gestures in the movement—to the A♭ that intrudes unexpect-
edly in the recapitulation of the first theme, for example, which
takes its meaning not only from other musical processes in this
piece but also from broader issues: from Beethoven's changing
uses of ♭VI across his career, from the relation of these to his
contemporaries' and predecessors' harmonic usage, from the
idea of surprise and even momentary incoherence in early
nineteenth-century artistic expression, and so on. The point is
that meaningful acts are what we make of them, not fixed and
permanent but rather perceived and temporarily defined according to their roles in the contextual structures we build for them.

An important corollary to our axiom holds that the meaning
of a work of art—let us specify a piece of music—is not wholly
inherent in it, but only partly so. Of course some portion of the
meaning of a work arises from the interactions of its constituent
signs as these create a context for and give significance to one
another. But extensive realms of meaning also arise from the
relation of the work and of its parts to things outside it. This is
what I take Leo Treitler to mean when he writes that 'music
engages multiple realms of order'.[13] The boundaries of meaning
of a work cannot be drawn at the edges of the score, but must be
located anew by each perceiver according to the work's
participation in his or her own context of meaning. We
understand works by incorporating them into our own personal
musical and extra-musical contexts, contexts for understanding
that involve elements reaching far beyond the work itself and
the particular features of it emphasized in any performance.
Depending on the listener, they might include elements as
diverse as the historical knowledge of a musicologist, the
technical and expressive skills of a performer, the sleep-inducing
dinner with too much wine consumed before the concert, or
even the 'goblin walking quietly over the universe' that Helen
pictured as she listened in Forster's *Howards End* to the Scherzo
of Beethoven's Fifth Symphony.

This leads to another corollary: since the meaning of a musical
work does not wholly reside in the work, it cannot be conveyed
fully by means of performance. The notion often encountered
that the performer 'brings out the meaning of the work' is an
oversimplification, for performance affords only a limited

[13] Leo Treitler, 'History, Criticism, and Beethoven's Ninth Symphony',
Nineteenth-Century Music, 3 (1980), 193–210; see p. 203.

access to the meanings of works. This follows from the preceding discussion in two ways.

First, all meanings, authentic or not, arise from the personal ways in which individuals, performers and audience, incorporate the work in their own signifying contexts. Clearly the performer can exert only so much influence on the personal context of the listener. The conductor in Forster's fictional account, we may presume, did not set out to evoke goblins in Helen's imagination; but she heard them anyway.

Second and more important, the authentic meanings of a work arise from our relating it to an array of things outside itself that we believe gave it meaning in its original context. These things are not inherent in the score—and most of them are not susceptible of presentation in concert. A performance can present little more of a work's original context than the portion of it that exists within the work itself: the internal interaction of its constituent signs and gestures. This is only a part of the conceptual worlds in which the work took on its first meanings: and any performance, therefore, amounts at best to a relatively thin context for authentic meaning. A thick context must result from an elaborate work of cultural interpretation, an interpretation that sketches a system of ideas about art, man, and the world—an ideology, in other words—that may have made the work meaningful to its creators or original audience. Such interpretation is the province especially of the cultural historian, and the authentic meanings gained through it are given fullest voice through his or her methods. The performer, in so far as he acts as performer and not as cultural historian, can only touch upon certain of these meanings.

An example will help clarify this point. Recent issues of *Early Music* have contained a series of attempts to construct an ideological context for John Dowland's songs, two articles by Robin Headlam Wells and one each by Anthony Rooley and Robert Toft.[14] Toft and Headlam Wells view this repertory from the perspective of Elizabethan rhetoric books, seeking to

[14] Anthony Rooley, 'New Light on John Dowland's Songs of Darkness', *Early Music*, 11 (1983), 6–21; Robin Headlam Wells, 'The Ladder of Love: Verbal and Musical Rhetoric in the Elizabethan Lute-Song', *Early Music*, 12 (1984), 173–89; Robert Toft, 'Musicke a Sister to Poetrie: Rhetorical Artifice in the Passionate Airs of John Dowland', *Early Music*, 12 (1984), 190–8; and Wells, 'John Dowland and Elizabethan Melancholy', *Early Music*, 13 (1985), 514–28.

understand from this context how the musical settings were meant to project the rhetorical tropes of their texts. This is interesting and generally unimpeachable work, following in the footsteps of earlier writers such as Bruce Pattison and Elise Bickford Jorgens. Headlam Wells is especially probing: he presents the lute-song as one facet of a humanistic excitement at the emotional power of eloquence typical of late Elizabethan literary culture.

Rooley takes a different tack. He proposes that we understand Dowland's darkest songs, songs like the famous 'Flow my tears', as reflections of their composer's participation in a hermetic or Neoplatonic cult of melancholy current in English culture and stemming from French and Italian philosophical traditions. Rooley's proposal is not altogether convincing, given the fragmentary nature of his evidence and its less-than-fully coherent presentation. Headlam Wells is quick to point up these flaws in one of his articles, an explicit response to Rooley's essay. But while it remains doubtful that Dowland was the hermetic philosopher, the John Dee of music, that Rooley makes him out to be, even Headlam Wells admits that Dowland 'shared the delight in the pleasures of melancholy which appealed to so many of his contemporaries' ('John Dowland,' p. 526). The interests of cultured Englishmen in melancholy, which around 1600 no doubt ranged from mere Continental affectation to the compendious occult and manifest philosophies found in Robert Burton's *Anatomy of Melancholy*, form an undeniable ingredient of the context for the composition and first appreciations of Dowland's songs of sadness.

What of all this material can be presented in a performance of Dowland's songs? Surely performers can reflect Toft's rhetorical observations in a sharpened awareness of Dowland's musical rhetoric and in more sensitive renderings of his texts. But performance alone cannot detail the new humanistic attitudes towards affective language in the 1580s and 90s, attitudes that Headlam Wells has begun to describe. Nevertheless authentic meanings of Dowland's songs arise from their relations to these new attitudes. Similarly, performances of Dowland's melancholic songs can and usually do project some affect of sadness. But they cannot begin to convey the varied and complex resonances of the concept of melancholy in the

Elizabethan mind. And, again, the songs gain many authentic meanings from these resonances.

Authentic meanings: throughout this discussion I have vacillated for rhetorical reasons between the singular 'meaning' and its plural. But it must be apparent by now that there can be no single authentic meaning for a work; the existence of multiple authentic meanings for any work is another corollary to our axiom. Such multiplicity results from two characteristics of the contexts the historian constructs. First, as I have said above, these are necessarily incomplete and are therefore provisional. One historian's partial context will always differ from another's and afford somewhat different meanings, even though both may be well developed and offer convincingly authentic meanings. Second, the original meanings of a work can be just as diverse as those we find in it today, and historical interpretation must recognize this diversity. Even a single historian will perceive various differently shaded meanings of a work depending on whether the subject of his enquiry—his companion in conversation—is the work's composer, the poet of its text (if it is vocal music), the patron who requested it, the ambassador who reported its première to his superiors, or a violinist in the band. All these overlapping and competing meanings may be more or less authentic depending on the historian's ability to elaborate their contexts. And all these meanings may join in the historian's mind to form a richer context in which each of them is deepened.

Up to this point I have attempted to explore the historical creed broached at the outset of this chapter. To summarize: the creed is based in the proposition that the authentic meaning of a work is the meaning we come to believe its creators and original audience invested in it. The creed is grounded in the contextual view of meaning expressed in our axiom and its corollaries; it is put into action by the metaphor regarding the historical act as conversation between the historian and his or her subjects.

This conception of history locates authentic meaning in the relation of a work to its original ideological context, conceived as broadly as possible, and seeks that meaning through a constructive act of historical cultural interpretation. The provisional nature of such interpretation rescues historical performers from the positivistic dead-end they have travelled down in their search for 'the original sound'. But it also reduces considerably their role in the discovery of authentic meanings. For musical performance is not normally an act of historical contextual construction. The meanings of a work conveyed in performance are at best bright reflections of meanings that can be portrayed in richer colour and more complex shading through the historian's art. At worst the meanings presented in performance are all but entirely irrelevant to the authentic meanings of a work.

All of this describes the historian's conversation, his dialogic construction of contexts, in abstract terms. I would like now to offer an example of its results, a case study that will underscore the breadth of meanings available to the historian and relevant to our authentic experience of music. My example was suggested by one of the more adventurous products of the historical performance movement in recent years, a complete recording of Angelo Poliziano's *Orfeo* by Paul van Nevel and the Huelgas Ensemble (RCA Seon RL 30856; 1982).

Poliziano's *Orfeo* is a small Italian *fabula*, or mythological play, of a sort in vogue at North Italian courts of the late fifteenth century. It was most likely written and first performed at Mantua in 1480. Like its namesake staged at Mantua more than a century later, the *Orfeo* of Alessandro Striggio and Claudio Monteverdi, it tells the story of Orpheus's loss of Euridice, her resurrection won through Orpheus's powerful appeal to the underworld gods, and her second death. It ends with Orpheus's dismemberment by the Bacchantes.

Music played a major role in early performances of *Orfeo*, so important a role, indeed, that Romain Rolland was led to call the work 'l'opéra avant l'opéra' in the title of an essay of 1908.[15] Recent considerations of the place of music in the play, notably those of Nino Pirrotta and Cynthia Pyle, have been more circumspect.[16] They have none the less affirmed that major portions of the work must have been sung in the first

---

[15] See Romain Rolland, *Musiciens d'autrefois* (Paris, 1908).
[16] Nino Pirrotta, *Li due Orfei: Da Poliziano a Monteverdi* (Turin, 1975), ch. 1 (trans. as *Music and Theatre from Poliziano to Monteverdi*, Cambridge, 1982); Cynthia Munro Pyle, 'Il tema di Orfeo, la musica, e le favole mitologiche del tardo Quattrocento', in *Ecumenismo della cultura*, 2 *La parola e la musica nel divenire dell'umanesimo*, ed. Giovannangiola Tarugi (Florence, 1981), 121–39.

performances, including at least a *canzone* for Aristaeus early in the action, the Bacchantes' frenzied song at the end, and much of Orpheus's role. That, for historians fascinated by the diverse ways in which music and drama have been joined over the centuries, is the good news.

The bad news is that no fifteenth-century musical settings of any passages from *Orfeo* survive. This is what makes the Huelgas recording so venturesome: for it van Nevel supplied a setting of all of Poliziano's text from various manuscripts and prints of frottola music. He could do so because much of Poliziano's text is structured in fixed poetic forms that recur again and again in the frottola books. His method is in keeping with musical practices of the time: music setting one text was commonly transferred to another text of the same form, so commonly, indeed, that some pieces in the music books are generic settings, explicitly designated for the setting of any poem in a particular form. The loss of the music of *Orfeo* is probably not due to the vagaries of manuscript transmission, but rather to the fact that it was never written down at all. It was improvisatory in nature, or at least semi-improvisatory, and supplied by the players whose parts involved singing. Such improvised music was much prized at Italian courts in this period and usually involved a singer accompanying himself in simple polyphony on an instrument like the *lira da braccio* or lute. Just such an improviser, it seems, sang to the *lira* the role of Orpheus in the première of Poliziano's play.

This singer, the first known Orpheus in modern dramatic history, was named Baccio Ugolini. But in what ways did Ugolini view his music? In what ideological context was it significant for him? What was his conception of the legendary musician Orpheus, and how did it interact with his more general ideas about music and its effects? Questions of this sort can set in motion our colloquy with Ugolini, and the answers we provide for them will be determined by the context we build around him. One such context follows.

What strikes us first in the fragmentary surviving reflections of Baccio Ugolini's career is the diversity of his talents. In Florence, Rome, Mantua, Naples, and other cities he was renowned as a poet and musician in the amorous courtly tradition of the *strambottisti*. His considerable philological talents led him to transcribe Latin elegies for Lodovico Gonzaga, Marquis of Mantua, and to accompany Poliziano on a manuscript hunt to Verona. His diplomatic skills encouraged Lorenzo de'Medici, ruler of Florence, to entrust to him embassies to Rome, Naples, Bruges, Basle, and elsewhere. And his knowledge of antiquities enabled Lorenzo to have him search, while on a mission to Naples, for ancient medals and other *objets* to add to Lorenzo's collection. No doubt in recognition of his services to the Medici, Ugolini received some lucrative ecclesiastic benefices, including the canonry of the cathedral of Florence and the episcopate of Gaeta.

All these activities made Ugolini a respected and valued member of the cultivated circle Lorenzo gathered around him. Indeed he was long an intimate of Lorenzo, an intimacy fostered by their common interest in poetry and music. The two men, we learn from a letter of 1490, passed evenings together in the exchange of songs and poems. Ugolini's friendship with Poliziano also was warm and of long standing; a letter of Poliziano in glowing praise of him, probably penned in 1489, attests eloquently to it.

Ugolini's various pursuits and his connections with Lorenzo and Poliziano are well known and were summarized almost a century ago by the historians Isidoro del Lungo and Arnaldo della Torre.[17] One final connection to another leader of Florentine culture, however, has received less attention than these, probably because it is less amply reflected in surviving documents. It may nevertheless be crucial in our attempt to reconstruct Ugolini's musical thought. This is Ugolini's relationship with Marsilio Ficino, translator of and commentator on Plato and the Neoplatonists, leader of an informal Platonic academy for the dispersion of their doctrines, and in general semi-official guru of Florentine culture through much of the late quattrocento.

Evidence of his relations with Ugolini is found in Ficino's correspondence. Two of Ficino's published letters are addressed to Ugolini, one more mentions him, and an unpublished letter to Baccio's brother Donato sends him greetings. The contents

---

[17] Isidoro del Lungo, *Florentia: Uomini e cose del Quattrocento* (Florence, 1897), 307–12; and Arnaldo della Torre, *Storia dell'Accademia platonica di Firenze* (Florence, 1902), 796–800.

of these few documents suggest that throughout the years of his maturity, at least from the late 1460s until his death in 1494, Ugolini looked upon Ficino as a teacher and respected him as a philosopher. We will examine these documents more closely in a moment; but first we may infer generally that the relations they reflect between Ugolini and Ficino included musical discussions and performance. The inference is safe for two reasons. First, music played important and diverse roles in Ficino's thought throughout his career. Any follower of his, especially a musician like Ugolini, could not help but encounter these. Second, Ficino also was a musician; like Ugolini, he was well known for his skill in singing to the *lira*, and he was a frequent musical companion of Cosimo de'Medici and most likely of his grandson Lorenzo as well. In a letter of 1492 Ficino even listed the revival of such 'ancient singing of songs to the Orphic lyre'—*antiquum ad Orphicam Lyram carminum cantum*—as one of the most glorious achievements of fifteenth-century Florentine culture.[18]

In another letter of 1492 Ficino recalled Ugolini's earliest known encounter with him.[19] This letter lists Ugolini among the audience of a series of public lectures on Plato that Ficino had delivered long before, in 1468 or, more likely, 1469. While the precise subject of these lectures seems to have been the dialogue *Philebus*, on which Ficino wrote a lengthy commentary in 1469, they most likely were imbued also with the ideas of Ficino's most influential work, his commentary on Plato's *Symposium*, written around the same time.[20] For our construction of Ugolini's musical context it is significant that music is a fundamental ontological element in Ficino's *Symposium* commentary. It appears there in various related roles.

[18] Marsilio Ficino, *Opera Omnia* (facs. repr. of Basle, 1576 edn.), ed. Mario Sancipriano (2 vols. in 4, Turin, 1959), 944. For a summary of Ficino's musical activities and thought see Paul Oskar Kristeller, 'Music and Learning in the Early Italian Renaissance', in *Renaissance Thought II: Papers on Humanism and the Arts* (New York, 1965), 142–62; esp. pp. 157–60.

[19] Ficino, *Opera Omnia*, 936–7.

[20] The substance of Ficino's public lectures is mentioned by his early sixteenth-century biographer Giovanni Corsi; see Raymond Marcel, *Marsile Ficin* (Paris, 1958), 683. On the date of the lectures see della Torre, *Storia*, 573; for the dates of Ficino's commentaries on *Philebus* and the *Symposium* see Michael J. B. Allen, ed. and trans., *Marsilio Ficino: The Philebus Commentary* (Berkeley, 1975), 48–56.

The most prominent of these is the poetic frenzy, one of Plato's four types of divinely inspired madness that lead the soul from inferior, worldly things back to the beauty and unity of god. In its earthly existence, Ficino writes, the soul is disturbed; its higher portions are asleep, its lower portions 'completely filled with discord and dissonance'. Therefore, he continues, 'we greatly need the poetic frenzy, which through musical sounds awakes the parts [of the soul] that sleep, through harmonic sweetness assuages those that are perturbed, and finally through the consonance of diverse things drives out the dissonant discord and tempers the various parts of the soul.'[21] This musically induced temperament is the first step in directing the soul back to its heavenly origins. Ficino had written about the poetic frenzy before the *Symposium* commentary, in a lengthy letter of 1457. There he characterized the ways in which men make music under its influence. 'Some', he wrote,

imitate the celestial music by harmony of voice and the sounds of various instruments, and these we call superficial and vulgar musicians. But some, who imitate the divine and heavenly harmony with deeper and sounder judgment, render a sense of its inner reason and knowledge into verse, feet and numbers. It is these who, inspired by the divine spirit, give forth with full voice the most solemn and glorious song. Plato calls this solemn music and poetry the most effective imitation of the celestial harmony. For the more superficial kind which I have just mentioned does no more than soothe with the sweetness of the voice, but poetry does what is also proper to divine harmony. It expresses with fire the most profound and, as a poet would say, prophetic meanings . . . .[22]

Apart from the poetic frenzy, music serves another, more general function in the *Symposium* commentary. The work as a whole, like Plato's dialogue on which it was based, takes as its subject love. This Ficino defined simply as the desire for beauty. Beauty itself is the echo of the divinity lost to the soul in its earthly exile. But on earth vestiges of this beauty that incites love are rare. Indeed it occurs in only three forms: beauty of

[21] I translate from the Italian version of the *Symposium* commentary, apparently by Ficino himself, entitled *Sopra lo amore o ver' Convito di Platone* (Florence, 1544); see oration VII, ch. 14.

[22] From the letter *De divino furore, Opera Omnia*, 612–15; trans. in *The Letters of Marsilio Ficino* I, trans. members of the Language Department, London School of Economics (New York, 1985), pp. 14–20; see p. 18.

souls, arising from the temperament of many virtues and perceived by the mind; beauty of bodies, born of the concord of lines and colours and perceived by the eyes; and beauty of sounds, arising from the consonance of many words and perceived by the ears. Here Ficino gave sounds and music an exalted status as one of the few earthly reflections of the divine.[23]

Finally, in the *Symposium* commentary Ficino adumbrated views of music he would later develop explicitly by connecting it and love to an animistic, magical conception of the universe. Magic, he said, is a drawing of one thing to another by virtue of their similarities, and in this it resembles love. In the same way the force by which a lover is drawn to the sweet songs and eloquent speeches of the beloved was, for Ficino, magical.[24] And both these forces operated in a hierarchic and animate cosmos, one shot through with influxes from on high that were first refracted through the stellar, planetary, and elemental spheres inhabited by benign demons and finally came to determine the dispositions of sublunar souls.

In Ficino's early writings, to summarize, music is a privileged reflection on earth of the divine, a powerful magical force, and an echo of heavenly beauty capable of tempering souls discordant in their earthly existence and inducing in them a mystical, frenzied gnosis. We are not certain, to be sure, that Ficino expounded all these doctrines in his lectures of 1469. But there is little doubt that Ugolini was familiar with them, because in 1474, some five years after the *Symposium* commentary, Ficino addressed a letter to him precisely on the subject of poetic frenzy.[25] The letter is shorter than Ficino's earlier one on all four divine frenzies, and straightforwardly adduces the Platonic reasons to believe that poetry springs from frenzy rather than from learned techniques. But in its easy references to Plato's *Phaedrus* and *Ion* and its casual remark that 'it is not necessary to give reasons where the matter is self-evident', the letter reveals clearly enough that Ugolini was an intitiate of Ficino's Platonic

---

[23] *Sopra lo amore*, i. 3.
[24] Ibid. vi. 10; see also ii. 8.
[25] *Poeticus furor à Deo est*, in Ficino, *Opera Omnia*, 634–5; trans. *The Letters*, 70–1. The letter is addressed to a second poet, Antonio Pelotti, along with Ugolini.

musical thought. And, though we have no record of Ugolini's reaction to this thought, his lasting ties with Ficino suggest that he carried Ficinian conceptions of music with some sympathy into his own music-making, including his portrayal of Orpheus in 1480.

We may pursue the matter slightly further with the help of Ficino's second letter to Ugolini. This confirms the durability of their relations and suggests once more Ugolini's immersion in the doctrines of his teacher. It is a wittily cordial note, written in 1493, with which Ficino sent Ugolini a copy of his most recent treatise, the *Liber de Sole*.[26] This *Book of the Sun* is one of the late treatises in which Ficino, under the influence of the works by Plotinus, Porphyry, Proclus, and other writers of late antiquity that he was currently translating, constructed on the foundations of his Platonic philosophy an elaborate superstructure of Neoplatonic mysticism and magic. These treatises include also the commentary on Plato's *Timaeus*, published in 1484, and *De vita*, a substantial medical treatise begun in 1480 and published in 1489.

Music plays a central part in Ficino's late metaphysics, as it had in his earlier thought. But a shift of emphasis is notable in his writings about it. It is no longer simply an earthly reflection of divine beauty, a straightforward ontological given, or a force attuning our discordant souls, the first step towards frenzied gnosis. Now the occult and magical powers of music, adumbrated in the *Symposium* commentary, grow more explicit. In the *Timaeus* commentary, for example, Ficino explored the sources of music's powerful effects, locating them, as he had in earlier writings, in the similarity of the airy substances making up both music and man's spirit. But by now Ficino had come to think of music as a living substance, almost a disembodied spirit. At the same time he conceived of a connection between the material of music and the airy quintessence of the superlunar world, so that the pulsing vitality of music was fortified by the animate celestial spheres. All of this gave sounds and music an occult power over man far greater than that of any medicine.[27]

By the time of the third book of *De vita*, entitled *De vita*

---

[26] Ficino, *Opera Omnia*, 951.
[27] Ficino, *In Timaeum commentarium* (*Opera Omnia*, 1438–66), ch. 29, 31.

coelitus comparanda (On Obtaining Life from the Heavens) and probably completed in 1489, music was for Ficino a means of self-consciously manipulating astrological influxes to preserve physical and psychological well-being. 'Remember', he wrote, 'that song is the most powerful imitator of everything. . . . When the heavens are imitated with [its] power it marvellously rouses our spirit to the heavenly influx, and indeed the influx to our spirit.'[28]

By the 1480s, in other words, Ficino regarded music as a pre-eminent medium of natural astrological magic. And, we know from his own account in *De vita coelitus comparanda*, he practised this magic in his musical performance. Few details of this music have come down to us, but D. P. Walker has argued convincingly that it took the form of sung recitation of hymns to the *lira da braccio*—that ancient singing to the Orphic lyre of which, we have seen, Ficino was so proud. For the texts sung Walker proposed a set of Greek hymns, thought in the Renaissance to be by Orpheus himself, that Ficino had translated into Latin many years before, in the early 1460s. This picture of Ficino practising natural magic by singing hymns of Orpheus to the lyre conforms well, Walker noted, with a series of Orphic theses propounded in 1486 by Pico della Mirandola, the brash and brilliant young philosopher who had studied with Ficino in 1484 and 1485. Pico's second thesis reads: 'Nothing is more effective in natural magic than the Hymns of Orpheus if there be applied to them a suitable music, proper disposition of the soul, and other circumstances known to the wise.' Ficino's magical Orphic music seems to have left here a deep impression.[29]

But what of Ugolini's own Orphic song in 1480? Was this suffused, at least in Ugolini's mind, with the ideology of Ficino's musical magic? Even though the clearest traces we have of Ficino's magical practices all post-date the performance of Poliziano's *Orfeo*, we know that Ficino had translated the Orphic hymns almost two decades before Ugolini sang the role of Orpheus. It is difficult to believe that he had not sung them

---

[28] Ficino. *De vita libri tres (Opera Omnia, 493–572)*, bk. iii, ch. 21.
[29] D. P. Walker, *Spiritual and Demonic Magic from Ficino to Campanella* (Notre Dame, 1975), 19–24. For Pico's Orphic theses see Giovanni Pico della Mirandola, *Conclusiones sive Theses DCCCC Romae anno 1486 publice disputandae, sed non admissae*, ed. Bohdan Kieszkowski (Geneva, 1973), 80–3.

well before 1480. And Ficino's magical and astrological conceptions of music grew gradually, we have seen, from seeds planted
already in the *Symposium* commentary of the late 1460s. The
notion that he sang his hymns with conscious magical intent
before 1480, then, is certainly likely. So is the idea that Ugolini
was aware of these practices by the time he played Orpheus. We
are left, finally, with an intriguing and illuminating context for
Ugolini's portrayal. The ideologies that he brought to Poliziano's *Orfeo* surely included Platonic and Ficinian conceptions of
poetic frenzy and of music as a reflection of divine beauty. They
may also have involved an élite Florentine cult of Orphic
musical magic.[30]

I have elaborated this example at some length because, as we
have seen, depth of understanding increases with the complexity and richness of the context in which we find it. Nevertheless
my case study by no means exhausts the possibilities for
historical interpretation of Ugolini's Orpheus. There is much
more to be said, for example, about Ficino's conception of
music. And Pirrotta constructs a context for Ugolini's song from
entirely different sources: from the possible place of the play in
fifteenth-century traditions of mythological banquet entertain-
ments, from Ugolini's and Poliziano's relations with the patrons
for whom the play must have been staged, from the stylistic
conventions within which Ugolini probably composed his
music, and so on.

The ideologies in my example may seem far-fetched, and the
example itself an extraordinary case of curious lore coming to
bear in limited and unique ways on musical thought and

---

[30] This can be said in spite of the lack of obvious Ficinian ideas in Poliziano's
text (remarked upon by Pirrotta, *Li due Orfei*, 15, and Vittore Branca, *Poliziano
e l'umanesimo della parola* (Turin, 1983), 63). For in the first place it is Ugolini's
ideology, not Poliziano's, that I have attempted to characterize here; he
brought his own personal meanings to the play, whatever Poliziano's may have
been. In the second place, it is difficult to believe that Poliziano himself was not
touched by Ficino's Orphism, even though *Orfeo* does not obviously convey
this (or any other) philosophy. The very decision to put Orpheus on stage was
a loaded act in the midst of a local philosophical culture that lionized him as
priscus theologus, teacher of Pythagoras (and indirectly of Plato), and musical
magician. For a Ficinian interpretation of *Orfeo* see Richard Cody, *The
Landscape of the Mind: Pictorialism and Platonic Theory in Tasso's* Aminta *and
Shakespeare's Early Comedies* (Oxford, 1969), 23–43.

performance. But is it so extraordinary? Not, I would say, in light of the numerological symbolism that we perceive more and more clearly in Renaissance music of all kinds.[31] Not, to invoke the central canon of western music, in light of the Neoplatonic mysteries of Mozart's Freemasonry or the embodiment of Schopenhauer's Platonism in *Tristan und Isolde*. And not, to glance beyond western culture, in light of the congeries of waterfall metaphors by which the Kaluli people of Papua New Guinea conceive of musical composition and performance.[32] We must, I think, see more clearly the cultural contingency of all the music we study and appreciate the ideological distance between ourselves and its creators—even composers whose ways of thought are ostensibly close to our own.

Perhaps my example may seem a case of special pleading, since it involves vocal music, music whose significance and expressive intent is at least partly dependent on its text. But we have seen that much of the meaning of a work arises from things outside it, from an ideological context external to all of its elements, in this case text as well as music. My example, if successful, should suggest realms of significance behind Ugolini's portrayal of Orpheus that are not manifested in Poliziano's text, just as they undoubtedly were not in Ugolini's music. I have tried, that is, to describe a state of mind in which Ugolini may have approached his music-making. Such states of mind condition the things we make and do, but are not wholly revealed in them.

And, finally, my example may seem somewhat perverse, since none of Ugolini's music for *Orfeo*, and little or no music of any sort by him, survives. I freely admit to some polemical mischief in choosing the example. For my point, stated in its most extreme form, is that there are deep and rewarding kinds of musical knowledge that involve neither the score nor its performance. The most profound and authentic meanings of music will be found not in musical works themselves but behind

[31] For a recent and convincing case in point see Richard Taruskin, 'Antoine Busnoys and the *L'Homme armé* Tradition', *Journal of the American Musicological Society*, 39 (1986), 255–93; see esp. pp. 271–3.
[32] See Steven Feld, '"Flow like a Waterfall": The Metaphors of Kaluli Musical Theory', *Yearbook for Traditional Music*, 13 (1981), 22–47.

them, in the varieties of discourse that give rise to them. The deepest interpretation of such meanings will spring from minds caught up in the mysterious and fundamentally human act of pondering the past.

6

THE PASTNESS OF THE PRESENT AND THE PRESENCE OF THE PAST

RICHARD TARUSKIN

Do we really want to talk about 'authenticity' any more? I had hoped a consensus was forming that to use the word in connection with the performance of music—and especially to define a particular style, manner, or philosophy of performance—is neither description nor critique, but commercial propaganda, the stock-in-trade of press agents and promoters. I note with some satisfaction that John Spitzer's entry under 'authenticity' in *The New Harvard Dictionary of Music* does not even mention performance.[1] It deals, rather, with 'the nature of the link between a composer and a work that bears his or her name', that is, with texts and transmission, the traditional and proper domain of scholarly authentication.

Satisfaction is somewhat diminished as the eye wanders up to the entry preceding Spitzer's, where we find, as the third of five definitions of the adjective 'authentic', the following: 'In performance practice, instruments or styles of playing that are historically appropriate to the music being performed'. There it is at last in all its purloined majesty, this word that simply cannot be rid of its moral and ethical overtones (and which always carries its invidious antonym in tow), being used to privilege one philosophy of performance over all others. While one certainly cannot fault a dictionary for reporting current usage—and the currency of the usage in question, alas, cannot be denied—there does seem to be some (perhaps unwitting) complicity in the perpetuation of the propaganda here, since the operative synonym, 'appropriate', is also an ineluctably value-laden term. One simply cannot dissent from the concept when it is defined in this way. One is hardly free to say, 'I prefer inauthenticity to authenticity,' or, 'I prefer inappropriateness to appropriateness'—at least if one is interested in maintaining

[1] Don Michael Randel (ed.), *The New Harvard Dictionary of Music* (Cambridge, Mass., 1986), 60–1.

respectability with the crowd that swears by the *Harvard Dictionary*. Once the terms have been equated in this way, commitment to the values they assign and the privileges they grant must necessarily follow.

The mischief is compounded when we turn to the article on 'performance practice', to which the definition of 'authentic' refers us. On its face the article is quite reasonable and sophisticated, especially when compared with its notorious predecessor in the 'old' *Harvard Dictionary*. Where the earlier entry began by defining the term as 'the study of how early music, from the Middle Ages to Bach, was performed and the many problems connected with attempts to restore its original sound in modern performance', and ended with what seems now the incredibly provincial observation that 'in the period after Bach the problems of performance practice largely disappear, owing to the more specific directions of composers for clearly indicating their intentions,'[2] its replacement starts out with a minor masterpiece of sweeping yet cautious generalization, defining performance practice as 'the conventions and knowledge that enable a performer to create a performance'. Very pointedly, the article goes on to emphasize the fact that although 'historically, the study of performance practice has concentrated on periods and repertories in which the gap between what was notated and what was thought necessary for a performance (especially a historically authentic performance) was greatest,' nevertheless 'the recent history of this study has seen the extent and importance of this gap recognized in repertories ever closer to the present.'[3]

What we have here is a rather subtle—and again, in all likelihood, benign and unwitting—Socratic bait-and-switch in which, first, the very recent concept of historical authenticity is implicitly projected back into historical periods that never knew it (this by the use of the past tense in the first of the quoted sentences for both of the phrases in apposition: 'what *was* notated and what *was* thought necessary for a . . . historically authentic performance', instead of 'what *is* thought necessary . . . ' or simply, 'what was performed'), and, second, the

    [2] Willi Apel (ed.), *Harvard Dictionary of Music*, 2nd edn. (Cambridge, Mass., 1969), 658–9.
    [3] *New Harvard Dictionary*, 624.

application of the loaded term to a virtually unlimited musical and historical terrain (effected by carrying over the word 'gap', which has been invested both with the notion of the problem and with that of its approved solution, into the second sentence). The definition has become authoritarian, and it signifies a definite encroachment of 'historically authentic performance' beyond areas of traditional historical concern into areas where it now threatens the status of artists not trained in 'historically appropriate instruments or styles of playing'. Which is why the 'classical music scene'—in the view of the editor who put the headline to Will Crutchfield's discussion of the so-called 'authentic performance movement' in the Sunday *New York Times*—has lately taken on the appearance of a 'battlefield',[4] and why we are fighting it out, in this book and elsewhere.

Many have realized that the battle is bloodier than it ought to be precisely because of that dread yet hollow shibboleth with which one of the armies insists on scourging the other. So some writers, myself among them, have proposed that talk of authenticity might better be left to moral philosophers, textual critics, and luthiers.[5] Gary Tomlinson, in his contribution to this symposium, wants to reserve it to historians such as himself: by his lights an 'authentic' performance would seem to be a performance accompanied by a good set of programme notes. Joseph Kerman calls 'authentic' a 'baleful term which has caused endless acrimony', for it 'resonates with unearned good vibrations'.[6] A retreat into euphemism can be observed. The American Musicological Society, in its guidelines to the Noah Greenberg Award, now uses the term 'historically-aware'.[7] The New York concert series 'Music Before 1800' has used 'historically accurate' in its promotional literature.[8] At Oberlin,

---

[4] Will Crutchfield, 'A Report From the Battlefield', *The New York Times* (Sunday, 28 July 1985), section II, p. 1. The headline on the article's continuation (p.8) reads, 'Musicians Are at War Over the "Right" Way to Play'.

[5] See R. Taruskin, contribution to 'The Limits of Authenticity: A Discussion,' *Early Music*, 12 (1984), 3–12.

[6] *Contemplating Music: Challenges to Musicology* (Cambridge, Mass., 1985), 192.

[7] *AMS Newsletter*, 16/2 (Aug. 1986), 5, 14.

[8] This phrase was also used as an interchangeable equivalent with 'historically authentic' (though not explicitly identified as such) by Donald J.

'historically informed' is the going phrase. But these ersatz shibboleths will not achieve a cease-fire, if that is their intent, for they still imply invidious comparison with what is unaware, inaccurate, and un- or misinformed. Whether we even have a right to use the word 'accurate' is grounds for a battle in itself; and I doubt whether history has much to do with it, as you will see.

Kerman proposes the Tomlinsonesque word 'contextual' as a 'value-free substitute', and while the word does pass the invidious–antonym test, it raises problems of its own. It seems to validate what is often cited as a major shortcoming of 'historical' performance, that it places the chief emphasis on factors external to the music performed and can actually subvert real interpretation, the value Kerman sets above all others. At the very least it seems to encourage what seems to me the naïve assumption that re-creating all the external conditions that obtained in the original performance of a piece will thus re-create the composer's inner experience of the piece and allow him to 'speak for himself', that is, unimpeded by that base intruder, the performer's subjectivity.[9] Doubtless Kerman would not construe contexts so narrowly as I fear, but others certainly have. Christopher Hogwood's recording of the *Eroica* Symphony, for example, is an express attempt to re-create the conditions that obtained at the first performance of that piece, at a private house, by 'a very powerful company (consisting almost entirely of amateurs)'.[10] These factors are cited to justify

Grout in his essay, 'On Historical Authenticity in the Performance of Old Music', in *Essays on Music in Honor of Archibald Thompson Davison* (Cambridge, Mass., 1957), 341–7. This thirty-year-old piece, the title of which seems to contain one of the earliest uses of the word 'authenticity' in the sense that has since become so widespread and cultish, can serve as a convenient benchmark by which to measure the subsequent progress of the field. Much that Grout wrote off as pipe-dreaming in 1957, particularly as regards mastering old instruments and singing techniques, is taken for granted as a fact of musical life today.

[9] R. Taruskin, 'On Letting the Music Speak for Itself: Some Reflections on Musicology and Performance', *Journal of Musicology*, 1 (1982), 341.

[10] Christopher Hogwood, 'Hogwood's Beethoven', *The Gramophone* (Mar. 1986), 1136. For details of this performance at the Vienna palace of Prince von Lobkowitz, and the rehearsals that led up to it, see Tomislav Volek and Jaroslav Macek, 'Beethoven's Rehearsals at the Lobkowitz's' *Musical Times*, 127 (1986), 75–80.

a performance practice that lacks the 'wider variety of nuance and tempo modification which were later to be considered the hallmarks of a conductor's interpretation', but instead features the 'uncomplicated, rhythmical' approach typical of amateur performances to this day.[11] I would like to think that Kerman would recoil along with me from such an abject and literalistic rejection of interpretive responsibilities, which arises not so much out of serious artistic conviction as out of Wellsian time-travel fantasies. But such performances do follow logically from the premises his word implies. The concept of contextuality seems especially paradoxical when you consider that practically all music composed before 1800, and a great deal composed since, is almost invariably heard out of context today—that is, in that most anachronistic of all settings, the concert-hall. But what am I saying? Now we can hear *Aida* on the patio and the St Matthew Passion in the shower—in anybody's performance. No, clearly, 'contextual' will not do.

How about 'verisimilar', then? Can we fairly say, without introducing spurious moral issues, that performances of a type described in days of yore as 'authentic' are actually aiming at nothing more controversial than historical verisimilitude? Not a chance. For one thing, it *is* controversial, and has been so from the beginning. Why should this be our aim? What does such an aim say about us? Robert Morgan's answer in Chapter 3 echoes a thesis put forward by Donald Grout some thirty years ago. If, Grout wrote, a composer of 'old music'

could by some miracle be brought to life in the twentieth century to be quizzed about the methods of performance in his own times, his first reaction would certainly be one of astonishment at our interest in such matters. Have we no living tradition of music, that we must be seeking to revive a dead one? The question might be embarrassing. Musical archaism may be a symptom of a disintegrating civilization.[12]

Besides, our conception of historical verisimilitude, despite all the strides that have been made in the three decades since Grout wrote, and despite any strides we are likely to make in the future, remains just as speculative and contingent—and hence, just as specious—as it was in 1957. It is true that some

---

[11] Clive Brown, notes to Oiseau-Lyre 414 338.
[12] 'On Historical Authenticity', 346.

performance styles that have arisen in the last quarter century under the banner of historical verisimilitude have proven extremely persuasive, influential, and (with the passage of time) authoritative—at least within the world of performance. One is the, shall we call it, 'Mediterranean' style of rendering the songs of the troubadours, pioneered in the 1960s by Thomas Binkley, Andrea von Ramm, and their colleagues in the Studio der frühen Musik in Munich. Another is the Netherlandish style of baroque string playing associated with names such as Jaap Schröder, Anner Bylsma, and the brothers Kuijken. An earlier example would be the style of Gregorian chant singing evolved at the Benedictine Abbey of Solesmes by Pothier and Mocquereau. The fact is, however, that in not one of these cases can the historicity of the style in question withstand the slightest scrutiny on any positive documentary basis. They are not fashioned out of whole cloth, to be sure, but not only are they unverifiable in all their aspects, they are each quite falsifiable in some. Does this invalidate them? Only from the point of view of historical data. Whatever the case a scholarly prosecutor might choose to bring against them, they will remain as persuasive and authoritative as ever, until a more persuasive style, as is inevitable, comes along to supersede them. What makes for persuasion, I want to emphasize—and hence, what makes for authority and authenticity, in a sense I would approve—has to do both with the persuaders and with the persuaded.

Those whose scholarly superego insists that everything they do must survive a trial-by-document are doomed to a marginal existence as performers. Strict accountability in fact reduces performance practice to a lottery,[13] for the performer can exercise no control over the state of evidence. If you construe your fragmentary evidence the way religious fundamentalists construe scripture—that is, if you believe that what is not permitted is prohibited—then you will find yourself in the position of the early music performer who happily averred that, when making records (which are themselves 'documents' of a special narcissistic kind), 'I personally try to restrain all the people who work with me . . . . I think it's best to be minimal about your additions,' lest the recording 'embarrass us for

---

[13] 'On Letting the Music Speak for Itself', 344.

another twenty years'.[14] There is logic in this position, but it is the logic of certain death. There is nothing you can do, after all, and be sure that someone will not say, 'Hey, you can't do that!' If you want no one to say it, you must do nothing—as many do in the name of 'authenticity'. Such an authenticity is worthy neither of the name nor of serious discussion.

The inadequacy of 'historical verisimilitude' as an umbrella concept to account for the style of performance we are trying to name is especially poignant in the case of certain performers and groups that explicitly eschew verisimilitude as a performance ideal yet are clearly within the pale of the so-called 'authenticity movement'. Peter Phillips, the director of the Tallis Scholars, one of the young English choirs whose work has set a new standard in the performance of Renaissance sacred polyphony, has come right out and said that 'we can guess at the type of sound produced by sixteenth-century choirs, and the evidence suggests that imitation of them would be highly undesirable.' Even more forthrightly, he continued: 'It is unlikely that any choir in the sixteenth century had at any one time a group of singers who were sufficiently young to perform in a manner which we should consider to be ideal—conditions then were not so favourable to experiment and choice as they are now, and it is for that very reason that we can be so bold as to say that we think we can do better.'[15] I dare say we ought to do better than the band of amateurs who thrashed their uncomplicated rhythmical way through the first performance of the *Eroica*, too.

The difference between the new English choirs and their sixteenth-century prototypes was a matter not only of age, but of gender as well. The new choirs use women rather than boys on the stratospheric treble parts in Tudor music. This was a decision consciously taken in the mid-1960s by David Wulstan, the founder and director of the Clerkes of Oxenford, the first of the new choirs, after five years in which the group had worked as a traditional men-and-boys choir. It is curiously revealing that Wulstan and his spokesmen were at first not so straight-forward as Phillips about methods and aims. 'The primary

---

[14] James Badal, 'On Record: Christopher Hogwood', *Fanfare* (Nov.–Dec. 1985), 90–1.
[15] 'Performance Practice in 16th-Century English Choral Music', *Early Music*, 6 (1978), 195.

object [was] to obtain as nearly as possible the sound of the great English Sixteenth Century Choirs,' we may read in the programme notes to one of Wulstan's early recordings. 'Because boys' voices now break early, they tend to find the high vocal parts of the period overtaxing: with proper training, however, girls' voices can produce exactly the right sound.'[16] But this is clearly a prevarication. Wulstan, obviously, had never heard a 'great English Sixteenth Century Choir'. He knew what he wanted, though, and knew he would never get it from boys as young as English choirboys now are. Since he had never heard a seventeen-year-old sixteenth-century choirboy, the sound to which his 'girls' ' voices 'came as nearly as possible' was one he had imagined, not heard. It was, in short, a creation of the twentieth century, not the sixteenth. And yet it somehow had to be passed off as a historical reconstruction.

Why? To placate ol' debbil musicology, I guess. Wulstan is an academic musicologist, Phillips is not. Their differing perspectives on what they were doing (or what they wanted to present themselves as doing) points up the ambivalences in the relationship between musical scholarship and musical performance (even 'performance practice'). Scholars tend to assume it is they who have furnished the major impetus for historical performance. Grout put this in terms of a rather unattractive joke: 'Historical Musicology, like Original Sin, has given everybody a bad conscience,' he wrote, putting an end to the 'days of innocence' when 'people did not bother about the original tradition, but simply assumed that the practice of their own nineteenth century was the universal rule and proceeded to apply it accordingly'.[17] While some performers do seem to be motivated by a bad conscience—and Grout's choice of simile accords well with what was said earlier about 'religious fundamentalism'—I believe he was dead wrong about the origins of the kind of performance we are considering today, and about what sustains it. A glance at the historical record, such as Howard Mayer Brown provides in Chapter 2, will show that musicology has been a Johnny-come-lately to the authentic performance movement, and I will make bold to assert that musicology has been responsible for more of what has gone

---

[16] W. A. Chislett, notes to Seraphim LP 60256 (works of Tallis).
[17] 'On Historical Authenticity', 342.

wrong with 'authentic' performance than what has gone right with it—though there are welcome signs that this may be changing.

It is the academic mind, not the performer's, that is trained to generalize and to seek normative procedures—even when this means elbowing off the table the difficulties and ambiguities that surround, for a notable example, the Renaissance mensural system.[18] Edgard Varèse once gloomily predicted that 'it will not be long before some musical mortician begins embalming electronic music in rules'.[19] Compare that with Christopher Hogwood, who looks forward to the day when we will be able, after digesting 'sufficient data', to make 'rules and regulations' to govern performances of nineteenth-century music.[20] The academic mentality tends to operate on the basis of authority ('objectivity') not identification ('subjectivity').

Let us consider in this light the vexed matter of the composer's intentions *vis-à-vis* the performer's responsibilities. Musicologists have characteristically assumed, to quote Donald Grout in 1957, that 'an ideal performance is one that perfectly realizes the composer's intentions',[21] or, to quote Howard Mayer Brown (Chapter 2), that 'the central question can be formulated very simply: should we play music in the way the composer intended it?' I have already had occasion to express my scepticism about such an ideal from standpoints both practical and philosophical.[22] We cannot know intentions, for many reasons—or rather, we cannot know we know them. Composers do not always express them. If they do express them, they may do so disingenuously. Or they may be honestly mistaken, owing to the passage of time or a not necessarily consciously experienced change of taste. If anyone doubts this, let him listen to the five recordings Stravinsky made of *Le Sacre du Printemps*, and try to decide how the composer intended it to

---

[18] Cf. Philip Gossett, 'The Mensural System and the *Choralis Constantinus*', in Robert Marshall (ed.), *Studies in Renaissance and Baroque Music in Honor of Arthur Mendel* (Kassel and Hackensack, 1974), 71–107.

[19] Edgard Varèse, 'The Liberation of Sound', in Benjamin Boretz and Edward T. Cone (eds.), *Perspectives on American Composers* (New York, 1971), 32.

[20] 'On Record: Christopher Hogwood', 89.

[21] 'On Historical Authenticity', 341.

[22] 'On Letting the Music Speak for Itself', 340–1.

go.[23] (For 'help', one may consult his published reviews of five other performances.[24]) The decision will have to be made either on the basis of one's preferences (in which case the recourse to authority has been entirely spurious), or on the basis of some arbitrary rule (the 'Fassung letzter Aufnahme?'), which comes down in any case to an appeal to an authority higher than the composer's, anyway. But all that is really beside the point. I continue to maintain that composers do not usually have intentions such as we would like to ascertain, and that the need obliquely to gain the composer's approval for what we do bespeaks a failure of nerve, not to say an infantile dependency. I have previously dismissed the appeal to intentions as an evasion of the performer's obligation to understand what he is performing. It is what Wimsatt and Beardsley, at the conclusion of their immortal (if usually misunderstood) 'Intentional Fallacy', called 'consulting the oracle'.[25]

Now compare Wanda Landowska: 'If Rameau himself would rise from his grave to demand of me some changes in my interpretation of his *Dauphine*, I would answer, "You gave birth to it; it is beautiful. But now leave me alone with it. You have

[23] They include three studio recordings: 1928 (with a Paris pick-up ensemble), 1940 (with the Philharmonic-Symphony Orchestra of New York), 1960 (with the Columbia Symphony Orchestra); a piano roll (Paris: Pleyela, c.1925); and a live performance (the last he would ever conduct of this work) with the Swedish Radio Symphony Orchestra, recorded on 24 September 1961 and recently issued on Discocorp RR–224 (with rehearsal sequences).

[24] 'Three Types of Spring Fever (Stravinsky Reviews *The Rite*)', in Igor Stravinsky and Robert Craft, *Retrospectives and Conclusions* (New York, 1969), 123–30 (performances by Karajan, Boulez, Craft); 'Spring Fever: A Review of Three Recent Recordings of *The Rite of Spring*', in Igor Stravinsky, *Themes and Conclusions* (Berkeley and Los Angeles, 1982) 234–41 (performances by Boulez, Mehta, and his own of 1960).

[25] W. K. Wimsatt, Jr. and Monroe C. Beardsley, 'The Intentional Fallacy', *Sewanee Review* (1946), 468–88; very widely anthologized, e.g., in Hazard Adams (ed.), *Critical Theory Since Plato* (New York, 1971), 1015–22; Frank A. Tillman and Steven M. Cahn (eds.), *Philosophy of Art and Aesthetics* (New York, 1969), 657–69. Gary Tomlinson is quite wrong to imply that all this essay propounds is the notion that 'knowledge of the expressive aims of past artists is irrelevant . . . and the search for it pointless'. For me its essential implication is that an author's *ex post facto* interpretation of his work is not privileged, and that the ontological status of a work of art is independent of its origins. I find it curious, in any event, that Tomlinson considers the 'intentional fallacy' an 'outmoded' notion, since the ideas he attempts to reintroduce are even older. Tomlinson's quest for 'authentic meanings' really amounts to little more than the old Germanic ideal of historical '*Verstehen*', as preached and practised by proponents of idealistic *Geistesgeschichte* in days of yore.

nothing more to say; go away!"[26] No consulting the oracle for her! But would the oracle demand to be consulted? In an earlier article I gave copious examples from the literature and from my own experience to show that 'once the piece is finished, the composer regards it and relates to it either as a performer if he is one, or else simply as a listener.'[27] To the examples cited there from Irving Berlin, Debussy, and Elliott Carter, I should like to add some comments George Perle voiced in private conversation. After recalling occasions on which he had edited or modified his compositions to reflect some of the better performances of them that he had heard, he reflected that the relationship between composer and performer is 'a complicated business' that performers who do not work directly with composers are not likely to understand. The greatest single source of bad performance, he averred, is literalism, adding, 'It's what you expect nowadays.'

I consider this matter settled. But whether or not you agree with me, I hope to persuade you that it is just a red herring, and cannot be used as a way of characterizing 'authenticity'. For adherents to the point of view we are dissecting here have no unique claim in the matter of fidelity to the composer's intentions. Everyone claims it. Landowska, in the very same essay from which I drew her defiant retort to Rameau, gave the following as her answer to the rhetorical question, 'On what do I base my interpretations?'

By living intimately with the works of a composer I endeavor to penetrate his spirit, to move with an increasing ease in the world of his thoughts, and to know them 'by heart' so that I may recognize immediately when Mozart is in good humor or when Handel wants to express triumphant joy. I want to know when Bach is raging and throwing a handful of sixteenths at the face of some imaginary adversary or a flaming spray of arpeggios, as he does in *The Chromatic Fantasy*. The goal is to attain such an identification with the composer that no more effort has to be made *to understand the slightest of his intentions* or to follow the subtlest fluctuations of his mind.[28]

Bruno Walter, in his 'Notes on Bach's *St Matthew Passion*', continually emphasizes his 'endeavors to be faithful to Bach's

---

[26] *Landowska On Music*, ed. Denise Restout (New York, 1981), 407.
[27] 'On Letting the Music Speak for Itself', 340.
[28] *Landowska On Music*, 406 (italics added).

intentions'[29]—often as a justification for his departures from eighteenth-century performance practice. More recently, Kenneth Cooper, representing the Chamber Music Society of Lincoln Center in its much-advertised joint appearance with Christopher Hogwood's Academy of Ancient Music in September 1984, admonished an interviewer in a televised intermission feature with the remark that 'We're no less concerned with Bach's intentions than Chris is.'

The difference between the point of view represented here by Landowska, Walter, and Cooper, and what from here on I shall in desperation call the 'authentistic' point of view (authentistic being to authentic as Hellenistic was to Hellenic), is that the former construes intentions 'internally', that is, in spiritual, metaphysical, or emotional terms, and sees their realization in terms of the 'effect' of a performance, while the latter construes intentions in terms of empirically ascertainable—and hence, though tacitly, external—facts, and sees their realization purely in terms of sound. Walter speaks explicitly of the performer's responsibility to gain 'intimate knowledge of the spiritual content of Bach's compositions', while Landowska, in a declaration already quoted by Howard Mayer Brown (Chapter 2), said, 'Little do I care if, to attain the proper effect, I use means that were not exactly those available to Bach.'[30] The difference, to put matters in historical perspective, is that between idealism on the one hand, which recognizes a sharp distinction between content and form and between spirit and letter, and positivism on the other, which denies the existence of any but sensory experience, and hence any knowledge not based on sensory data. To a positivist content is a function of form, spirit a function of letter. Content and spirit as concepts in themselves are illusions born of reifying subjective sensation.

Both of these viewpoints go back to the nineteenth century— under different names, of course, they go back to the Greeks— and both are still with us today, though clearly the positivists are wielding the bigger guns. There seems to be a wall of misunderstanding between them. Brown surely misconstrues Landowska when he says, with reference to the passage just

---

[29] Bruno Walter, *Of Music and Music-Making*, trans. Paul Hamburger (New York, 1961), 183.
[30] *Landowska On Music*, 356.

cited, that she 'believed more strongly in her own personal understanding of the music and her commitment to it than in any more dispassionate quest for what the composer would have wanted or expected'. As we have seen, she believed she had reached a point of identification with the composers she played that was so close that she could divine what they wanted and expected, though she did not think of these desires and expectations primarily ('merely', she would have said) in terms of sound. When she says 'the proper effect', she means 'the effect intended by Bach', pure if not so simple.

Early in her career Landowska wrote an essay on transcriptions as intransigent as any modern textualist or authenticist might be today. And just like today's writers, she began by taking aim at her predecessors. She quoted Hans von Bülow: 'The harpsichord works of Bach are the Old Testament; Beethoven's Sonatas the New. We must believe in both.' And then she commented: 'While saying that, he added several bars to the *Chromatic Fantasy*, changed the answer of the Fugue, and doubled the basses; thus he impregnated this work with an emphatic and theatrical character. A true believer must not change anything in the New or the Old Testament.'[31] Yet if we compare her recorded performance of the *Chromatic Fantasy* (see Appendix, Recording No. 1) with one by a present-day authenticist, we shall, many of us, be tempted to level the same strictures at her as she levelled at von Bülow (listen, particularly, to her renditions of the passages in block chords with the laconic instruction, '*arpeggio*'). But if this means we misunderstand her now, she would have had a hard time understanding us as well. She would have wondered, for one thing, what anything 'dispassionate' had to do with art.

The wall of misunderstanding was evident in the Kenneth Cooper–Christopher Hogwood TV exchange, too, even though the participants affected comradely agreement. Cooper, responding to the interviewer's remarks on historical evidence as justifier of performance practice, said: 'It should be remembered about history . . . that what we know about history was only a small part of what was done, so that when we represent what we know about it, we are distorting it; and therefore to try

----

[31] Ibid. 101.

and fill in a little of the creative energy—even if it's not exactly the same creative energy (because we'll never know what that is)—[helps us in] getting closer to a fuller picture'. For Cooper, then, to realize Bach's intentions one needs not only knowledge but a vital impetus born of intuition to fill the gaps between the facts. This alone can convert knowledge into action.

To this Hogwood rejoined: 'That's the wonderful thing, I think, about coming across new versions of pieces or new evidence. Suddenly that gives you this extra energy: "Ah, a new set of instructions for embellishment . . . ah, wonderful!"' No *élan vital* here. What enables action on this view is a green light from the boss. The gaps between the facts can only be filled by new facts. Gaps will ever remain.

As I have suggested, the positivist viewpoint is ascendant today—obviously so among authenticists. One tends to patronize the idealistic viewpoint for naïvely confusing subject with object and for its mystical reliance on illusory non-knowledge. What a variety of sins such thinking may rationalize, we are apt to say today. Yet the positivistic viewpoint can lead to positions just as ludicrous and untenable, and just as potentially mischievous. It makes things rather easy for reviewers, for one thing. It is now possible to pass judgement on a performance one has not yet heard. One very prominent critic, conspicuously allied with academic musicology, recently announced an impending series of recitals, at which two prominent New York musicians would perform the Beethoven sonatas for piano and cello, by sniffing: 'They are fine artists, but [!] they play modern instruments . . . I look forward to [their] recitals but will know them . . . for what they are: transcriptions, in effect, in which Beethoven's tone colors, textures, attacks, and sonic durations are inevitably altered.'[32] Pity the poor fine artists, thus consigned, as Dante consigned the Greek philosophers, to the upper reaches of Hell. Elsewhere our critic contrasted their 'transcriptions' with a performance on 'original instruments', in which 'Beethoven's music rang out more bravely, more beautifully, and in better balance' than modern instruments could achieve, and (it follows) with Beethoven's tone colours, textures, attacks, and sonic durations unaltered.

[32] Andrew Porter, 'Musical Events', *The New Yorker*, 3 Nov. 1986, 142–3.

But a moment's reflection will unmask this ploy. In neither case did the critic hear Beethoven's tone colours or sonic durations. He heard the tone colours and sonic durations of a cello and a piano. Nor did he hear Beethoven's attacks. He heard the attacks of a cellist and a pianist. We have here a particularly egregious instance of what has become a widespread and obnoxious fallacy: taking the instrument for the player and (in this case) even for the composer. Facile intransigence like this smacks of snobbery; the critic has absolved himself from the exercise of his proper function, which is to evaluate specific cases, not legislate class distinctions. Performances, even when they are not evaluated, as here, in advance, are often evaluated nowadays not for their accomplishment but for their class connections.

In any event, I hope it may be agreed that fidelity to the composer's intentions cannot be used as a yardstick by which the value of a performance may be measured, and that it is not in expressions of such fidelity that the essential nature of authentistic performance resides. Perhaps that essence can be located in the domain of hardware—in the 'original instruments' we prize. But this can only be the case in so far as historical verisimilitude is the validator; and we have seen that that extent is not nearly as far as is often imagined. Besides, I sometimes wonder whether the craze for original instruments has anything much to do with historicism at all. One prominent advocate of 'historical performance' (his term) for nineteenth-century music had this to say about an 'original instruments' recording of the *Missa Solemnis*:

I would be hard pressed to point up any significant difference between the vocal styles applied here and those in any of a half dozen representative modern recordings. There is something specious about arguing for instrumental authenticity while largely ignoring the vocal domain. It is certainly true that we know less about vocal techniques and performance styles in the eighteenth and nineteenth centuries than we do about instrumental performance. But that is no reason to abandon the search.[33]

Many, I'm sure, would wish to debate the contention

---

[33] Robert Winter, 'The Emperor's New Clothes: Nineteenth-Century Instruments Revisited', *Nineteenth-Century Music*, 7 (1984), 255.

advanced here about the relative state of knowledge. But that is beside my point. What chiefly interests me is the idea that an indispensable earnest of authenticity is strangeness. Let us not abandon the search, the critic admonishes, simply because we have little idea of what we are searching for. He wants change, though he knows not what change he wants. Make it different, he seems to be saying, because difference is what counts. Make It New.

Who said that before? Why, Ezra Pound, of course, in the title to a testamentary book of essays, in its day a bible of modernism. And now we have come at last to the nub and essence of authentistic performance, as I see it. It is modern performance.

This may take a deal of explaining, since the vocabulary of conventional criticism opposes modern performance to what I wish to call by that name. Yet the ideal of authentistic performance grew up alongside modernism, shares its tenets, and will probably decline alongside it as well. Its values, its justification, and, yes, its authenticity, will only be revealed in conjunction with those of modernism. Historical verisimilitude, composers' intentions, original instruments, and all that, to the extent that they have a bearing on the question, have not been ends but means; and in most considerations of the issue they have been smokescreens. To put my thesis in a nutshell, I am convinced that 'historical' performance today is not really historical; that a thin veneer of historicism clothes a performance style that is completely of our own time, and is in fact the most modern style around; and that the historical hardware has won its wide acceptance and above all its commercial viability precisely by virtue of its novelty, not its antiquity.

In my essay, 'On Letting the Music Speak for Itself', I raised the matter of modernism tangentially, chiefly in connection with the ideal of impersonality—'depersonalization' to use T. S. Eliot's word[34]—that links modernist thinking to the values implicit in authentistic performance. Both regard the individual 'as he is at the moment'—that is, as an ephemeral carbon-based,

---

[34] 'Tradition and the Individual Talent' (1917), in Frank Kermode (ed.), *Selected Prose of T. S. Eliot* (New York, 1975), 40.

oxygen-breathing organism soon to expire, decay, and disappear, and who is prey to all the mundane subjective pleasures and pains that flesh is heir to—as a thing of no consequence. Eliot's *envoi* to what he called 'the responsible person interested in poetry', reads as follows:

To divert interest from the poet to the poetry is a laudable aim: for it would conduce to a juster estimation of actual poetry, good and bad. There are many people who appreciate the expression of sincere emotion in verse, and there is a smaller number of people who can appreciate technical excellence. But very few know when there is an expression of *significant* emotion, emotion which has its life in the poem and not in the history of the poet. The emotion of art is impersonal. And the poet cannot reach this impersonality without surrendering himself wholly to the work to be done. And he is not likely to know what is to be done unless he lives in what is not merely the present, but the present moment of the past, unless he is conscious, not of what is dead, but of what is already living.[35]

For a gloss on this beautifully gnomic text let us turn to Pound's *Make It New*, which, its title notwithstanding, consists mainly of studies of very old poetry, from the Troubadours to the Elizabethans. Under the heading of 'A Few Dont's' for poets, we find this:

Consider the way of the scientists rather than the way of an advertising agent for a new soap.

The scientist does not expect to be acclaimed as a great scientist until he has *discovered* something. He begins by learning what has been discovered already. He goes from that point onward. He does not bank on being a charming fellow personally. He does not expect his friends to applaud the results of his freshman class work. Freshmen in poetry are unfortunately not confined to a definite and recognizable class room. They are 'all over the shop'. Is it any wonder 'the public is indifferent to poetry?'[36]

What is only personal is irrelevant. What is sought is a contribution of something valuable to the common wealth of art. And that means becoming well acquainted with that common wealth, which in turn means knowing history, or, in Eliot's terms, possessing 'the historical sense', defined as 'what

[35] Ibid. 44.
[36] Ezra Pound, *Make It New* (London, 1934), 339.

makes a writer most acutely conscious of his place in time', and what impels him towards the 'extinction of personality'.[37]

It is no accident that both Eliot's maxims and Pound's were written during the First World War, the convulsion that truly ended the nineteenth century—ended the Renaissance, as people were fond of saying then—and that posed a hitherto inconceivable threat to all security and stability, whether of individual lives or of Culture and Civilization writ large. Refuge in order and precision, hostility to subjectivity, to the vagaries of personality, to whatever passes and decays—these were the inevitable reactions of all who were committed to the preservation of the high culture. The threat has only intensified since the days of Eliot and Pound, and high modernism has become even more intransigent, objectivist, élitist, and fearful of individual freedom of expression, which leads inexorably to the abyss. Examples can be found everywhere. A convenient one has appeared in the newspaper on the day I happen to be writing this. Lincoln Kirstein, comrade of Balanchine and sometime collaborator with Stravinsky, takes up the cudgels against 'postmodernism', the code for whatever beleaguers the high culture today, with an attack on Isadora Duncan, dead these sixty years. She it is who, by personifying and glorifying the 'exposure of a private personage's unique sensibility', led the way to the depravity of the present moment, when 'exquisite care in craftsmanship, elegant spareness, historic obligation and humane responsibility are conveniently ignored by a generation of dance dilettantes'. Isadora's legacy, writes Kirstein, 'was reputation, not repertory'. She was the antithesis of Nijinsky, whose 'intense personifications used the broad language of a received academic vocabulary' and whose '"self" remains mysterious'. The peroration is borrowed from St Augustine: 'I understand with complete certainty that what is subject to decay is inferior to that which is not, and without hesitation I placed that which cannot be harmed above that which can, and I saw that what remains constant is better than that which is changeable.'[38]

We might already wish to draw an analogy with authentistic performance, which upholds a comparable goal—to arrest the

---

[37] Eliot, 'Tradition', 38, 40.
[38] Lincoln Kirstein, 'The Curse of Isadora', *The New York Times* (Sunday, 23 Nov. 1986), section II, pp. 1, 28.

decay of the music of the past by reversing the changeable vagaries of taste and restoring it to a timeless constancy. This would be a facile analogy, and one that accepted at face value what I hope I have shown to be a specious, or at least a debatable claim.

Let us instead press on. Shortly after I drew my first parallels between authentistic performance and modernist aesthetics, an extremely clever article by Daniel Leech-Wilkinson appeared in *Early Music*, as part of that journal's symposium on 'The Limits of Authenticity'. As a result of an experiment in which pairs of recordings (one authentistic, the other not) encompassing a wide range of repertory (from plainchant to Schubert) were compared, the author was able to report that

in every case . . . the stylistic contrast between the earlier and the 'authentic' performance is essentially the same. The earlier performance—in accordance with the fashions of its time—shows greater variation of dynamics, speed and timbre, amounting to a performance which is more 'emotional', more a personal 'interpretation' of what the performers believe the composer to be 'saying'; while the more recent, 'authentic' performance is characterized by relatively uniform tempo and dynamics, a 'clean' sound and at least an attempt to avoid interpretive gestures beyond those notated or documented as part of period performance practice. In a nutshell, the difference is that between performer as 'interpreter' and performer as 'transmitter'.

Leech-Wilkinson concluded that 'the remarkable uniformity of approach which dominates early music performance . . . is nothing more than a reflection of current taste.'[39]

I believe these observations may be considerably extended. For the most part, Leech-Wilkinson compared recordings of the 1950s and 1960s with recordings of the 1970s and 1980s. Had he compared recordings of the 1920s and 1930s with those in his earlier group, his conclusions would have been substantially the same, as they would have been were he to have compared early 'electrics' with turn-of-the-century acoustic discs. Moreover, what he found to be true of performances involving repertory falling under the general—and ever-expanding—umbrella of 'early music' would have been equally true of performances of virtually any repertory, including current repertory. Modern

[39] *Early Music*, 12 (1984), 14.

performance gets moderner and moderner, as Alice might say. Many who have made the comparison will tell you that Gary Graffman's Prokofiev, for example, sounds more like Prokofiev than Prokofiev's (ditto Sándor's Bartók or Tacchino's Poulenc). Changes in performing style in the twentieth century, no less than in past centuries, have been allied with changes in composing style, and with more general changes in the aesthetic and philosophical outlook of the time. Changes of this kind moreover, are never sudden, always gradual. To contemporaries, all periods are transitional and pluralistic. A multiplicity of styles is always available in any present, of which some are allied more with the past and others with the future. Only when the present becomes the past and the future becomes the present can we see which was which.

For a forcible reminder of this, we can listen today to Bach's Fifth Brandenburg Concerto, recorded at the Salzburg Festival in the Bach Bicentennial year, 1950, by Willi Boskovsky on violin, Gustav Neidermayer on flute, and the string section of the Vienna Philharmonic under Wilhelm Furtwängler, who also plays the piano solo (Appendix, Recording No. 2a). It seems incredible that this performance happened so recently. It visits us now like the ghost of Jacob Marley, weighted down by generations of accrued tradition (some might wish to continue the Marley metaphor and call them accrued misdeeds), made crushingly palpable in Furtwängler's unforgettably hamfisted continuo chords, banged out at full Bechstein blast with left hand *coll'ottava*. By comparison, *any* performance we may hear today will seem virtually weightless, reminding us of Karl Marx's definition of the modern experience as one in which 'all that is solid melts into air'.[40] This is Bach interpreted by a musician who still regarded Bach as Beethoven did—'not a brook but an ocean', and the fountainhead of contemporary music. The performance is a kind of sacramental act, a communion that renews contact with the source and strengthens the 'perception, not only of the pastness of the past but of its presence . . . a sense of the timeless as well as the temporal and of the timeless and the temporal together', of which Eliot

---

[40] Karl Marx and Friedrich Engels, *Manifesto of the Communist Party* (1848), trans. Samuel F. Moore, in *Introduction to Contemporary Civilization in the West*, ii, 3rd edn. (New York, 1961), 683–4.

speaks. It embodies not an ahistorical vision of Bach, as we might be inclined to call it before reflecting, but the very opposite: a profoundly historical one in which the present actively participates. The pastness of the present is as much implied by it as the presence of the past. 'Whoever has approved this idea of order will not find it preposterous', wrote Eliot, 'that the past should be altered by the present as much as the present is directed by the past,' and this because

what happens when a new work of art is created is something that happens simultaneously to all the works of art which preceded it. The existing monuments form an ideal order among themselves, which is modified by the introduction of the new . . . work of art among them. The existing order is complete before the new work arrives; for order to persist after the supervention of novelty, the *whole* existing order must be, if ever so slightly, altered; and so the relations, proportions, values of each work of art toward the whole are readjusted; and this is conformity between the old and the new.[41]

So Furtwängler's Bach is no smug or mindless adaptation of Bach to the style of Wagner. It is a reaffirmation of the presence of Bach *in* Wagner and the simultaneous, reciprocal presence of Wagner in Bach. Without that perception, and its affirmation in the art of performance, Bach would fall out of the tradition, and so, deprived of their fount, would Beethoven, Brahms, and Wagner. All would become alien to all; the centre would cease to hold.

Artists who feel themselves heir to tradition in this way have a very exigent sense of canon. What is canonical is kin; what is not is alien. For German musicians of Furtwängler's generation, Bach was canonical but Handel was not. Schoenberg, who (as Robert Morgan has eloquently reminded us in Chapter 3) possessed these perceptions and was possessed by them to a rare degree—and who, according to his biographer, 'was furious if one mentioned Handel in the same breath as Bach'[42]—made a 'free transformation' of one of Handel's Concerti Grossi, Op. 6, that illustrates perfectly what Adorno (who hated the very idea of what we now call 'authenticity') meant by calling the

[41] Eliot, 'Tradition', 38–9.
[42] H. H. Stuckenschmidt, *Arnold Schoenberg: His Life, World and Work*, trans. Humphrey Searle (New York, 1978), 365.

arrangements of Schoenberg and Webern 'loyal . . . in being disloyal'.[43] By violating every aspect of its sound and structure, Schoenberg sought to give Handel's music an 'intensification of motival development', and especially a 'solidity of form' that would prevent it from melting into air. By remedying an 'insufficiency with respect to thematic invention and development [that] could satisfy no sincere contemporary of ours',[44] Schoenberg sought to save at least this work of Handel's for the canon. The resulting 'Concerto for String Quartet and Orchestra' was a rather extreme example of 'the alteration of the past by the present'. Webern's arrangement of the six-part Ricercar from the *Musical Offering*, of course, was another.

It would be a great mistake to call either Furtwängler's or Schoenberg's approaches naïve. What can make them appear so is the fact that they rely on a sense of continuity—and hence direct transmission—of tradition that many in the twentieth century believe to be lost. Eliot stated this sense of loss—or perhaps we should say, of rejection—quite explicitly, and in this rejection lies the challenge and the curse of modernism.

If the only form of tradition, of handing down, consisted in following the ways of the immediate generation before us in a blind or timid adherence to its successes, 'tradition' should positively be discouraged. We have seen many such simple currents soon lost in the sand; and novelty is better than repetition. Tradition is a matter of much wider significance. It cannot be inherited, and if you want it you must obtain it by great labour.[45]

Eliot was attempting an end run around the age of Romanticism and its catastrophic disorders. 'It was romanticism that made the revolution,' wrote T. E. Hulme, who would die on the battlefields of Flanders in 1917. 'They [who] hate the revolution . . . hate romanticism.'[46] His 'they', of course, meant 'we'. In Hulme's view, Romanticism was the culminating phase of humanism, that fatal hubris 'which is the opposite

[43] Theodor W. Adorno, 'Bach Defended Against his Devotees', in *Prisms*, trans. Samuel and Shierry Weber (Cambridge, Mass., 1981), 146.

[44] Arnold Schoenberg, programme note for Janssen Symphony Orchestra of Los Angeles, reprinted on sleeve of Columbia ML4406 (1951).

[45] Eliot, 'Tradition', 38.

[46] 'Romanticism and Classicism', in T. E. Hulme, *Speculations: Essays on Humanism and the Philosophy of Art*, ed. Herbert Read (London, 1936), 115.

of the doctrine of original sin: the belief that man as a part of nature was after all something satisfactory.' He went on:

The change which Copernicus is supposed to have brought about is the exact contrary of the fact. Before Copernicus, man was not the centre of the world; after Copernicus he was. You get a change from a certain profundity and intensity to that flat and insipid optimism which, passing through its first stage of decay in Rousseau, has finally culminated in the state of slush in which we have the misfortune to live.[47]

That slush seeped into art through an excess of 'vitality', Hulme's term for a view of art that equates its beauty with its power to evoke a pleasurable empathy:

Any work of art [of this kind] we find beautiful is an objectification of our own pleasure in activity, and our own vitality. The worth of a line or form consists in the value of the life which it contains for us. Putting the matter more simply we may say that in this art there is always a feeling of liking for, and pleasure in, the forms and movements to be found in nature.[48]

And human nature above all.

Like Eliot, and like his mentor Wilhelm Worringer,[49] Hulme chose all his examples from the visual arts or literature, where there is no problem defining the natural forms and movements that serve as models for art. But explicit statements of a vitalistic aesthetic of music are far from uncommon. Hanslick, though an early and implacable opponent of such a view, nevertheless summed it up well when he admitted the analogy (to him a misleading analogy and irrelevant to what is beautiful in music) between the dynamic properties of music—'the ideas of intensity waxing and diminishing; of motion hastening and lingering'—and the 'forms' with which emotion presents itself to our consciousness.[50] Later writers have formulated the idea in more general terms. Susanne Langer's way of putting it is that

[47] Hulme, 'Modern Art and Its Philosophy', in *Speculations*, 80.
[48] Ibid. 85.
[49] See his *Abstraktion und Einfühlung* (Munich, 1908); a sizeable extract from the introduction to this work, which furnished Hulme with his thesis, may be found (trans. M. Bullock) in Francis Frascina and Charles Harrison (eds.), *Modern Art and Modernism: A Critical Anthology* (New York, 1982), 150–64.
[50] Eduard Hanslick, *The Beautiful in Music*, trans. Gustav Cohen (Indianapolis and New York, 1957), 23.

music reflects 'the morphology of feeling',[51] or, more loosely (after Carroll C. Pratt), that music may 'sound the way moods feel'. Even so recent a writer as Roger Sessions adhered to the notion, and expressed it more sweepingly than anyone else I have read: 'What music conveys to us—and let it be emphasized, this is the *nature of the medium* itself, not the consciously formulated purpose of the composer—is the nature of our existence, as embodied in the movement that constitutes our innermost life: those inner gestures that lie behind not only our emotions, but our every impulse and action, which are in turn set in motion by these, and which in turn determine the ultimate character of life itself.'[52]

None of the musical writers I have just quoted were professed vitalists, rather the contrary. They were all more or less opposed to the prevalent layman's notion of music as a 'language of emotions', or a medium for concrete propositional expression. The vital quality they all point to is a potentiality that may or may not be harnessed (legitimately or otherwise) by a composer or performer. Any music that does seek to harness it will perforce emphasize the qualities to which Hanslick drew attention—the dynamic qualities of music, as expressed in fluctuations of tempo and intensity. That is why romantic music—and romantic performance practice—are more richly endowed than any other kind with crescendos and diminuendos, accelerandos and ritardandos, not to mention tempo rubato and a highly variegated timbral palette.

For a vitalist interpretation of Bach one could do no better than Furtwängler's rendition of the harpsichord 'cadenza' in the first movement of the Fifth Brandenburg (Appendix, Recording No. 2*a*). It would be ridiculous to call it a 'modern' performance. By 1950 it was already an anachronism, conclusive evidence that the performer had reached his artistic maturity before the First World War. That nobody plays Bach like Furtwängler any more goes without saying. But does anyone play Schumann like that any more? Chopin? Tchaikovsky?

Or consider Leopold Stokowski's interpretation of the opening of the Fifth Brandenburg (Appendix, Recording No.

---

[51] *Philosophy in a New Key* (New York, 1948), 193.
[52] *Questions About Music* (New York, 1971), 45.

2*b*). The presence of the harpsichord in this performance ought to show how far the use of 'original instruments' will assure 'authenticity'. Stokowski had also reached his majority by the time of the First World War, and he was also brought up in an atmosphere where 'vitalist' performance of all repertoires was the norm. And yet in this recording, made in 1961, an elephantine allargando at the end of the first ritornello has become less an expressive gesture than a purely formal one—or, to use a word that was being derided by some literary critics as 'sanctified'[53] before I was born (so when will we musicologists wise up?), it has become a 'structural' device of an offensively didactic kind, and the performance therefore is of a kind I believe we can all agree to call 'mannered'—and doubly anachronistic, because it has lost its connection with the vitalistic aesthetic that had provided its justification.

To vitalist art (again following Worringer) Hulme opposed 'geometrical' art, the kind which, he predicted, was going to gain ascendancy in the twentieth century. His brilliant description and account of it deserves to be quoted at some length:

It most obviously exhibits no delight in nature and no striving after vitality. Its forms are always what can be described as stiff and lifeless. . . . [It embodies] the *tendency to abstraction*.

What is the nature of this tendency? What is the condition of mind of the people whose art is governed by it?

It can be described most generally as a feeling of separation in the face of outside nature.

While a naturalistic art is the result of a happy pantheistic relation between man and the outside world, the tendency to abstraction, on the contrary, occurs in races whose attitude to the outside world is the exact contrary of this. . . .

In art this state of mind results in a desire to create a certain abstract geometrical shape, which, being durable and permanent, shall be a refuge from the flux and impermanence of outside nature. The need which art satisfies here, is not the delight in the forms of nature, which is a characteristic of all vital arts, but the exact contrary. In the reproduction of natural objects there is an attempt to purify them of their characteristically living qualities in order to make them necessary and immovable. The changing is translated into something fixed and necessary. This leads to rigid lines and dead crystalline forms, for pure

---

[53] Cf. Robert Penn Warren, 'Pure and Impure Poetry' (1942), in John Crowe Ransom, (ed.), *The Kenyon Critics* (Cleveland and New York, 1951), 33.

geometrical regularity gives a certain pleasure to men troubled by the obscurity of outside appearance. The geometrical line is something absolutely distinct from the messiness, the confusion, and the accidental details of existing things. [54]

Hulme's examples of 'races' that inclined towards geometrical art included 'primitive people', who 'live in a world whose lack of order and seeming arbitrariness must inspire them with a certain fear'; but also the Egyptian, the Byzantine, and the post-classical pre-Renaissance western civilization, all of them intent on an afterlife and hence full of religious contempt for the natural world. He did not mention—because, in an essay entitled 'Modern Art' he did not need to—his own contemporaries, traumatized and dislocated first by the Industrial Revolution, then by war and political upheaval. As Yeats put it, 'Nature, steel-bound or stone-built in the nineteenth century, became a flux where man drowned or swam.'[55] Forster, less metaphorically, called it 'this continual flux even in the hearts of men'.[56] The feeling these images described was the great twentieth-century abjectness, the sense of 'withdrawal, marginality, parasitism, and opposition—what we now call alienation'.[57] Translate withdrawal into Latin roots and you get abstraction.

Escape from the flux led many early twentieth-century artists to primitive and archaic art, which shared the geometrical quality Hulme described: recall Picasso and his African ritual masks, or Pound and his medieval poetry with its literally fixed forms. The great labour Eliot spoke of in connection with attaining to Tradition involved the deliberate seeking of points of contact with the Necessary and the Immovable, a determined quest to recover what in another essay Hulme called the 'dry hardness which you get in the classics'.[58] All of this resonates with some of the famous passages in Stravinsky's *Poetics of Music* already quoted in Chapter 3 by Robert Morgan, as where the great paradigmatic musical modernist avers that 'the artist imposes a culture upon himself' and that 'tradition results from

[54] Hulme, *Speculations*, 85–7.

[55] W. B. Yeats, 'Introduction', *The Oxford Book of Modern Verse* (London, 1936), p. xxviii.

[56] E. M. Forster, *Howards End*, 143.

[57] Roger Shattuck, 'Catching Up with the Avant-Garde', *New York Review of Books* (18 December 1986), 66.

[58] Hulme, *Speculations*, 126–7.

a conscious and deliberate acceptance'.[59] And you can be sure that it is to Stravinsky that we shall return.

But first let us return to Bach. A comparison of the beginnings of five different recordings of the Fifth Brandenburg Concerto, recorded over a fifty-year period from 1935 to 1985 (see Appendix, Recordings 2*c*–*g*), will show the change-over from the vital to the geometrical in twentieth-century performance practice. They display their individual uniquenesses and mutual differences, to be sure; but what they all have spectacularly in common is a fundamentally inelastic approach to those very dynamic properties that were so richly and purposely varied by Furtwängler. They all differ from Furtwängler's rendition infinitely more than they differ among themselves; the transition among them between what we are accustomed to call 'modern' performances and authentistic ones on 'original instruments' is in this context no thing of great moment. The earliest of them, by the Adolf Busch Chamber Orchestra— recorded in 1935 with Busch on violin, Marcel Moyse on flute, and the young Rudolf Serkin on piano—exhibits a bit more variation in loudness than the others (though even here the variations are more between the concertino and the tutti than within either group singly), and its tempo is noticeably slower than the others. The tempo is no less steady, though, which already forces attention away from the music's iconicity—that is, its capacity for analogizing human behaviour and feeling— and on to the reiterative rhythmic patterns, wherein resides music's closest analogy with geometry. The second and third in the sampling are virtually identical in tempo and in levelness of intensity, although the former was made in 1950 (the same year as Furtwängler's!) under Fritz Reiner and the latter was made about a decade and a half later by the Collegium Aureum—one of the earliest on 'original instruments' and heavily touted as such in its day. The differing recording ambiences—very dry for Reiner, very live for the Collegium—almost make up for the radical difference in the size of the ensembles: in Reiner's recording there was a ripieno of two players to a part (for a total of ten) in addition to the soloists; in the Collegium Aureum

[59] Igor Stravinsky, *Poetics of Music*, trans. Arthur Knoedel and Ingolf Dahl (Cambridge, Mass., 1947), 56–7.

version there were solo ripienists, and the violin soloist was also the first violin of the tutti, so that only seven players in all participated. The last pair of recordings are recent British contributions: the English Concert under Trevor Pinnock (1982) and the Academy of Ancient Music under Christopher Hogwood (1985). Their approach does not differ appreciably from the others, save perhaps in the lightness of tone, though as the performances grow progressively lighter as the sample progresses, lightness as such represents not a departure but rather the opposite. There is another way, however, in which the last pair of recordings do differ from their predecessors: the first three, in common with almost all recordings I have heard, whatever the vintage or the instrumentarium, slow down very slightly (imperceptibly to me without the use of a metronome) for the solo section, while Pinnock and Hogwood inflexibly maintain tempo. In Pinnock's case the players are obviously working at it against what appears to be a natural tendency, so that they actually seem subjectively to rush a bit.

In any case, there can be no disputing the fact that, in terms of Hulme's categories and compared with Furtwängler's perform-ance, these are all of them geometrical renditions, not vitalistic ones, and they become more and more geometrical as they go along. What I do dispute, and emphatically, is that the concept of this style of performance had its origins in historical research or in aspirations towards historical verisimilitude, let alone respect for the composer's intentions. Wanda Landowska, decrying what she called the 'objective' style of performing early music, wrote: 'As for Bach, reducing to straightforward-ness his involved, ornate and baroque lines would be like transforming a gothic cathedral into a skyscraper.'[60] I am not sure about the gothic cathedral, but when she said *skyscraper* she hit the nail on the head. What we have here is a case of what Virgil Thomson called 'equalized tensions . . . the basis of streamlining and of all those other surface unifications that in art, as in engineering, make a work recognizable as belonging to our time and to no other'.[61]

---

[60] *Landowska On Music*, 401.
[61] 'Modernism Today' (1947), in Virgil Thomson, *Music Reviewed 1940–1954* (New York, 1967), 233.

The historical research came later. Aspirations towards historical verisimilitude and (especially) appeals to the composer's intentions, were special pleading, rationalizations *ex post facto*. Virgil Thomson was under no illusions when he reviewed the performances of Landowska—who, he felt, 'plays the harpsichord better than anybody else ever plays anything'[62] — in terms Landowska might have neither recognized nor approved. For him, it was the most modern playing around, precisely because it was the most geometrical. 'Her especial and unique grandeur is her rhythm,' he declared, after hearing her perform the *Goldberg Variations* in 1942:

It is modern quantitative scansion at its purest. Benny Goodman himself can do no better. . . . Only in our day, through the dissemination of American and South American popular music, which differs from European in being more dependent on quantitative patterns than on strong pulsations, has a correct understanding of Bach's rhythm been possible and a technique invented for rendering it cleanly and forcibly. . . . The final achievement is a musical experience that clarifies the past by revealing it to us through the present.[63]

So by the time Schoenberg brought out his updated Handel Concerto Grosso, many if not most of his 'sincere contemporaries' undoubtedly found it antiquated in concept.

By 1933 most modern musicians were well used to Hulme's categories—if not by his names, then by their own—and knew very well where they stood on the matter. Here is how Stravinsky summed it up in the *Poetics of Music*, relying on an article by his friend Pierre Souvtchinsky (who himself had relied upon Bergson, one of Hulme's mentors):

Mr. Souvtchinsky . . . presents us with two kinds of music: one which evolves parallel to the process of ontological time, embracing and penetrating it, inducing in the mind of the listener a feeling of euphoria and, so to speak, of 'dynamic calm.' The other kind runs ahead of, or counter to, this process. It is not self-contained in each momentary tonal unit. It dislocates the centers of attraction and gravity and sets itself up in the unstable; and this fact makes it particularly adaptable to

---

[62] Virgil Thomson, *The Musical Scene* (New York, 1945), 203.
[63] Ibid. 202.

the translation of the composer's emotive impulses. All music in which the will to expression is dominant belongs to the second type. . . .

Music that is based on ontological time is generally dominated by the principle of similarity. The music that adheres to psychological time likes to proceed by contrast. To these two principles which dominate the creative process correspond the fundamental concepts of variety and unity. . . . For myself, I have always [!] considered that in general it is more satisfactory to proceed by similarity rather than by contrast. Music thus gains strength in the measure that it does not succumb to the seductions of variety. What it loses in questionable riches it gains in true solidity.[64]

True solidity—again the rage against flux and impermanence, the same refuge in fixity and necessity, the same fear of melting into air. I would go so far as to suggest that all truly modern musical performance (and of course that includes the authentistic variety) essentially treats the music performed as if it were composed—or at least performed—by Stravinsky.

If this seems an overly bold assertion, let us ask ourselves where a conductor such as Fritz Reiner, whose 1950 recording of the Fifth Brandenburg we have considered, would have got his very modern ideas about baroque period style. You can be sure he never read his Dolmetsch. In the 1910s, when Dolmetsch's great guidebook came out, Reiner was in Dresden, hobnobbing with Nikisch, Muck, Mahler, and Strauss, vitalists to a man, the latter pair leaving us, in their compositions and arrangements, ample testimony to their utterly sentimentalized, fairyland vision of the eighteenth century. It must have been from the music of his own time from which Reiner (as great musicians do in all periods) formed his ideas about the music of other times. Closely identified with Stravinsky's music in America (he conducted the Metropolitan première of *The Rake's Progress* shortly after recording the Brandenburgs), '*l'amico Fritz*' earned a grudging accolade from the Old Man—no lover of interpreters—in one of the late books of conversation.[65] I believe it was Stravinsky who taught Reiner—and the rest of us—about

---

[64] Stravinsky, *Poetics of Music* (Bilingual edn., Cambridge, Mass. 1970), 41, 43.
[65] Stravinsky, *Themes and Conclusions*, 225.

Bach the geometrist, as it may have been Landowska—whom he heard as early as 1907—who taught Stravinsky.

The best theoretical formulation of the twentieth-century 'geometrical' Bach style our recordings have documented can be found in Edward T. Cone's treatise on *Musical Form and Musical Performance*:

Certainly the style of . . . the age of Bach and Handel is most memorably characterized by an important rhythmic feature: the uniformity of its metrical pulse. This is in turn but one facet of a regularity that pervades the texture of the music. As a result the typical movement of this period is indeed a *movement*, i.e., a piece composed in a single unvarying tempo. . . . Even when a movement juxtaposes two or more such units in clearly contrasted tempos, there is often an underlying arithmetical relation that, if observed in performance, unifies them. In this music, events of the same kind tend to happen either at the same rate of speed, or at precisely geared changes of rate. . . . In the best of this music, the contrapuntal texture, either actual or implied, sets up a hierarchy of events, each proceeding at its own rate, yet all under a strict metric control that extends from the entire phrase down to the smallest subdivision of the beat. . . . The beats seem to form a pre-existing framework that is independent of the musical events that it controls. One feels that before a note of the music was written, the beats were in place, regularly divided into appropriate sub-units, and regularly combined into measures; and that only after this abstract framework was in place, so to speak, was the music composed on it. . . . In performance, the result should be a relative equalization of the beats.[66]

The first point to observe about this fascinating document of twentieth-century taste is that it is profoundly anti-historical. What is presented as a self-evident feature of baroque music and an evaluation of its equally self-evident importance for determining the essential nature of baroque style, is in fact a set of opinions uncorroborated by any contemporary witness. In fact, these are points no seventeenth- or eighteenth-century theorist or treatise writer ever made, to my knowledge. With respect to Bach, they can be traced back no further than Virgil Thomson and his 'modern quantative scansion'. In the second place we may note the close congruence between Cone's description of

---

[66] Edward T. Cone, *Musical Form and Musical Performance* (New York, 1968), 59, 62, 70.

temporal and metrical regularity and Stravinsky's description of 'a music based on ontological time'. The critic pronounces the same positive value judgement on it as the composer: there is even the suggestion of the old 'refuge from flux and imperman- ence' when Cone speaks of the abstract framework that pre- exists (and, implicitly, outlasts) the individual composition. Where Cone actually goes even further than Thomson or Stravinsky is where he claims that the greater the pervasiveness of regularized metrical pulse at multiple levels of texture, the better the music is—and this because through the multilevelled rhythmic structure a unifying hierarchy is made manifest. Now if 'structural' was the sanctified shibboleth of the 'new critical' 1930s and 1940s, surely 'hierarchy' and 'unifying' were the sanctified words of the Schenkerian 1950s and 1960s, at least in academic bastions of logical positivism, among which Cone's alma mater occupied the premier position. This is Bach strictly as viewed through Princetonian eyes.

And this ahistorical viewpoint led Cone into making a downright erroneous prescription for performers: the equalized beat, reminiscent once more of streamlining and skyscrapers. The author elaborates:

We can best understand such metric play if we assume that in this style the primary metric unit is not the measure [bar] but the beat. This is not to say that the measure is unreal or purely conventional; but it is only one step in the hierarchical subdivision and combination of beats, which remain the unchanging elements. (Even the Late Baroque is, after all, not so far away from the Renaissance!) . . . Our orientation within the measure should be effected more by the actual musical profile than by applied accentuation (which, after all, was unavailable on two of Bach's favorite instruments).[67]

Harpsichordists and organists who have invested gallons of sweat and tears in learning successfully to belie the concluding canard may smirk or wince at pleasure. But the main point is that had the author actually looked into any baroque musical primer, from Quantz onwards he would have found precious little about equalized beats, but page upon page about metres and their allied dance rhythms, about prosody, about good notes and bad—in short, about the bar as primary metric unit

[67] Ibid. 66, 70.

and the concomitant necessity for applied accentuation. (And it is precisely in this that the late Baroque is in fact light years from the Renaissance!) What Cone describes—and what all the recordings in our batch, from Reiner to Hogwood, exemplify— is a specifically twentieth-century style of baroque performance that is often linked with a certain invention of Mr Elias Howe.

But if the sewing-machine style cannot be historically associated with Bach, it can certainly be associated with the 'neo-classic' Stravinsky. It is what Stravinsky and his spokes- men at one time called 'monometric' rhythm.[68] Edward Cone's prime exhibit of the hierarchized metrical texture of baroque music at its best comes from one of the episodes in the first movement of Bach's Concerto in D minor for harpsichord. Simultaneous patterning of steady semiquavers, steady quavers, crotchet attacks, and syncopated minim attacks (plus, later, syncopated crotchets) does indeed make up an entrancing texture of time (ontological, that is) (Example 1). There is no reason to assume that Bach or his contemporaries thought this fairly mechanistic passage noteworthy, let alone exemplary of the highest qualities of his style; but there can be no doubt that Stravinsky, on the lookout for models of geometrical solidity and equalized tensions, was struck by this very movement (and for the same reasons that Edward Cone was struck)—so struck, in fact, that he modelled the first movement of his Concerto for Piano and Winds on it. One clue of his dependency on this particular movement of Bach's is his adoption of the violinistic *bariolage* effects so uniquely endemic to these two keyboard concertos (the one by Bach obviously a transcription of a lost violin concerto that has been occasionally reconstructed) (Examples 2(a) and (b)).

---

[68] See Nicolas Nabokov, 'Stravinsky Now', *Partisan Review*, 11 (1944), 332: 'Look at any one of [Stravinsky's] bars and you will find that it is not the measure closed in by bar lines (as it would be in Mozart, for example), but the monometrical unit of the measure, the single beat which determines the life of his musical organism.' The term goes back directly to the composer. A sketchbook dated 1919–22, which pertains to some of the earliest 'neo-classic' pieces (*Octuor*, *Sonate*), also contains notations for a set of 'Cinq Pièces monométriques'. See description of 'Sketchbook G' in John Shepard, 'The Stravinsky *Nachlass*: A Provisional List of Music Manuscripts', *MLA Notes*, 40 (1984), 743.

Ex. 1   *Bach, Concerto in D minor for harpsichord, 1st movt.*

Ex. 2a   *Bach, Concerto in D minor for harpsichord, 1st movt.*

Ex. 2b   *Stravinsky, Concerto for Piano and Winds, figs. [39]–[40]*

Another is the peroration of Stravinsky's movement, the *Largo del principio*, where he sets up a rigid metrical matrix just like the one Cone admired in Bach, only more complex: sextolets in the piano right hand (beginning note-for-note identical to Bach's semiquaver figuration in Example 1), large triplets in the left hand extracted hemiola-fashion from the sextolets by sampling every fourth note, crotchet pulsations in the bass instruments, all against a theme in dotted rhythms (Example 3).

Rigidly mechanical metrical structures like this one would characterize a number of influential Stravinsky compositions of the middle 1920s, including the *Sonate* (1924) and *Serenade* (1925) for piano, both of which he recorded—the former on a Duo-Art pianola roll in 1925, the latter on a set of ten-inch electrical discs issued by Columbia in 1934. Stravinsky's

Ex. 3 *Stravinsky, Concerto for Piano and Winds, Largo del principio*

performance style gained an enormous prestige among progressive musicians in the 1920s and 1930s, when he was at the height of his career both as performer and as publicist, not only on behalf of his music, but on behalf of his philosophy of music, too. In newspaper *avertissements*, in pamphlets, in public orations on both sides of the Atlantic, and in his autobiography, Stravinsky propounded a philosophy of 'pure music', and the properly 'objective' manner of performance required to realize its purity. This he called 'execution', and by defining it (in the *Poetics of Music*) as 'the strict putting into effect of an explicit will that contains nothing beyond what it specifically commands', Stravinsky invoked the doctrine of quasi-religious fundamentalism alluded to before: what is not permitted is prohibited. 'Execution' is contrasted, of course, with 'interpretation', that old Stravinskian bugaboo. The whole 'sixth lesson' of the *Poetics* is a sustained invective—perhaps exorcism would be an apter word—directed against the bugbear, for as Stravinsky puts it, 'it is the conflict of these two principles—execution and interpretation—that is at the root of all the errors, all the sins, all the misunderstandings that interpose themselves between the musical work and the listener and prevent a faithful transmission of its message.'[69] Stravinsky's ideal performer, then, is a 'transmitter'—the very term Daniel Leech-Wilkinson used to distinguish authentistic performers from their 'interpreter' forebears.

Stravinsky permits himself to couch the issue in sternly moralistic terms: 'Between the executant . . . and the interpreter . . . there exists a difference in make-up that is of an ethical rather than of an esthetic order, a difference that presents a point of conscience.' The point is that of scrupulous fidelity to the letter of the text, and an ascetic avoidance of unspecified nuance in the name of expression, or as Stravinsky stigmatizes it, in the name of 'an immediate and facile success that flatters the vanity of the person who obtains it and perverts the taste of those who applaud it'.[70] Worst of all are interpretations based on extramusical ideas; these are the real 'criminal assaults' and 'betrayals'.[71] The highest quality in an executant, on the other hand, is

---

[69] *Poetics of Music*, Bilingual edn., 163.
[70] Ibid. 165.   [71] Ibid. 167.

'submission', defined in terms that seem as if borrowed from T. S. Eliot: 'This submission demands a flexibility that itself requires, along with technical mastery, a sense of tradition and, commanding the whole, an aristocratic culture that is not merely a question of acquired learning.'[72] Ultimately Stravinsky boils it down to 'good breeding' (*savoir-vivre*)—'a matter of common decency that a child may learn'. The opposite of good breeding, of course, is vulgarity.

Stravinsky's illustrative example is uncannily pertinent to our present concern:

> *The Saint Matthew's Passion* by Johann Sebastian Bach is written for a chamber-music ensemble. Its first performance in Bach's lifetime was perfectly realized by a total force of thirty-four musicians, including soloists and chorus. That is known. And nevertheless in our day one does not hesitate to present the work, in complete disregard of the composer's wishes, with hundreds of performers, sometimes almost a thousand. This lack of understanding of the interpreter's obligations, this arrogant pride in numbers, this concupiscence of the many, betray a complete lack of musical education.[73]

We need not enter into a debate over the assumptions that inform this paragraph. We need not point to the epistemological difficulties Stravinsky skirts with the bland phrases 'perfectly realized', and 'the composer's wishes'. Nor need we hire a psychologist to investigate what the phrase 'concupiscence of the many' would have meant to a Russian aristocrat uprooted by the Bolshevik revolution. What interests us here is the early enunciation of principles that have become articles of faith in our age of authentistic performance: to wit, that the first performance of a work possesses a privileged authority, and that the composer's wishes are to be gauged in material rather than spiritual terms, to be measured, that is, in terms of sound, not 'effect', precisely because sound, not effect, is measurable. Stravinsky goes on for the next five paragraphs to discuss the sound qualities of the St Matthew Passion; he never stops to consider its effect, let alone its religious meaning.

It is of course not only noteworthy but inevitable that every instance of exaggeration, distortion, or malfeasance cited by

---

[72] Ibid. 171.
[73] Ibid. 173.

Stravinsky in his lesson on performance ethics has to do with the same dynamic features, the nuances of tempo and intensity, we discussed earlier when, using T. E. Hulme's terminology, we distinguished vitalist performance from geometrical. Stravinsky's categories are the same: what Hulme calls vital Stravinsky condemns as interpretation; what Hulme calls geometrical Stravinsky upholds as execution. For both of them the vital is vulgar, the geometrical élite. We may detect an echo of these categories, and also of Stravinsky's faith in the performance medium as guarantor of breeding, when Joseph Kerman tells us that 'it is almost impossible to play Mozart emotionally on a modern piano without sounding vulgar'.[74] We may put these categories to the test by reference to a pair of recordings. An unabashedly vitalist (vulgar?) performance of the slow movement from Mozart's Sonata for two pianos in D major, K448, by Béla and Ditta Bartók (Appendix, Recording No. 4) features any number of tiny, unnotated, and hence (in Stravinskian terms) criminal and treacherous crescendi and diminuendi, accelerandi and ritardandi, and that most heinous of 'sins' and 'follies', according to Stravinsky's explicit designation in the *Poetics*: 'a *crescendo* . . . is always accompanied by a speeding up of movement, while a slowing down never fails to accompany a *diminuendo*.'[75] The recording was made in 1939, the year of Stravinsky's *Poetics*. Not all modern composers shared Stravinsky's ideas on performance, which only goes to show us yet again that all times and places, past and present, are ideologically heterogeneous. On the other hand, Stravinsky's own performance (with his son Soulima) of Mozart's Fugue in C minor, K426 (Appendix, Recording No. 4) is execution, pure and simple. You could not hope to find a drier, harder—in a word, more geometrical—performance of any music. You cannot say that the man did not practise what he preached.

It would be absurd to ask which of these two performances is the more authentic, or which is more faithful to Mozart's intentions. And the question would remain equally irrelevant and absurd had the renditions been played on fortepianos instead of modern grands. The difference between them is

[74] *Contemplating Music*, 211.
[75] *Poetics*, 165.

clearly an aesthetic and an ideological one, historical only to the extent that one exhibits a style of performance we take to be emblematic of nineteenth-century music making, while the other is obviously and wholly of the twentieth century. And we all know which of them lies closer to the norms of 'authentistic' performance today.

Stravinsky's performance of Mozart's Fugue furnishes a perfect illustration of what Ortega y Gasset called a dehumanized art. The term was not meant to, nor should it, conjure up images of robots or of concentration camps. It meant an art purged of those 'human, all too human' elements that to artists in the early twentieth century suggested ephemerality, inconstancy, mortality, in favour of abstract patterns and precisions suggesting transcendence of our muddy vesture of decay. Ortega's word 'human', in this narrowly defined context, is once more a cognate to what Hulme had denoted by the word 'vital'. In his classic essay, 'The Dehumanization of Art', first published in 1925, Ortega gave a startlingly complete and prescient description of the new twentieth-century aesthetic of what he felt the need pleonastically to dub 'artistic art'—'an art for artists and not for the masses, for "quality" and not for hoi polloi'.[76] It is a description that can be applied equally well to the performance style of new music sixty years ago and that of old music today. His description sounds many notes that have already been heard in our discussion so far: élitism, purism, insistence on scrupulous realization, and what Ortega calls 'iconoclasm', that is, literally, the avoidance of iconicity and the kind of facile expressivity the latter often entails. He adds, and properly emphasizes, another dimension, though, one without which our discussion will never be complete. That is the element of demystification and irony. 'The new style', he writes, 'tends . . . to consider art as play and nothing else, . . . a thing of no transcending consequence.'[77]

Beginning at least as far back as Hanslick, writers espousing a modern or anti-romantic view of art have decried its abuse as an ersatz religion or narcosis. The fundamental mistake, on this view, was to confuse the idea of beauty—the legitimate domain

[76] José Ortega y Gasset, *The Dehumanization of Art and Other Essays on Art, Culture and Literature*, trans. Helene Weyl (Princeton, 1968), 12.

[77] Ibid. 14.

of art, appealing, in Hanslick's words, to 'the organ of pure contemplation, our *imagination*'[78]—with that of sublimity, formulated long ago by Longinus with respect to rhetoric, and associated by more recent writers with nature. The sublime consisted in 'boldness and grandeur', and manifested itself in 'the Pathetic, or power of raising the passions to a violent and even enthusiastic degree', in the words of William Smith, Longinus's eighteenth-century translator, for whom 'enthusiasm' meant *intoxication*.[79] Eighteenth-century writers insisted on carefully distinguishing the sublime from the beautiful. For Edmund Burke they presented 'a remarkable contrast', which he detailed as follows:

Sublime objects are vast in their dimensions, beautiful ones comparatively small: beauty should be smooth and polished; the great is rugged and negligent . . . beauty should not be obscure; the great ought to be dark and gloomy: beauty should be light and delicate; the great ought to be solid and even massive. They are indeed ideas of a very different nature, one being founded on pain, the other on pleasure.[80]

The history of music in the nineteenth century could be written in terms of the encroachment of the sublime upon the domain of the beautiful—of the 'great' upon the pleasant—to the point where for some, with Wagner at their head, the former all but superseded the latter as the defining attribute of the art of tones. Not only that, but for Wagner, who more than any other musician invested his art with aspects of redemptive and ecstatic religion, the sublime was associated particularly with the fluctuant, dynamic aspects of his music—its waxing and waning, its harmonic fluidity, its oceanic, infinitely evolving *forma formans*—and its power and appeal, fundamentally wild and irrational, lay precisely in its 'pathetic', intoxicant, and psychically contagious properties. All of this was profoundly repugnant to the early generation of modernists whose thought we have been dissecting. Ortega, speaking on their behalf, proclaimed that 'art must not proceed by psychic

---

[78] Hanslick, *The Beautiful in Music*, 11.
[79] Quoted in Peter le Huray and James Day, *Music and Aesthetics in the Eighteenth and Early-Nineteenth Centuries* (Cambridge, 1981), 4.
[80] *A Philosophical Enquiry into the Origin of our Ideas of the Sublime and the Beautiful* (1757), in Le Huray and Day, 70–1.

contagion, for psychic contagion is an unconscious phenomenon, and art ought to be full clarity, high noon of the intellect'.
And, 'aesthetic pleasure must be a seeing pleasure; for pleasures
may be blind or seeing.'[81] One thinks of Freud's famous dictum
on the goal of psychoanalysis: 'Where id was, there ego shall
be.'

It became a mission for twentieth-century artists to restore
the distinction between bright, wide-awake beauty and blind,
irrational sublimity, to reserve the former for art, and to give
the latter back to life, nature, and religion. In this way neither
art nor life would be degraded. Proponents of 'Die neue
Sachlichkeit'—the 'new actuality'—attacked the vaunted autonomy of the art work, along with the philosophy that put the
creator and his personality at its centre. It is significant that
theorists of the new actuality insist once again on the primacy of
the ontological over the psychological, and emphasize (here we
have perhaps a lingering echo of Futurism) quickness of tempo
and mechanical uniformity of movement. Thus Boris Asafiev:

Contemporary life, with its concentration of experience, its capricious
rhythms, its cinematographic quality, its madly fast pace—-the quality
of this life has weaned us away from slow and leisurely contemplation.
. . . [In] the field of music . . . responses can be seen in the striving for
severity of construction, for clarity of writing, for concentration of the
greatest tension within the shortest possible time, for the attainment of
the greatest expression with the most economical expenditure of
performing forces. As a result, there is a growing contrast in
contemporary music between works built on the principle of maxi-
mum concentration, economy, and conciseness, and those which
dispose their materials in breadth and employ the largest possible
number of performers. The former are notable for emotional and
formal conciseness, for intensity of expression. . . . Emotional
outpourings and formal breadth characterize the latter. . . . In the first
case, the music asserts the dynamics of life; in the second it is ruled by
an emotional hypnosis and a sterile hedonism. It is natural, therefore,
that the new chamber music should have chosen the first style. . . . It
has been unavoidably influenced by the impetuous current of our lives
with its resilient rhythms, its flying tempi, and its subordination to the
pulse of work. . . . The new chamber style is nearer to the street than
to the salon, nearer to the life of public actuality than to that of
philosophical seclusion. . . . Its style is essentially dynamic, for it is

---

[81] Ortega, *The Dehumanization of Art*, 27.

rooted in the sensations of contemporary life and culture and not merely in personal sentiments and emotions. Its style is energetic, active, and actual, and not reflectively romantic.[82]

This vivid description of an art debunked and off its pedestal was made in connection with Hindemith and Stravinsky.[83] How well it applies not only to twentieth-century composition, but to twentieth-century performance, will be evident if we return for a moment to the recordings of the Fifth Brandenburg Concerto we considered a while ago. The Furtwängler reading can be well described by invoking all the adjectives Burke associated with the sublime: vast, great, rugged, negligent, obscure, solid, massive. It exemplifies Asafiev's categories of slow and leisurely contemplation, emotional hypnosis, and formal breadth. The more recent the later performances, the more closely they conform to the attributes of Asafiev's 'new chamber style': resilient rhythms, flying tempi, energy, activity, actuality, clarity, concision, the absence of subjective reflection. The metronome tells part of the story. Every performance described thus far has been faster than the last (figures give approximate metronome mark for a crotchet):

Furtwängler	*c.*72
Stokowski	*c.*84
Busch	*c.*88
Reiner	*c.*94
Collegium Aureum	*c.*94
Pinnock	*c.*96
Hogwood	*c.*98

In addition, the performances grew progressively lighter and more buoyant: from a full symphonic string complement plus soloists (Furtwängler) to a mere half dozen players (Hogwood). Furtwängler sought to invest the work with an imposing gravity—an importance, in short—of which modern performers have sought just as deliberately to divest it. After

[82] Boris Asafiev, *A Book about Stravinsky* (1926), trans. Richard F. French (Ann Arbor, 1982), pp.97–99. Translation slightly adjusted in accordance with the original (Leningrad, 1929).

[83] The paragraph cited from *A Book about Stravinsky* had originally appeared in the Leningrad journal *Novaia muzyka*, in an article on 'The New Chamber Style'.

Hogwood's rendition, at once the lightest and the quickest, the piece seems ready virtually to blow away, or in Marx's phrase to melt into air.

And with this lightening, both material and spiritual, comes the element of irony, what Ortega called the 'ban on all pathos' that inevitably arises as a 'first consequence of the retreat of art upon itself'. He even goes so far as to say 'the modern inspiration . . . is invariably waggish.' That may have been going too far, and Ortega immediately retreats a bit: 'It is not that the content of the work is comical—that would mean a relapse into a mode or species of the "human" style—but that, whatever the content, the art itself is jesting. To look for fiction *as* fiction—which . . . modern art does—is a proposition that cannot be executed except with one's tongue in one's cheek.'[84]

I believe this to be true both of modern creation and modern performance, but to avoid the potential misunderstanding to which Ortega calls attention, I would prefer to view modern irony not as a crisis of seriousness, but as a crisis of sincerity, of speaking truly and in one's own voice. So pervasive has this crisis become for music that a book has been devoted to it, which opens with a very provocative question:

Music is a language. Such, at least, is the implicit assumption, if not the explicit assertion, of many who talk and write about it. . . . For we are told that music has meaning, although no two authorities seem able to agree on what that meaning is. There is consequently a great deal of discussion concerning just what music says and how, indeed, it can sav anything. But in all this argument one question is seldom, if ever, asked: If music is a language, then who is speaking?[85]

This is a question, I submit, that could only have occurred to a musician in the twentieth century. Put to any pre-modern composer (of whatever century), it would have elicited an unhesitating, if unreflective (and philosophically perhaps untenable) reply: 'Why, I am, of course!' And many performers would claim as much, too. The composer Schumann even allowed of the performer Liszt that his art was 'not this or that style of pianoforte playing; it is rather the outward expression of

    [84] Ortega, op. cit. p. 47.
    [85] Edward T. Cone, *The Composer's Voice* (Berkeley and Los Angeles, 1974),
1.

a daring character'.[86] Asked among the modernists, however, Cone's question would produce a chorus akin to that elicited by the Little Red Hen: "'Not I," said the composer; "Not I," said the performer.' When art turns back on itself and its human content is denied, there is nothing left to express, as Stravinsky put it so bluntly in his autobiography. After the famous fighting words to the effect that 'music, by its very nature, is essentially powerless to *express* anything at all,' Stravinsky tried somewhat less successfully to formulate an alternative. Though a murky passage, its preoccupations are clear enough, and familiar: it takes us right back to the ontology of time, and to the idea that the content of art is its form.

The phenomenon of music is given to us with the sole purpose of establishing an order in things, including, and particularly, the coordination between *man* and *time*. To be put into practice, its indispensable and single requirement is construction. Construction once completed, this order has been attained, and there is nothing more to be said.[87]

To ask 'who is speaking', then, is to propound an irrelevancy, for it presupposes the existence of a speaker, a ghost in the machine. To the proponent of a dehumanized, geometricized art, literally no one is speaking. There is, I would suggest, no aspect of today's authentistic performance practice more pertinent to twentieth-century aesthetics, and none harder to justify on historical grounds, than its ambience of emotional detachment, its distancing of voice from utterance. This is easiest to observe, of course, when actual voices are present, singing words that possess an emotive import that has been embodied in the music. To a vitalist performer such as Otto Klemperer, for example, the Crucifixus of the B minor Mass is a statement about a matter of great human concern, emotionally intensified by Bach's rhetoric of chromaticism, dissonance, and melodic descent. Bach speaks of Christ's suffering and death, and the performers, identifying with Bach and Christ alike, speak directly to the listener out of their experience both lived and musical (Appendix, Recording

---

[86] Quoted in Irving Kolodin (ed.), *The Composer as Listener* (New York, 1962), 262.

[87] Stravinsky, *An Autobiography* (New York, 1962), 54.

No. *5a*). To a modernist like Johannes Martini (Appendix, Recording No. *5b*) the Crucifixus is a musical construction, some elements of which have generic semantic connotations—e.g., the tetrachordal ground bass, an 'emblem of lament'[88]—and for that very reason may 'speak for themselves,' independent of the composer, who has not created but merely chosen them and set them in motion, and—needless to say—without any assistance from the executants.

The exceedingly lightweight sonority and quick tempo of Martini's recording further serve the modernist aim of emotional distancing. I am quite convinced that this performance would have occasioned bewilderment on the part of any musician brought up with the doctrine of the affections. He would indeed have found it waggish. It comes, of course, from an album that advertises its fidelity to historical performance practice. That 'performance practice' and expression can be divorced like this is a perfect symptom of modernist irony, and amply confirms Ortega's contention that to modern artists art is 'a thing of no consequence'.

If there is a historical resonance here, it is with something remoter than Bach and alien to him: we are transported back to the castle at Urbino, where Castiglione's courtiers sat discussing *sprezzatura*, that 'certain noble negligence in singing', that marks the true aristocrat.[89] These sentiments found echo once again at the high tide of the Enlightenment, when Bach had been forgotten. Burney assures us that 'music is an innocent luxury, unnecessary indeed, to our existence, but a great improvement and gratification of the sense of hearing';[90] while for Kant, it 'merely plays with sensations'.[91] Modernism has

[88] Cf. Ellen Rosand, 'The Descending Tetrachord: An Emblem of Lament', *Musical Quarterly*, 65 (1979), 346–59.

[89] Cf. Baldesar Castiglione, *The Book of the Courtier* (*Il Libro del cortegiano*, 1528), trans, Charles S. Singleton (Garden City, N Y , 1959), 104. The phrase quoted in the text is from Giulio Caccini's *Nuove musiche* of 1601, trans. Piero Weiss, in Piero Weiss and Richard Taruskin, *Music in the Western World: A History in Documents* (New York, 1984), 170. Ultimately the Italian Renaissance insistence on aristocratic detachment derives from Aristotle, who in the *Politics* (Book viii) cautioned that too enthusiastic an involvement with musical performance compromises the status of a 'free man'.

[90] Charles Burney, *A General History of Music* (1776), ed. Frank Mercer (New York, 1957), i. 21.

[91] Immanuel Kant, *Critique of Judgment* (1790), trans, J. H. Bernard (New York, 1951), 171.

been a new Enlightenment, reacting to the romantic as its predecessor had reacted to the baroque. Virgil Thomson echoed Burney and Kant when, voicing what he made bold to call 'the only twentieth-century musical aesthetic in the Western world', he asserted that 'the only healthy thing music can do in our century is to stop trying to be impressive'.[92] And in an introduction to one of Thomson's books, Nicolas Nabokov sounded off in a similar vein, and at the top of his lungs:

In order to become meaningful again music must rid itself of nineteenth-century habits, the clutches of historicism, and its immortality machine. Music should get itself defrocked like present-day priests and nuns who want to serve their community and enjoy life. It should forget about its nineteenth-century 'beatification' (foretold by Goethe and accomplished by Wagner). The composer should stop being a public idol like a TV singer or a cinema actor. He should be again a juggler, a gamester, a trickster, and use all the newly developed techniques for his tricks and games. He should not compose for eternity, but for fleeting occasions and for the fun of it. He should then let his work disappear in Lethe, just as the thousands of seventeenth- and eighteenth-century operas, cantatas, and oratorios have fortunately disappeared. Only musicologists regret their absence.[93]

Surely many if not most of our recorded examples have already illustrated the applicability of these dicta to authentistic performance, and may begin to suggest a reason for the movement's burgeoning commercial success. The art works of the past, even as they are purportedly restored to their pristine sonic condition, are concomitantly devalued, decanonized, not quite taken seriously, reduced to sensuous play. And as the thousands of ephemerae at which Nabokov sneered have been resurrected, the classics of the repertory have been made to recede into their midst. Adorno decried this a generation ago, when he complained of the levelling tendency of what he called 'objectivist' performances of Bach. 'They say Bach, mean Telemann,' he thundered at their perpetrators, accusing them of a blind refusal to recognize that 'Bach's music is separated from the general level of his age by an astronomical distance'.[94]

[92] Virgil Thomson, 'French Music Here' (1941), in *A Virgil Thomson Reader* (New York, 1981), 207.
[93] Nicolas Nabokov, 'Twentieth-Century Makers of Music', Introduction to Virgil Thomson, *American Music Since 1910* (New York, 1971), p. xv.
[94] 'Bach Defended Against his Devotees', 145.

Authentistic performers do seem determined to close this gap, which, if I may say it without necessarily embracing Adorno's moral indignation, testifies rather conclusively to their modernity.

Indeed, in pursuit of this goal they can go to lengths nowadays such as Adorno never dreamed of. Hogwood's text for the Fifth Brandenburg, for example, is not the standard, canonical one. His recording has sought to restore what is billed on the album as the *Urfassung*, the original version of the set, bringing with it a promise of hitherto unprecedented 'authenticity'. In practical terms this meant that the concerti were performed not from the text preserved in Bach's famous fair copy dedicated to the Margrave of Brandenburg, but from variant texts preserved in various manuscripts copied in Leipzig after Bach's death, which, to quote Mr Hogwood's notes, 'reveal the earlier forms of the Brandenburg Concertos'. By subtle and (in my opinion) devious arguments, the authority of these miscellaneous secondary sources is elevated above that of the fair copy, 'which carries a specious authority stemming more from its Dedication and calligraphy than from its value as source material'. The two concertos that differ the most under this dispensation from their canonical forms are the First and the Fifth. Mr Hogwood waxes positively indignant at the poor taste and opportunism that impelled Bach to revise them:

His desire to impress the Margrave with variety above all is apparent, alarmingly in Concerto 1 where the revised version adds a new *concertante* third movement for the *violino piccolo* to a work that opens with a strongly *ripieno* movement; and in Concerto 5, where a harpsichord episode of nineteen bars is inflated out of all proportion to produce what is currently mistermed a 'cadenza' of sixty-five bars.[95]

Let us recall Stravinsky's strictures, quoted above, about the 'seductions of variety'. In his recording, Mr Hogwood has rectified Bach's lapse by reinstating the original nineteen-bar solo. Let me suggest that this conglomeration of shallow fireworks and harmonic barbarities, however 'in proportion', and however it may conform to the performer's idea of the stylistic norms of its day, is poor music by any standard, and that by replacing it Bach judged it so. As a snapshot of Bach the

---

[95] Notes to Oiseau-Lyre 414 187-1 (Bach: Brandenburg Concertos 1-6).

improviser, it has its human interest to be sure, but it is unfinished composition at best. It is amusing to hear it as a once-only curio, but to offer it as a viable substitute for what Bach offered as representative of his best and most fully elaborated work is manifestly to devalue both that work and the critical sensibility that impelled its revision. Bach is indeed reduced here to the level of Nabokov's transitory gamester and trickster, as is Beethoven in Hogwood's 'rhythmical, uncomplicated' renditions. And if I am not succeeding in keeping my indignation at bay, it is because I see here the ultimate perversion of the idea of authenticity: the elevation of what amounts to a rejected draft to the status of a viable alternative—and even a preferable one— because it is earlier, more in keeping with *ex post facto* historical generalizations, and less demanding on the listener. The utter spuriousness of the ploy is revealed in the fact that Hogwood's collection of early drafts is none the less being marketed as a rendition—and a particularly 'authentic' one—of 'The Brandenburg Concertos', a designation that has meaning only in conjunction with the canonical six in the calligraphic fair copy with dedication.

But even those less offended than I will have to agree that the immoderate reverence for the canon exemplified by Furtwängler and Schoenberg has been replaced by an equally immoderate irony. By being rendered so much less impressive than Furtwängler's, Hogwood's Bach is rendered correspondingly more modern.

To sum up the argument thus far, I hold that discussions of authentistic performance typically proceed from false premises. The split that is usually drawn between 'modern performance' on the one hand and 'historical performance' on the other is quite topsy-turvy. It is the latter that is truly modern performance—or rather, if you like, the avant-garde wing or cutting edge of modern performance—while the former represents the progressively weakening survival of an earlier style, inherited from the nineteenth century, one that is fast becoming historical. The distinction between the two, as far as I can see, is best couched in terms borrowed from T. E. Hulme: nineteenth-century 'vital' versus twentieth-century 'geometrical'. In light of this definition, modern performance, in the sense I use the term, can be seen as modernist performance, and its conceptual and aesthetic congruence with other manifestations of musical modernism stand revealed. What Carl Dahlhaus calls the 'postulate of originality' and defines as 'the dominant esthetic of [Wagner's] day' is still with us even if Wagner is not, and still decrees that music, both as to the style of its composition and the style of its performance 'should be novel in order to rank as authentic'.[96] When this is understood, it will appear no longer paradoxical but, on the contrary, very much in the nature of things that the same critics who can be counted upon predictably to tout the latterday representatives of High Modernism in music—Carter, Xenakis, Boulez—and who stand ready zealously to defend them against the vulgarian incursions of various so-called post-modernist trends, are the very ones most intransigently committed, as we have already observed, to the use of 'original instruments' and all the rest of the 'historical' paraphernalia. For we have become prevaricators and no longer call novelty by its right name.

But if the natural alliance between high modernism and authentistic performance can be thus readily discerned today, in the period of the senescence and decline of the former (and—who knows?—possibly the latter as well), it is just as conspicuous at the other end of their dual history, when both movements were in their fledgling years. Back in 1918 Ezra Pound wrote this:

I have seen the god Pan and it was in this manner: I heard a bewildering and pervasive music moving from precision to precision within itself. Then I heard a different music, hollow and laughing. Then I looked up and saw two eyes like the eyes of a wood-creature peering at me over a brown piece of wood. Then someone said: Yes, once I was playing a fiddle in the forest and I walked into a wasps' nest.

Comparing these things with what I can read of the Earliest and best authenticated appearances of Pan, I can but conclude that they relate to similar occurrences. It is true that I found myself later in a room covered with pictures of what we now call ancient instruments, and that when I picked up the brown tube of wood I found that it had ivory rings upon it. And no proper reed has ivory rings on it, by nature. Also, they told me it was a 'recorder', whatever that is.[97]

---

[96] *The New Grove Wagner* (London, 1984), 104.
[97] *Literary Essays of Ezra Pound*, ed. T. S. Eliot (New York, 1968), 431.

It is the beginning of an essay entitled 'Arnold Dolmetsch', which goes on to adumbrate very nearly every point I have been making about authentistic performance and the modern aesthetic. Here are a few more passages:

This is the whole flaw of impressionist or 'emotional' music as opposed to pattern music. It is like a drug: you must have more drug, and more noise each time, or this effect, this impression which works from the outside, in from the nerves and sensorium upon the self—is no use, its effect is constantly weaker and weaker. . . .

The early music starts with the mystery of pattern; if you like, with the vortex of pattern; with something which is, first of all, music, and which is capable of being, after that, many things. What I call emotional, or impressionist music, starts with being emotion or impression and then becomes only approximately music. . . .

As I believe that [Wyndham] Lewis and Picasso are capable of revitalizing the instinct of design so I believe that a return, an awakening to the possibilities, not necessarily of 'Old' music, but of pattern music played on ancient instruments, is, perhaps, able to make music again a part of life, not merely a part of theatricals. The musician, the performing musician as distinct from the composer, might again be an interesting person, an artist, not merely a sort of manual saltimbanque or a stage hypnotist. It is, perhaps, a question of whether you want music, or whether you want to see an obsessed personality trying to 'dominate' an audience. . . . It is music that exists for the sake of being music, not for the sake of, as they say, producing an impression.

They tell me 'everyone knows Dolmetsch who knows of old music, but not many people know of it'. . . . Why is it that the fine things always seem to go on in a corner? Is it a judgment on democracy? Is it that what has once been the pleasure of the many, of the pre-Cromwellian many, has been permanently swept out of life? . . . Is it that the aristocracy, which ought to set the fashion, is too weakened and too unreal to perform the due functions of 'aristocracy'? . . . Is it that real democracy can only exist under feudal conditions, when no man fears to recognize creative skill in his neighbor?[98]

It is all here: hatred of the revolution and the mob, the avoidance of living forms, the purity of art, art as scrupulous play of pattern, as wide-awake precision, as reflector of life as socially experienced. And over all, the twinkling ironic eye of Pan. Ortega, who knew not Dolmetsch, invoked the wood

[98] Ibid. 434–6.

god, too: 'The symbol of art is seen again in the magic flute of
the Great God Pan which makes the young goats frisk at the
edge of the grove. All modern art begins to appear comprehensible and in a way great when it is interpreted as an attempt to
instill youthfulness into an ancient world.'[99] And so, at its best,
does authentistic performance.

An interest in 'early music', meaning anything earlier than the
Viennese classics, was taken as a sign of avant-gardism in
Stravinsky's youth, something regarded with great scepticism
by more conservative artists, Stravinsky's teacher among them.
Rimsky-Korsakov's diary for 9 March 1904 contains the
following entry:

This evening, together with Glazunov, I listened to the Johannes
Passion [of Bach] at the Lutheran Church. Beautiful music, but it is
music of an altogether different age and to sit through an entire
oratorio at the present time is impossible. I am convinced that not only
I, but everyone is bored, and if they say they enjoyed it then they're
just lying through their teeth.[100]

Landowska was fond of quoting Eugène d'Albert's preface to
his turn-of-the-century edition of the *Well-Tempered Clavier*: 'I
know there are people who can listen for hours to [Bach's]
cantatas without showing any apparent boredom. These people
are either hypocrites or pedants.'[101] Those of us who know
better than to be seduced by such quotations into a complacent
sense of our own superiority to Rimsky-Korsakov and d'Albert
will surely agree that Bach's lack of headway among such
eminent musicians must have had something to do with the
relationship between the kind of performances he was getting
then and the expectations of his hearers. The fact that Bach's
music has made such a fantastic, unprecedented headway in the
eighty-odd years since then obviously has to do with changes
both in the performances and in the expectations. In light of
such reflections, consider now the candid reaction of an ideally
competent and sensitive listener to a recent performance of the
St Matthew Passion that was billed as a historical reconstruction
of the work (as it happens, very much along the lines proposed
by Stravinsky half a century ago):

---

[99] Ortega, *The Dehumanization of Art*, 50.
[100] Mark Yankovsky *et al.* (eds.), *Rimskii-Korsakov: Issledovaniia, materialy, pis'ma* (Moscow, 1954), ii. 16–17.
[101] Quoted in *Landowska On Music*, 85.

Since my early teens I have heard many renditions of Bach's *St Matthew Passion*, covering the full spectrum of twentieth-century performance practice, from traditional versions with enormous choirs and piano continuo through various realizations according to the ever-changing notions of 'authenticity,' and I have never failed to be intensely moved by this work. But, in every earlier performance I always found the piece long and heavy, and, in spite of the frequent cuts in the traditional performances, my reserves of concentration were sooner or later exhausted. In the uncut Bach Ensemble version I found myself for the first time totally involved to the very end, and I left the performance without the sense that the piece was overly long.[102]

The review goes on to emphasize many of the points we have dwelt upon in the present discussion: energetic tempi, clarity of texture, buoyant sonorities vouchsafed by small but variegated performing forces. These qualities would have been appreciated by Rimsky-Korsakov, too, who complained in his diary that it all sounded alike, that the choral writing was clumsy, that the tone colour was uniform owing to 'this incessant organ', and so on, all of which prevented the music from making an effect comparable to what he called '*our* music—a free music, music that plays with a succession of varied moods, music that employs all the most varied technical means, music that flows in varied and interesting forms'.[103]

What can all this mean, except that in modern performances, including those modernistic ones I call authentistic, modern audiences have been discovering a Bach they *can* call their own—or, in other words, that Bach has at last been adapted with unprecedented success to modern taste. Our authentistic performers, whatever they may say or think they are doing, have begun to accomplish for the twentieth century what Mendelssohn *et al.* had accomplished for the nineteenth. They are reinterpreting Bach for their own time—that is, for our time—the way all deathless texts must be reinterpreted if they are in fact to remain deathless and exempt from what familiarity breeds.

That is why I wish to register my complete dissent from Robert Morgan's gloomy diagnosis of the twentieth-century cultural

[102] Alexander Silbiger, 'Conference Report: Johann Sebastian Bach: 300th Anniversary Celebration', *Journal of Musicology*, 4 (1985–6), 119.
[103] *Rimskii–Korsakov: Issledovaniia*, 17.

impasse that the 'authenticity movement' supposedly reveals. We have got our purposes, all right, and our stylistic preferences, and they are well and truly represented—authentically represented!—in our performances of music of all ages. This was quite dramatically illustrated at that much-touted Battle of the Bands in September 1984, when the Chamber Music Society of Lincoln Center and the Academy of Ancient Music faced off on the stage of Alice Tully Hall. It was—despite the advance publicity and the differences in the ways Messrs Cooper and Hogwood expressed themselves at intermission time—by no means the expected case of the Schleps vs. the Prigs. One heard dash and vigour from the British fiddles, and poise and clarity in the New Yorkers' playing. Both groups started their trills from above and neither eschewed string vibrato. Simon Standage played with the panache of the Galamian pupil he is, and Kenneth Cooper brought down the house with the unforgettable glitter and drive of his splendiferously embellished Fifth Brandenburg (replete with sixty-five bar 'cadenza'). This was first-rate modern Bach from all hands. All of it was fleet, buoyant, and eminently geometrical. And it was not simply a matter of 'convergence', nor one of the 'mainstream' aping the 'historians'. The geometrical Bach, as we now know, was in place before the 'historians' ever began to ply their wares.

So why all the bloodshed and recriminations? Why not simply recognize our modern Bach for what he is, and stop the nonsense about authenticity? As I see it, there are three reasons: (i) some enduring Dolmetsch-inspired mythology; (ii) the belated intervention of positivist musicology; and (iii) the ideology of our museum culture.

As Pound observed, Arnold Dolmetsch began his pioneering work 'in a corner', and stayed there all his life. Though a muckraking critic like Shaw might, as we would now say, co-opt him as a stick with which to beat the Establishment,[104] the professional musicians of his day by and large wrote Dolmetsch off as a rustic crank. Unlike Landowska, who was only vaguely aware of him, Dolmetsch never toured the world. He was a local phenomenon, and once removed to Haslemere an isolated

---

[104] See Shaw's reviews of Dolmetsch's historical concerts in the early 1890s, collected in Bernard Shaw, *Music in London 1890–94* (New York, 1973), vols ii and iii *passim*.

one. Nor was the level of his performance, or his family's, of a technical quality that could effectively challenge the musicians of the mainstream. Thus Dolmetsch and the musicians of his age stood as it were back to back; and as his life went on he adopted more and more the embattled and embittered tone of a voice crying in the wilderness—a tone that has remained characteristic of many of his heirs. In the Introduction to his magnum opus, *The Interpretation of the Music of the Seventeenth and Eighteenth Centuries*, published in 1915, Dolmetsch inveighed against the 'prejudice and preconceived ideas' of 'intolerant modernity'. What he meant by modernity, however, was the musical world on which he had turned his back in the 1880s, still preserved in aspic by Furtwängler in 1950. That world could indeed be characterized as a monolithic mainstream. Even by 1915, though, it had changed into a divided world, one faction of which (though probably unbeknown to Dolmetsch) was growing quite receptive to his message.

Or was it? From what we can gather from this very book, from Dolmetsch's attitudes towards 'original instruments',[105] and from the handful of recordings he made near the end of his life, it appears that Pound might have, as the saying lately goes, creatively misunderstood the subject of his fascinating essay of 1918. Where Pound waxed enthusiastic over pattern and precision, Dolmetsch emphasized 'what the Old Masters *felt* about their own music, what impressions they wished to convey, and, generally, what was the *Spirit of their Art*', and he purported to 'show how erroneous is the idea, still entertained by some, that expression is a modern thing, and that the old music requires nothing beyond mechanical precision'.[106] Dolmetsch's use of the word 'modern' here is already a symptom of the confusion he has sown. But more to the point, it transpires that he was still a musician whom we might call an idealist and a vitalist, and he played little or no role in establishing the modernist style of performance that sustains early music playing today.

[105] See the account of Dolmetsch's harpsichord by Robert Donington, quoted by Laurence Dreyfus in 'Early Music Defended Against its Devotees: A Theory of Historical Performance in the Twentieth Century,' *Musical Quarterly* 69 (1983), 305–6.
[106] Arnold Dolmetsch, *The Interpretation of the Music of the Seventeenth and Eighteenth Centuries* (London, 1915; 2nd edn. 1946; repr. 1969), p. xiii (italics original).

But be all that as it may, Dolmetsch bequeathed a mythology, to which many still unreflectingly subscribe, that cast a hated 'present' that even by the time of its casting was receding into the past, against a 'past' that was actually a constructed dogmatic fiction created in the present—for surely I need remind no one how many of the tenets of Dolmetsch's 'historical style' (his overdotting, for one thing) have been seriously modified and in some cases overturned by subsequent research.

Meanwhile a seismic shift in musical sensibilities, brought on by the advent of modernism, was effecting a change in performance style for all music. It did not happen overnight, but after a couple of generations, say by the middle of the twentieth century, it was done. Anyone who still adheres to the division 'modern' style versus 'historical' style, then, is implicitly taking Furtwängler's Bach for the norm; which is to say, he is still living with Dolmetsch in the 1880s.

Now it was just around the time that the shift to what I call authentically modern performance was completed that academic musicologists began turning their attention in a conspicuous way to performance practice. This can be viewed as part of a larger picture, the modernist take-over of the universities. In academic music studies, it was the heyday of logical positivism, symbolized, if you will, by the Princeton music department, which in the 1950s and 1960s was presided over by Milton Babbitt in composition and theory, and by Arthur Mendel in musicology.[107] Mendel (1905–79) had started his musical career in the 1920s as a composition pupil of Nadia Boulanger. In the 1930s he had been a prominent critic of new music (for *The Nation*, *Modern Music*, etc.). In the 1940s he was a choral conductor specializing in the music of Schütz and Bach. It is not surprising, given his background, that when he became an academic musicologist he should have made performance practice his speciality. He was among the earliest to do so; since his time, the number of such scholars has become legion.

Performance research as Mendel practised it was a vastly different kind of enterprise from what it had been with

---

[107] For stimulating, partly autobiographical, reflections on this phase of academic music study and its consequences, see chap. 2 ('Musicology and Positivism: the Postwar Years') of Kerman, *Contemplating Music*.

Dolmetsch or Landowska. Positivist scholarship is interested in letter, not spirit. It sets up research experiments—'problems'— to be solved by applying rules of logic and evidence, the goal being avowedly to determine 'What was done', not 'What is to be done', let alone 'How to do it'. Direct application to actual performance is not the primary aim of such studies. They are not 'utilitarian' but 'pure research'. Howard Mayer Brown has accurately characterized the nature of such scholarship in Chapter 2 of this book, especially where he insists upon the 'dispassionate' suspension of 'personal commitment' in the quest for a truth that ultimately represents—in the words of Leopold von Ranke, the father of *Historismus*—'the way it really was' (*wie es eigentlich gewesen*). A perfect example of positivistic historicism in the realm of performance practice is Mendel's classic article, 'Some Ambiguities of the Mensural System', which questions the prescriptive tempo relationships that have been established by modern editors in a wide range of fifteenth- and sixteenth-century music, demonstrates that contemporary theorists disagreed too often to be trusted uncritically, and ends with fully seven closely-packed pages detailing dozens of individual unsolved problems in need of attack by future inductive research. The list is preceded by a more general prospectus that merits quoting at some length:

> What is needed, it seems to me, is not more articles advocating this or that interpretation of this or that theorist, or of a group of theorists arbitrarily selected, but rather an orderly method of gathering and sorting evidence from both the theorists and (particularly) the music itself. We do not know for most composers how consistent they were in their own mensural practice. We do not know what degree of consistency may have been imposed by publishers or copyists on different composers. We need to gather evidence of the mensural practice of each of the principal composers, each of the principal publishers, perhaps each of the principal anthologies.[108]

In one sense this agnosticism is quite salutary. It deconstructs the historiographical dogmas of the Dolmetsches, and throws some cold light on their rejection of the unloved specious 'present'. But as Howard Mayer Brown has pointed out

---

[108] Arthur Mendel, 'Some Ambiguities of the Mensural System', in Harold Powers (ed.), *Studies in Music History: Essays for Oliver Strunk* (Princeton, NJ, 1968), 153.

(tongue, one hopes, in cheek), a performer 'seems to need the psychological protection of actually believing in what he is doing'. He cannot settle for a survey of the problem, he must, by performing, propose a solution. A performance simply cannot merely reflect the sketchy state of objective knowledge on a point of performance practice, it must proceed from the conviction that a full working knowledge is in the performers' (subjective) possession. While generations of scholars chew over Mendel's seven pages of problems, what is the poor performer who wants to sing some Josquin des Prez to do? Wait till all the evidence is in and all the articles are published? He will probably never open his mouth. Rejoice that the answers have not been found and he is free to do as he likes? That is certainly one solution—but he who would do so risks rebuke these days from scholars whose implicit attitude seems to be, 'Shut up until we can tell you what to do.' This kind of destructive authoritarianism is rampant in reviews of performances of medieval and Renaissance music, where just about any performance at all is open to the charge of 'mixing . . . musicology and make-believe',[109] if that is the kind of tack the reviewer wishes to take. Professor Mendel himself, sad to say, made a habit of giving performers, in Grout's words quoted earlier, a 'bad conscience' about what they were doing, by challenging them to justify it on hard evidence. He presided over a terrifying workshop at the Josquin Festival Conference in 1971 on the performance of Josquin's Masses,[110] and used the positivistic inductive method as a veritable stick to beat modern performers. No matter what they did, Professor Mendel could find some theorist or source to say them nay. Nor can I ever forget the time Professor Mendel travelled up to New York to hear Nikolaus Harnoncourt lecture at Columbia about his ideas on Bach performance. The professor played the grand inquisitor: 'But Mr Harnoncourt, do you *know* that's true?' he intoned again and again. Mr Harnoncourt could only splutter.

That is not the way. Joseph Kerman has chided me for 'perpetuat[ing] old-fashioned stereotypes' of the musicologist

[109] David Hiley, record review in *Early Music*, 13 (1985), 597.
[110] A heavily edited transcript is available in Edward Lowinsky, in collaboration with Bonnie J. Blackburn (eds.), *Josquin des Prez* (London, 1976), 696–719.

versus the performer in my essay 'On Letting the Music Speak for Itself'.[111] I would like to think them outmoded, too, and as more scholars perform and more performers 'schol', perhaps one day they will be. But the spectre of Arthur Mendel continues to dance before me, and I feel we must still keep our guard up against holding the performer, as I put it then, 'to the same strict standards of accountability we rightly demand of any scholar'.[112] For performers cannot realistically concern themselves with *wie es eigentlich gewesen*. Their job is to discover, if they are lucky, *wie es eigentlich uns gefällt*—how we really like it.

Really talented performers are always curious, and curious performers will always find what they need in the sources and theorists—what they need being ways of enriching and enlivening what they do. I have saved for discussion till now my favourite recording of the Fifth Brandenburg Concerto, the one directed by Gustav Leonhardt, recorded in Holland in 1976 (Appendix, Recording No. *2h*). When discussing Edward Cone's model of baroque performance practice, I observed that where he speaks of beat, musicians of the period invariably spoke of metre. Taking this aspect of historical evidence seriously has been the special distinction of the Dutch and Belgian early music performers of the last couple of decades. Their efforts have occasionally met with scorn, and in truth, when applied literalistically, their zealous downbeat-bashing can turn into self-parody. But applied with discretion and wit, what a lilt due attention to metre can impart! Leonhardt's performance is still squarely within the domain of the geometrical, as we have defined it, and in tempo it is on a par with Pinnock, who 'placed' in our previous sampling at $\bold{\downarrow}$ =96. But the larger metrical units and the broader pulses lend a hint of iconicity to the performance—a sense of human gait. Hardnosed modernism here relaxes a bit, as well it might, its battle long since won. Leonhardt's recording also demonstrates the joyful results of thoroughly passionate and committed experiment with original instruments. His players have truly understood what I see as the inestimable and indispensable heuristic value of the old instruments in freeing minds and

---

[111] *Contemplating Music*, 203.
[112] 'On Letting the Music Speak For Itself', 343.

hands to experience old music newly.[113] What the result of such liberation will be, however, is unpredictable; and to presume that the use of historical instruments guarantees a historical result is simply preposterous.

Just how preposterous we can judge by comparing Leonhardt's recording with the recent one by the equally authentistic Concentus Musicus under Harnoncourt (Appendix, Recording No. 2*i*). We will not have heard such a tempo since Stokowski's, nor nuances such as these since Furtwängler. It is vitalism *redux*. Nikolaus Harnoncourt shared with Leonhardt the Dutch government's Erasmus Prize in 1980 for their recreations of baroque music. Clearly, though, if one of them should happen to be re-creating the music of the baroque, the other is baying at the moon. And if we think we know who is doing which, it is because we have accepted an authority, not because we are in possession of the truth. It is a fair guess that most early music connoisseurs today will side with Leonhardt in the matter of verisimilitude, and look upon Harnoncourt as a rebel. And in a way they would be right. Leonhardt's performance is well within the accepted canons of modernism, while Harnoncourt's is a challenge to them, not unlike the challenge lately issued by the so-called neo-romantics to modernist canons of composition. We are in the midst of what may yet be another major shift in aesthetic and cultural values, and the fact that 'early music' is reflecting it testifies to its vitality and its cultural authenticity.

As long as we speak of re-creations we can accept this kind of pluralism with equanimity and tolerance—which need not mean, of course, without a preference. It is when we talk about restoration that the trouble begins, and 'authenticity' turns ugly.

Ever since we have had a concept of 'classical' music we have implicitly regarded our musical institutions as museums and our performers as curators.[114] Curators do not own the artefacts in

---

[113] See 'The Limits of Authenticity: A Discussion', 11.

[114] For illuminating reflections on this theme, see three articles by William Weber: 'Mass Culture and the Reshaping of European Musical Taste', *International Review of the Aesthetics and Sociology of Music*, 8 (1977), 5–21; 'The Contemporaneity of Eighteenth-Century Musical Taste', *Musical Quarterly*, 70 (1984), 175–94; 'Wagner, Wagnerism, and Musical Idealism', in David C. Large and William Weber (eds.), *Wagnerism in European Culture and Politics* (Ithaca and London, 1984), 28–71; and two by J. Peter Burkholder: 'Museum

their charge. They are not free to dispose and use up at pleasure. They are caretakers, pledged to preserve them intact. Hence the negative value that lately attaches to the word 'transcription'. It has acquired a specious ring of vandalism, even forgery.

And hence the magical aura that has attached, in the minds of many, to 'original instruments'; for they are artefacts as concretely, tangibly, and objectively authentic as an Old Master painting, and those who use them can claim *ipso facto* to be better curators than those who do not. But though the instruments are objects, the pieces they play are not. And hence the falseness, nay the evil, of the notion, so widespread at the moment, that the activity of our authentistic performer is tantamount to that of a restorer of paintings, who strips away the accumulated dust and grime of centuries to lay bare an original object in all its pristine splendour. In musical performance, neither what is removed nor what remains can be said to possess an objective ontological existence akin to that of dust or picture. Both what is 'stripped' and what is 'bared' are *acts* and both are interpretations—unless you can conceive of a performance, say, that has no tempo, or one that has no volume or tone colour. For any tempo presupposes choice of tempo, any volume choice of volume, and choice is interpretation.

But that is not the worst of it. What is thought of as the 'dirt' when musicians speak of restoring a piece of music is what people, acting out of an infinite variety of motives over the years, have done with it.[115] What is thought of as the 'painting' by such musicians is an imaginary rendering in which 'personal

---

Pieces: The Historicist Mainstream in the Music of the Last Hundred Years', *Journal of Musicology*, 2 (1983), 115–34; 'Brahms and Twentieth-Century Classical Music', *Nineteenth-Century Music*, 8 (1984), 75–83.

[115] Here. too, there is a *bona fide* modernist resonance. One of the last prose pieces to be published under Stravinsky's name contains this bit of heavy-handed ironizing about Leonard Bernstein: 'Publicity often seems to be about all that is left of the arts. . . . Hence the spectacle, *also* almost the only one left, of the prisoners of publicity relentlessly driven to ever more desperate devices, as the condemned, in the Fifth Canto, are blown eternally by the unceasing winds. Recently one of music's superdamned (in this sense) was actually reduced to 'cleaning up' the score of . . . *Cavalleria Rusticana*, obvious as it must have been even to him that the accumulated dirt of bygone 'interpreters' was also the protective makeup that had kept the ghastly piece going this long.' 'Performing Arts', *Harper's* (June 1970), 38.

choices' have been 'reduc[ed] to a minimum',[116] and, ideally, eliminated. What this syllogism reduces to is: *people are dirt.*

And with that, of course, we return to our starting-point, for this is another, less attractive way of stating the premise that underlies the whole modern movement. It is the dark side of dehumanization, the side that does evoke robots and concentration camps. We will not forget where Ezra Pound ended up, and why.

But we are not there yet, and Leonhardt's quirky Bach, to say nothing of Harnoncourt's, gives reassurance that the restoration ideal is far from universally shared. It is not the elimination of personal choice from performance that real artists desire, but its improvement and refreshment. And for this purpose original instruments, historical treatises, and all the rest have proven their value.

The best indication of all that sterile restoration has not become the general ideal is that we have not acted upon our best means of achieving it, namely sound recordings. We have a much better idea of what music sounded like in Tchaikovsky's day than we will ever have of what it sounded like in Bach's day, and yet we do not hear performances of Tchaikovsky in our own day that sound like the Elman Quartet, for example, whose recorded interpretation of the famous 'Andante cantabile' surely represents the kind of approach the composer expected (intended?) (Appendix, Recording No. 6).

Why not? Because it does not please us. Modern performance is an integrated thing. Our performances of Tchaikovsky are of a piece with our performances of Bach. That is what proves that they are of and for our time. And that is why, within the terms of the definition the foregoing statement implies, I do regard authentistic performances as authentic. As soon as a consensus develops that we must restore Tchaikovsky to his scoops and slides simply because that is what the evidence decrees,[117] I shall be the first to join Robert Morgan in a chorus of lament for our

[116] Christopher Hogwood, quoted in Will Crutchfield, 'A Report From the Battlefield' (see n. 4 above), 28.
[117] For a harbinger of such a viewpoint, see Jon Finson, 'Performing Practice in the Late Nineteenth Century, with Special Reference to the Music of Brahms', *Musical Quarterly*, 70 (1984), 457–75. Sure enough, an attempt is made to rationalize (and sanctify) *portamenti* by calling them 'structural'.

Alexandrian age and the doom that it forebodes. It will mean we no longer care personally what we do or what we hear. Osip Mandelstam was revolted by nothing so much as what he called 'omnivorous' or 'haphazard' taste; to him it signified nihilism, an absence of values.[118] But as long as we know what we do want and what we do not want, and act upon that knowledge, we have values and are not dirt. We have authenticity.

[118] Nadezhda Mandelstam, *Hope Against Hope*, trans. Max Hayward (London, 1983), 268.

APPENDIX
Recordings referred to in Chapter 6

1. Bach, *Chromatic Fantasy* (Landowska) RCA LCT 1137
2. Bach, Fifth Brandenburg Concerto, 1st movement
   (*a*) Vienna Philharmonic Orchestra
   Wilhelm Furtwängler, cond. and piano soloist
   Willi Boskovsky, violin
   Gustav Neidermayer, flute
   (Salzburg Festival, 1950)
   RECITAL RECORDS 515 (distributed by Discocorp,
   Berkeley CA)

   (*b*) Philadelphia Orchestra, Leopold Stokowski, cond.
   Fernando Valenti, harpsichord
   Anshel Brusilow, violin
   William Kincaid, flute
   COLUMBIA MS 6313 (1961)

   (*c*) Busch Chamber Orchestra
   Adolf Busch, violin and leader
   Marcel Moyse, flute
   Rudolf Serkin, piano
   ANGEL COLC 14 (originally recorded 1935)

   (*d*) Fritz Reiner, cond. a pick-up ensemble
   (ripieno: 2 on a part)
   Sylvia Marlowe, harpsichord
   Hugo Kolberg, violin
   Julius Baker, flute
   COLUMBIA ML 4283 (1950)

   (*e*) Collegium Aureum (ripieni soli)
   Franzjosef Maier, violin and leader
   Hans-Martin Linde, flute
   Gustav Leonhardt, harpsichord
   RCA VICTROLA 6023 (orig. Harmonia Mundi, *c*1965)

   (*f*) The English Concert (ripieno: 1 [plus solo], 2,2,1,1)
   Trevor Pinnock, harpsichord and leader
   Simon Standage, violin

Lisa Beznosiuk, flute
DG ARC 2742003 (1982)

(*g*) Academy of Ancient Music (ripieno:
1 vn., 1va., violone [no cello])
Christopher Hogwood, harpsichord and leader
Catherine Mackintosh, violin
Stephen Preston, flute
OISEAU-LYRE 414 187-1 (1985)

(*h*) Gustav Leonhardt, harpsichord and leader
(ripieni soli)
Frans Brüggen, flute
Sigiswald Kuijken, violin
PRO-ARTE 2PAX-2001 (1976)

(*i*) Concentus musicus Wien, Nikolaus Harnoncourt,
dir. (ripieni soli)
Leopold Stastny, flute
Alice Harnoncourt, violin,
Herbert Tachezi, harpsichord
TELEFUNKEN 6.42840 AZ (1982)

3. Mozart, Sonata in D, K448
Béla and Ditta Bartók, pianos
HUNGAROTON LPX 12334-38 (orig. recorded
Budapest, 1939)

4. Mozart, Fugue in C minor, K426
Igor and Soulima Stravinsky
FRENCH COLUMBIA LFX-951/3 (rec. Paris, *c.*1938)

5. (*a*) Bach, Crucifixus (B minor Mass)
Otto Klemperer, cond.
Angel S-3720   (*c.*1963)

(*b*) Bach, Crucifixus (B minor Mass)
Johannes Martini, cond.
MUSIKPRODUKTION DABRINGHAUS U. GRIMM 1146-47
(*c.*1985)

6. Tchaikovsky, Quartet No. 1, Op. 11 (Andante
cantabile)
Elman Quartet
VICTOR RED SEAL 745575 (*c.*1918)

INDEX OF NAMES